Emotional Vampires

Dealing with People Who Drain You Dry

Second Edition

Albert J. Bernstein, Ph.D.

NEW YORK   CHICAGO   SAN FRANCISCO
LISBON   LONDON   MADRID   MEXICO CITY
MILAN   NEW DELHI   SAN JUAN   SEOUL
SINGAPORE   SYDNEY   TORONTO

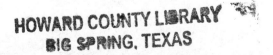

To the Girls,
Luahna, Jessica, and Clara

Contents

CONTENTS

CONTENTS

CONTENTS

Acknowledgments

Without the following people's help and support, this book could never have materialized:

Mindy Ranik, who came up with the title and provided about 10,000 miles worth of support during the writing of the original *Vampires* and this new edition.

My esteemed colleagues Luahna Ude and Bob Poole, clinicians of rare wisdom and rarer wit, who shared countless insights into the minds of vampires.

My agent, Janet Rosen of Sheree Bykofsky Associates, who is always there with an idea when I need one.

My editors, Leila Porteous, Casey Ebro, and Peter McCurdy who have shepherded me through the process of writing and production.

My friends Peter Bessas, Sundari SitaRam, Jenna Eckert, Donna Sherwood, and Janine Robbins, who have helped and supported me through various aspects of this project.

Most of all, I want to thank my family—Luahna, Jessica, Josh, and Clara—for putting up with me while writing, a feat requiring as much courage and forbearance as visiting Dracula's Castle at midnight.

About the Author

Albert J. Bernstein, PhD, is a clinical psychologist and business consultant who lives in Portland, Oregon, with his wife, Luahna, who is also a psychologist. Their grown children, Jessica and Josh, and their granddaughter, Clara, also live in Portland. Al is the author of a number of books on psychology and business. To find out more about him and his work, visit his website, albernstein.com.

1 Children of the Night

Who Are These Emotional Vampires?

Vampires stalk you, even as we speak. On broad daylit streets, under the blue pulsations of your office fluorescents, and maybe even in the warm lights of home, they're out there, masquerading as regular people until their internal needs change them into predatory beasts.

It's not your blood they drain; it's your emotional energy.

Make no mistake, we aren't talking about everyday annoyances that swarm around you like bugs in a porch light, easily whisked away with affirmations and assertive *I* statements. These are authentic creatures of darkness. They have the power not only to aggravate you, but to hypnotize you, to cloud your mind with false promises until you are tangled in their spell. *Emotional vampires draw you in, then drain you.*

At first, emotional vampires look better than regular people. They're as bright, talented, and charming as a Romanian count. You like them; you trust them; you expect more from them than you do from other people. You expect more, you get less, and in the end you get taken. You invite them into your life, and seldom realize your mistake until they've disappeared into the night, leaving you drained dry with a pain in the neck, an empty wallet, or perhaps a broken heart. Even then, you wonder—is it them or is it me?

It's them. Emotional vampires.

Do you know them? Have you experienced their dark power in your life?

Have you met people who seemed so perfect at first, but later turned out to be a perfect mess? Have you been blinded by brilliant bursts of charm that switched on and off like a cheap neon sign? Have you heard promises whispered in the night that were forgotten before dawn?

Have you been drained dry?

Emotional vampires don't rise from coffins at night. They live down the street. They're the neighbors who are so warm and cordial to your face, but

1

spread stories behind your back. Emotional vampires are on your softball team; they're star players until a call goes against them. Then, they throw tantrums that would embarrass a three-year-old.

Emotional vampires could be lurking within your family. Consider your brother-in-law, the genius who can't hold down a job. What about that vague, almost invisible aunt who takes care of everybody else until her strange and debilitating illnesses force you to take care of her? Do we even need to mention those loving, infuriating parents who are always telling you to please yourself, then expecting you to please them?

A vampire may even share your bed, a loving partner one minute and in the next, a cold, distant stranger.

ARE THEY *REALLY* VAMPIRES?

Though they act like creatures of darkness, there's nothing supernatural about emotional vampires. The melodramatic metaphor is nothing more than clinical psychology dressed up in a Halloween costume. Emotional vampires are people who have characteristics of what psychologists call *personality disorders*.

In graduate school, I learned this simple distinction: when people are driving themselves crazy, they have neuroses or psychoses. When they drive other people crazy, they have personality disorders. According to the diagnostic manual of the American Psychiatric Association, a personality disorder is:

> An enduring pattern of inner experience and behavior that deviates markedly from the expectations of the individual's culture. The pattern is manifested in two (or more) of the following areas:
>
> 1. Ways of perceiving and interpreting self, other people, and events.
> 2. Range, intensity, lability, and appropriateness of emotional response.
> 3. Interpersonal functioning.
> 4. Impulse control.*

The manual describes diagnostic patterns of thoughts and behavior for eleven different personality disorders, of which we will consider the five that are most likely to cause you trouble in your daily life: *Antisocial*, *Histrionic*, *Narcissistic*, *Obsessive-Compulsive*, and *Paranoid*. I chose these five because

---

*American Psychiatric Association: *Diagnostic and Statistical Manual of Mental Disorders*, 4th ed. (Washington, DC: American Psychiatric Association, 1994).

they occur most frequently in the population, and, more often than the others, they may be present to a subclinical degree. Day to day, you are far more likely to meet people who are a little bit Narcissistic or Histrionic, say, than people who are slightly Borderline or Schizoid.

The main reason I chose these five is that each of the types discussed here, although pathological and draining, also has characteristics that people find very attractive. Over the course of more than 40 years as a psychologist and business consultant, I have seen that these five disorders consistently cause the most trouble for the most people, at home, at work, and everywhere in between.

The bulk of the emotional vampires discussed in this book are not severely disturbed enough to qualify for an official diagnosis of personality disorder, but the ways they think and act still correspond to the patterns described in the diagnostic manual. Think of the patterns as a catalog of the ways in which difficult people can be difficult, ranging from severe enough to be hospitalized to mild enough to behave normally until the person is subjected to significant stress. In the world of psychology, everything is on a continuum.

All the patterns derive from the fact that emotional vampires see the world differently than other people do. Their perceptions are distorted by their cravings for immature and unattainable goals. They want everybody's complete and exclusive attention. They expect perfect love that gives but never demands anything in return. They want lives filled with fun and excitement, and to have someone else take care of anything that's boring or difficult. Vampires look like adults on the outside, but inside, they're still babies.

Emotional vampires don't go around wearing capes and snapping at people with their fangs. Usually, the difficult people discussed in this book are indistinguishable, both physically and psychologically, from everybody else. Vampires' immature tendencies usually come out only in threatening situations. The rest of the time, emotional vampires act like normal, responsible adults. That said, I'll also point out that vampires tend to be threatened by things that don't bother ordinary people. If you use your own experience as a guide, you wouldn't expect anyone to have problems with crosses, garlic, or holy water. Just as real vampires cringe in the presence of those traditional banes, emotional vampires are inordinately threatened by common adult experiences, including boredom, uncertainty, accountability, and having to give as well as receive. In the rest of the first section, we will more fully discuss the ways of vampires, the subtle differences in their personalities that make them both dangerous and seductive.

The easiest way to classify emotional vampires is according to the personality disorders to which their thoughts and actions are most similar. Each vampire type is driven by a particular immature and impossible need that, to the vampire, is the most important thing in the world. Vampires themselves are usually not aware of the childish needs that drive them. That's all the more reason you should be.

ANTISOCIAL VAMPIRES

Antisocial vampires are addicted to excitement. They're called antisocial, not because they don't like parties, but because they're heedless of social rules. These vampires *love* parties. They also love sex, drugs, rock 'n' roll, and anything else stimulating. They hate boredom worse than a stake through the heart. All they want out of life is a good time, a little action, and immediate gratification of their every desire.

Of all the vampires, Antisocials are the sexiest, the most exciting, and the most fun to be around. People take to them easily and quickly, and just as quickly get taken. Aside from momentary fun, these vampires don't have much to give back. Ah, but those moments! Like all the vampire types, Antisocials present you with a dilemma: they're Ferraris in a world of Toyotas, built for speed and thrills. You're apt to be very disappointed if you expect them to be reliable.

> *"What's wrong, honey?" Vampire Adam asks.*
>
> *Elise's jaw swings open on its own. "Adam, I cannot believe you'd ask me that. You think it's okay with me that you go around kissing other women right in front of my face?"*
>
> *Adam puts an arm around Elise's shoulder and she knocks it off.*
>
> *"Honey," Adam says, "it was a party, and I was drunk. Anyway, it was just a little peck."*
>
> *"A little peck that lasted five minutes?"*
>
> *"Sweetheart, you know that didn't mean anything. You're the one I really love. The only one. Come on, baby, trust me."*

Without Antisocial vampires, there would be no country-and-western music. If you think the only people susceptible to their charms are dewy-eyed romantics, you haven't seen them do a job interview or a sales pitch. Your best protection against these vampires is to recognize them before they turn on the charm. When you see them coming, hold on to your heart and hide your wallet until you've checked their references. What Antisocial vampires have done in the past is the best predictor of what they'll do in the future.

HISTRIONIC VAMPIRES

Histrionic vampires live for attention and approval. Looking good is their specialty. Everything else is an unimportant detail. Histrionics have what it takes to get hired into your business or your life, but be careful. Histrionic means dramatic. What you see is all a show, and definitely not what you get.

Vampires can't see their reflections in a mirror. Histrionics can't even see the mirror. They're experts at hiding their own motivations from themselves. They believe that they never do anything unacceptable, like making mistakes or having bad thoughts about anyone. They're just nice people who only want to help. If you question that, you're likely to suffer. It's amazing how much damage nice people can do.

> *Vampire Leanne calls her friend Melissa. "I was just talking to Patti, and she's thinking she might not go on the girls' weekend."*
> *"Why not?"*
> *"She has some issues with you. Maybe you ought to talk to her."*
> *"What kind of issues?"*
> *"Oh, she says you're a control freak, and that if everything doesn't go the way you want it to, you get all upset."*

If you were to ask Leanne why she is telling one of her friends about the negative things another friend has said, she would say she is only trying to help the two of them get along. The important thing to understand about Leanne and other Histrionics is that she won't be lying, at least not to you. Histrionics fool themselves; fooling other people is merely a side effect. Though Leanne seems to delight in stirring up conflict, she sees herself as a sweet, helpful person who is always getting accused of things she would never even consider. You will not be able to change her perception of herself. If you accuse her of creating trouble on purpose, you'll be in for a real drama, which will probably end with you looking far worse than she does.

Protect yourself by never telling a Histrionic vampire like Leanne anything you wouldn't want posted on Facebook.

Forget trying to get Histrionics to admit to their real motivation. Instead, take advantage of their acting ability by devising a less destructive role for them to play. The chapters on Histrionics will show you how. With a little creativity, you may be able to avoid being helped to death.

NARCISSISTIC VAMPIRES

Have you ever noticed that people with big egos tend to be small everywhere else? What Narcissistic vampires want is to live out their grandiose fantasies of being the smartest, most talented, and all-around best people in the world. It's not so much that they think of themselves as better than other people as they don't think of other people at all.

Narcissists are legends in their own minds. Surely, you don't expect them to live by the rules of mere mortals.

> *Vampire Lewis Hunter III, the CEO, is speaking to his management team: "I don't like to call it downsizing," he says. "It's more like right-sizing. There can be no question in anybody's mind that our overhead is simply unacceptable for these market conditions." He pauses to let the implications of his words sink in. "It is with heavy heart, then, that I'm forced to announce that each of you will have to submit a budget that reflects a 25 percent reduction from present spending levels. There is no other viable choice. In the spirit of teamwork, I think it's only fair that the adjustments be spread evenly, throughout all the departments."*
>
> *What Vampire Lew's managers don't know is that earlier in the day, Lew asked the board for a raise for his efforts in leading the company through what he called "the times that try men's souls." Lew got the raise. His salary increase will cancel out about 10 percent of the reductions.*

Narcissists present a difficult dilemma. Although there is plenty of narcissism without greatness, there is no greatness without narcissism. Without these vampires, there wouldn't be anyone with the chutzpah to lead.

Regardless of what they say, Narcissists seldom do anything that isn't self-serving. As long as you can tie your interests in with theirs, they'll think you're almost as great as they are.

Narcissists need to win. Don't compete with them unless you can just about kill them. Even then, watch out. They've been known to rise from the grave to wreak vengeance. Better you should sneak up on their blind side with an ego massage and learn how to give them the adulation they need without giving in.

OBSESSIVE-COMPULSIVE VAMPIRES

Obsessive-Compulsives are addicted to safety, which they believe they can achieve through scrupulous attention to detail and complete control over *everything*. You know who they are: anal-retentive people who can't see the forest because of the excessive number of superfluous, overabundant, and redundant trees. What you may not know is that all that attention to detail is designed to keep the Antisocial vampire inside safely contained.

Without Obsessive-Compulsives, none of the world's difficult and thankless tasks would ever get done, nothing would ever work the way it should, and none of us would do our homework, ever. For good or ill, Obsessive-Compulsives are the only people watching to see that the rest of us don't go too far astray. We may not always like them, but we need them.

For Obsessive-Compulsives, the most important conflicts are internal. They take no joy in hurting others, but they will hurt you if your actions threaten their sense of control. To Obsessive-Compulsives, surprises—even pleasant ones—feel like an ice-cold spray of holy water. They don't mean to retaliate, but they do feel compelled to state their opinion.

> *"Ta-da!" Kevin says as Vampire Sarah walks through the front door. "After all these months, I finally painted the living room!"*
>
> *He waits a minute for Sarah to react, but she says nothing.*
>
> *"Well, what do you think?"*
>
> *"It's wonderful. But . . ."*
>
> *"But what?"*
>
> *"It's just that, well, I didn't think we had decided on a color yet."*

The second-longest wait in the world is for Obsessive-Compulsives to make a decision. The longest wait is for them to speak even a single word of praise.

Perfectionism, over-control, and attention to detail—Obsessive-Compulsive vampires indulge in vices that masquerade as virtues. They habitually confuse process with product, and the letter of the law with its spirit. Your best protection from these vampires lies in continuing to keep your own eyes on the big picture and not getting lost with them in the dark forest of obsessive detail.

PARANOID VAMPIRES

In common parlance, *paranoid* means thinking people are after you. On the face of it, it's hard to imagine that there could be anything attractive about delusions of persecution. The lure of Paranoids is not their fears, but what lies behind them. Paranoia is really a supernatural simplicity of thought that enables these vampires to see things that others can't. Their goal is to know the Truth and banish all ambiguity from their lives.

Paranoids live by concrete rules that they believe are carved in stone. They expect everybody else to live by these rules as well. They're always on the lookout for evidence of deviation, and they usually find it. Think of them as the detectives of the vampire world. You feel safe and secure in their certainty—until you become a suspect.

> *Vampire Jamal strolls into the kitchen, wiping his hands on a paper towel. "I just changed your oil, and I noticed that your gas tank was almost empty."*
>
> *Theresa shrugs. "So?"*
>
> *"I just filled it up on Saturday."*
>
> *"Well, duh. I've been driving the car all week."*
>
> *Jamal throws away the paper towel. "You know," he says, "it's kind of funny. I don't ever remember you using a whole tank of gas in a week. Your car gets, what, 35 miles to the gallon? So that's about 450 miles."*
>
> *Theresa smiles and shrugs. "Busy week, I guess."*
>
> *Jamal looks directly into Theresa's eyes. "Where did you go?"*

The only thing Paranoids can't see is that it's their own behavior that makes other people go after them.

Paranoids see below the surface of things to hidden meanings and deeper realities. Most great moralists, visionaries, and theorists (and any therapists worth their salt) have a touch of the paranoid, or else they would merely accept everything at face value. Unfortunately, paranoia makes no distinction between theories of unseen forces in physics and those of unrecognized aliens trying to take over the world. The same motivation that led to the great religious truths of the ages leads also to burning heretics at the stake.

If you have anything to hide, a Paranoid will find it. Your only protection is the plain, unvarnished truth. Tell it once, and never submit to cross-examination. Easy to say, hard to do. The chapters on Paranoid vampires will show you how.

2 Maturity and Mental Health

If Emotional Vampires Are Children, What Does It Take to Be a Grown-Up?

So far as I'm concerned, maturity and mental health are the same thing. Both are made up of three essential attitudes.

1. The Perception of Control

To be psychologically healthy, we have to believe that what we do has some effect on what happens to us. Even if the perception of control is delusional, it usually leads to more productive action than believing that what we do makes no difference.

Over time and with reflection, our choices get better, and we perceive ourselves as having even more control over our fate. This is the main benefit of growing up.

Emotional vampires never grow up. Throughout their lives, they see themselves as victims of fate and the unpredictability of others. Stuff happens, and they just respond to it. As a result, they have no opportunity to learn from their mistakes, and they just keep on making the same ones over and over.

2. The Feeling of Connection

Human beings are social creatures. We can experience our full humanity only in the context of connection to something larger than ourselves. It is our connections and commitments that give meaning to our lives.

Becoming an adult human being means learning to live by social rules that become such a part of our reality that most of us follow them without even thinking.

Other People Are the Same as I Am As normal people grow, they come to appreciate more and more their similarity to others. Empathy is what maturity is all about.

Vampires just don't get this concept. To them, other people are there to supply their needs.

What's Fair Is Fair Social systems are based on reciprocity in everything, from back-scratching to telling the truth. Adults develop a sense of fairness and use it as a yardstick for measuring their behavior. Vampires don't; their idea of fair is that they get what they want when they want it.

What You Get Is Equal to What You Put In Adults understand that the more you give, the more you get. Vampires take.

Other People Have the Right to Deny Me Human relationships depend on a clear perception of the psychological line between what's mine and what's yours. Robert Frost said it well: "Good fences make good neighbors."

Vampires have a hard time seeing this all-important boundary. They believe that whatever they want should be given to them immediately, regardless of how anyone else might feel about it.

Social creatures trust each other to follow these basic rules, and emotional vampires betray that trust.

Their lack of connection to something larger than themselves is also the reason for vampires' internal pain. The universe is a cold and empty place when there is nothing in it bigger than your own need.

3. The Pursuit of Challenge

To grow is to do things that are difficult. Without challenge, our lives shrink to safe but unsatisfying routines. Challenges come in all shapes and sizes. The ones that help most force us to face our fears, back them down, and widen the scope of our existence. Vampires are sometimes better at this than we are. In addition to being pains in the neck, emotional vampires are artists, heroes, and leaders. Because of their immaturity, they can do things that we can't. The forces of darkness always swirl at the edges of creativity and great deeds. A world without vampires would be less stressful, but deadly dull.

To deal effectively with vampires, we have to think new thoughts and take unaccustomed actions. At times that may be scary, but facing fear is the kind of challenge that makes us grow.

WHAT CAUSES PEOPLE TO BECOME EMOTIONAL VAMPIRES?

Just as some of the newer stories about real vampires ascribe their delicate condition to a blood-borne virus, so there are many theories about the personality disorders that afflict their emotional cousins. At present, some of the most fashionable involve unbalanced brain chemistry, early trauma, or the long-term deleterious effects of growing up in a dysfunctional family.

Forget the theories; they will hurt you more than they will help you in your quest to understand vampires. There are two reasons for this. First, understanding where a problem comes from is not the same as solving it. Second, emotional vampires already see themselves as the innocent victims of forces beyond their control. If that's how you see them, their past can distract you from paying attention to the choices that you and they are making in the present.

Many self-help books have long sections about how difficult people got to be that way. This one doesn't. After years in the therapy business, I have come to believe that it is far more important to understand the mechanics of human problems—how they operate and what to do about them—than it is to speculate about what causes them.

IMMATURITY VERSUS EVIL

Emotional vampires are not intrinsically evil, but their immaturity allows them to operate without thinking about whether their actions are good or bad. They see other people as potential sources for whatever they happen to need at the moment, not as separate human beings with needs and feelings of their own. Rather than being evil itself, vampires' perceptual distortion is a doorway through which evil may easily enter.

The purpose of this book is not to consider the morality of emotional vampires, but to teach you how to spot them in your life and give you some ideas about what to do when you find yourself under attack by the forces of darkness.

Understanding emotional vampires' immaturity is your ultimate weapon. Many of their most outrageous actions would make perfect sense if they were done by a two-year-old. Don't let vampires' chronological age or positions of responsibility fool you. They are two-year-olds, at least when they're acting up. *The most successful strategies for dealing with emotional vampires are precisely the same ones you'd use with young children—setting limits, arranging contingencies, being consistent, keeping lectures to a bare mini-*

mum, rewarding good behavior and ignoring bad, and occasionally putting them in time-out.

You probably know these techniques already, but you may not have known that they were applicable to adults. Or perhaps you thought you shouldn't *have* to use them with grown-ups. You do, at least if you want to keep from being drained dry. Vampires are difficult enough to handle already; there's no point in ignoring effective strategies just because you think they're only for kids.

THE EVERYBODY AND NOBODY RULE

Human beings don't fit neatly into diagnostic categories, no matter how elegant or well conceived. As you read further, you'll probably discover that everybody you know, including yourself, has some characteristics of each of the vampire types. Everybody has some; nobody has all. *Most difficult people are a blend of two or more vampire types.* The chances are good that you will find your bullying boss or your supercilious former spouse scattered all over the pages of this book. Feel free to use the techniques that seem most appropriate, regardless of which chapter they appear in. Many of the techniques are introduced in the earlier chapters and refined later in the book. You'll probably find it most helpful to read straight through, so that by the time you reach the later, more complex types of vampires, you'll have a whole arsenal of techniques from which to choose.

WHAT IF YOU SEE YOURSELF?

If you see yourself among the vampires, take heart; it is a very good sign. We all have some tendencies in the direction of personality disorders. If you recognize your own, they are apt to be less of a problem than if you have no insight. Each section ends with a description of treatment approaches for the various vampire types. These should help you in working on your vampire issues yourself, or in selecting an appropriate therapist or therapy technique for yourself or for the vampires in your life.

Emotional vampires have a tendency to prefer therapy approaches that make them worse rather than better. People who throw tantrums like two-year-olds hardly need to be encouraged to get their feelings out into the open or, God forbid, get in touch with their inner child.

The opinions about therapy are, of course, my own, and certainly not shared by all psychologists. No opinions are shared by all psychologists. I believe that emotional vampires can grow up and become healthy human beings, but it takes a real effort on their part. And yours.

I hope you'll find this book useful, both at home, at work, and everywhere else in your life. Beyond that, I wouldn't be in the least upset if it gave you a chuckle here and there—and, if it would not be too much to wish for, the occasional glimmer of hope for the human condition that comes with understanding.

3 The Way of Vampires

How Emotional Vampires Are Different from and
More Dangerous than Other Annoying People

In an earlier chapter, I defined emotional vampires as people who have tendencies toward various personality disorders. Some readers may be wondering why I continue with all this "creatures of darkness" horror movie
business when we already know that we're talking about people who have
subdiagnosable traces of a psychological disorder. These people are sick, if
only mildly so. Why not just describe them in clinical terms, give suggestions
about how to deal with them, and be done with it?

It's not that simple, believe me.

Clinical psychology may wear the trappings of science, but underneath,
it still involves a fair measure of art and a bit of superstition as well. When
we talk about mental illnesses, and personality disorders in particular, we
aren't talking about diseases in any conventional sense. How many diseases
do you know that drive their sufferers to create art, succeed in business, or
have almost supernatural skill at persuasion? As we'll see throughout this
book, personality disorders are the impetus for all sorts of behaviors, some
destructive and some quite positive. To say that emotional vampires are sick
doesn't begin to explain their successes, or the control they can exert over
other people.

If they aren't sick, how do we characterize these people? I've called
them immature, which is accurate as far as it goes, but it still fails to capture
their essence. Emotional vampires aren't really children, even if parts of
their personalities are decidedly infantile. They may be your parents, your
bosses, or even the leaders of your country, so it's hard to think of them as
babies. The people we're talking about are usually perceived as grown-ups,
whether they deserve to be or not.

Both in the clinic and out in the real world, it's common to both overestimate and underestimate the people I'm calling emotional vampires. When

they do stupid things themselves, it's easy to see their immaturity, or to consider them sick. When they lure otherwise normal and intelligent people into stupid behavior, it's harder to imagine how a deficiency in their personalities could confer such dark and destructive power.

Even people with small traces of personality disorders can show the same pattern of being alluring, draining, and fiendishly difficult to understand. That's the real reason for the vampire metaphor. It's easier to see both such people's strengths and their weaknesses by pretending they're supernatural creatures who stalk the night, using their hypnotic powers to seduce normal people and drain them of their life forces. It does kind of make you pay attention, and helps you think of these people as something more than everyday annoyances.

VAMPIRES ARE DIFFERENT

This is the crux of the matter. In the movies and horror stories or in your everyday life, the most dangerous mistake you can make is believing that, underneath it all, vampires are really regular people, just like you. If you interpret what they say and do according to what you would feel if you said or did the same thing, you'll be wrong most every time. And you'll end up drained dry.

In the previous chapter, I listed the social rules that most of us have been following since childhood without so much as a thought. Vampires play by different rules entirely. They're not fair, but they're fairly consistent. Here are the social rules that vampires follow. Study them well so that you won't be blindsided.

My Needs Are More Important than Yours

Vampires operate with the selfishness of predators and young children. Regardless of what they say, most of what they do is guided by their desires of the moment rather than by any moral or philosophical principles. As we'll see in later chapters, if you understand the momentary need, you understand the vampire.

If your needs coincide with theirs, emotional vampires can be hard workers, caring companions, and all-around good company. That's why most of the annoying people in this book seem relatively normal most of the time. Everything changes when your needs come into conflict with theirs. That's when the fangs come out.

The Rules Apply to Other People, Not Me

The technical term for this belief is *entitlement*, and it is one of the most exasperating characteristics of emotional vampires. At work, on the road, in relationships, or wherever, most people follow the basic rules of fairness that they learned in kindergarten. They take turns, wait in line, clean up after themselves, and listen while other people talk. What emotional vampires learned in kindergarten is how easy it is to take advantage when you're not bound by the rules that other people follow.

It's Not My Fault, Ever

Vampires never make mistakes, they're never wrong, and their motives are always pure. Other people always pick on them unfairly. Vampires take no responsibility for their own behavior, especially when it leads to negative consequences.

I Want It Now

Vampires don't wait. They want what they want when they want it. If you get in their way or try to delay their gratification, they'll come at you snapping and snarling.

If I Don't Get My Way, I Throw a Tantrum

Emotional vampires have elevated the tantrum to an art form. When they don't get their way, they can create a sumptuous array of miseries for the people who tell them no. As we'll see in later chapters, each type of vampire specializes in a particular kind of manipulative emotional explosion. Many of the annoying and draining things that vampires do make complete sense when you see them as tantrums.

Emotional vampires may look like ordinary people. They may even look better than ordinary people, but don't be fooled. Vampires are, first and foremost, different. To keep from being drained, you must always be aware of what those differences are.

VAMPIRES PREY ON HUMANS

Night-stalking vampires will drain your blood. Emotional vampires will use you to meet whatever needs they happen to be experiencing at the moment. They have no qualms about taking your effort, your money, your love, your attention, your admiration, your body, or your soul to meet their insatiable cravings. They want what they want, and they don't much care how *you* feel about it. They are not thinking about you at all. If you get angry at them because you think they are deliberately trying to hurt you, your misunderstanding will make you even more vulnerable. They will see themselves as victims of your attack. Then you *will* become the target.

Vampires prey on unsuspecting people who assume that everyone is playing by the same set of social rules.

> *Vampire Jennifer calls at nine in the morning. She is obviously upset. "Sandy, I really need your help. My daycare is closed, and I've got to go in to work for a couple of hours. Can you watch my kids? I'd be willing to pay you."*
>
> *"You don't need to pay," Sandy says, "Bring them over." Jennifer's kids are pretty wild, but it's only two hours, and Jennifer did watch her children a few weeks ago when Sandy had to go to the dentist.*

Like most normal people, Sandy believes in helping a friend in need. She also believes in reciprocity, meaning that she feels obligated to return Jennifer's favor. She thinks that Jennifer is asking for a favor of approximately equal value.

> *By three in the afternoon, Sandy has texted Jennifer three times and left two voice mails with no response.*
>
> *At seven, Jennifer finally shows up.*
>
> *"Where have you been?" Sandy's exasperation is clear in her voice. "I called and texted ..."*
>
> *"Sorry about that. My phone doesn't work sometimes."*
>
> *"But you said a couple of hours, and ..."*
>
> *"There was an emergency, and we had to stay late, okay? There's no need to get pissy about it. It's not like I never take care of your kids."*
>
> *Sandy wants to remind Jennifer that she had watched her kids only one time for an hour and a half. She wants to ask Jennifer why she didn't call or text. She wants to say something, but Jennifer is already irritated. The Merlot on her breath suggests that the emergency was at happy hour.*
>
> *Sandy doesn't want to make a scene, so she says nothing.*

In addition to being heedless of social rules, emotional vampires all seem to have unreliable cell phones.

Electronics aside, this vignette illustrates the most common way that people get drained. You expect vampires to play by the rules, and when they don't and you say something, all of a sudden you're the bad guy.

Your best defense lies in knowing in advance how people with personality disorders think and behave.

Let's say that Jennifer has never taken advantage of Sandy before. Is there anything that might arouse her suspicion? There are some subtle clues.

First, everything was happening at the last minute in a highly emotional state. Sandy probably felt pressured to answer right away, without thinking things through. Vampires thrive in emotional situations. In the next section, on Histrionics, we will see how they create drama as a way of getting you to do their bidding.

Then, there is the offer to pay. Friends don't ask friends to pay for babysitting. If Sandy declines the money, she is automatically saying that she will babysit, and will do it for free.

The next clue is that Jennifer is not asking for something specific. To normal people, "a couple of hours" means two. To a vampire like Jennifer, it means whatever amount of time she needs. With vampires (or with anyone, for that matter), it's never a good idea to enter into a contract without knowing the terms. Normal people can be imprecise, but they seldom object if you ask them to be more specific. Vampires will continue to keep things vague.

Yet another thing to remember is that when emotional vampires offer to help you or give you something, they usually have a hidden agenda. The creatures of darkness are most dangerous when you need something and your guard is down. What other people might see as a friend in need, vampires see as a golden opportunity. They *always* get back more than they give. Don't let their predatory nature jump out and take you by surprise.

A final thing to remember is that vampires' favorite prey is people who have difficulty saying no. If you are one of those, make a habit of never answering right away. Always ask for time to think, even if you only say that you will call back in five minutes. Normal people will understand and give you time. Vampires will press you for an answer right away. If they do, the answer should probably be no. To keep from falling prey, you need courage as well as knowledge.

VAMPIRES CAN'T SEE THEMSELVES IN A MIRROR

If you want to know whether someone is a vampire, hold up a mirror and see if there's a reflection. If you want to know whether someone is an emotional vampire, hold up a self-help book that describes his personality perfectly and see if there's a spark of recognition. With both kinds of vampires, there will be nothing there. Night-stalking vampires have no reflections; emotional vampires have no insight.

You can describe vampires to themselves a thousand times, and they still won't see what's plain and obvious to everyone else. You can show them the chapter in this book that describes them perfectly, and they'll think it's about you. Or worse, they'll tell you that through the brilliance of my characterization, they've finally understood themselves and, by so doing, have changed. I'd like to believe that this book is that good, but I know better.

Vampires can learn about themselves and make real changes, but it takes years of hard work. It absolutely never happens in a single moment of blinding realization. If you believe you see a sudden blaze of self-understanding in a vampire's eyes, you're likely to be the one who gets burned.

VAMPIRES ARE MORE POWERFUL IN THE DARK

Both kinds of vampires thrive on darkness. Blood-hungry vampires stalk the night. Emotional vampires lurk in the darker side of human nature.

Emotional vampires are far more comfortable with their own immaturity than you are with yours. Also, they have absolutely no shame.

> *In the midst of a discussion with Susan, Vampire Cleve pulls over to the side of the freeway. "That's it!" he says as he opens the door. "If that's the way you feel about it, you can just go without me." He gets out of the car and starts to walk down the narrow shoulder of the road.*
>
> *Susan slides over into the driver's seat. Anger, hurt, and fear swirl around in her head. The kids in the backseat are crying pitifully as speeding cars whip by within inches of their father.*
>
> *Susan lets out a long sigh, turns on the emergency flasher, and puts the car in gear. Slowly, she pulls up behind Cleve and beckons him to get back in.*

Any psychologist will tell you that any action that is rewarded will happen more often. By giving in, Susan is rewarding Cleve for being a jerk, but what can she do? It's one of those devil's bargains in which she's damned because the little angel on her shoulder won't let her endanger her husband.

PROTECTING YOURSELF FROM VAMPIRES

Dealing with emotional vampires requires a lot of effort. They may be worth it; they may not. Only you can decide. Sometimes it's better to run away, or not get involved in the first place. I hope this book will help you choose the best approach with the vampires you face in your day-to-day life. Each chapter offers both tactics for fighting and suggestions about how to retreat.

4 Lovable Rogues

The Antisocial Types

Antisocials are the simplest of vampires, but also the most dangerous. All they want out of life is a good time, a little action, and immediate gratification of their every desire. If they can use you to accomplish these goals, nobody is more exciting, charming, or seductive. If you stand in their way, you're dog meat. Antisocials, like all vampires, are immature. On their best days, they function at the level of early teenagers. On their worst, they can give infants a run for their money (which, come to think of it, is true of teenagers also).

To be technically accurate, we're talking about people who have tendencies in the direction of an antisocial personality disorder. Antisocial, in this case, means unsocialized, or heedless of normal social constraints. The name is unfortunate. Like its predecessor, *sociopath*, it harks back to the days when psychiatric diagnoses were moral judgments rather than personality descriptions. A hundred or so years ago, when this diagnosis was first formulated, it was considered to be the personality type of criminals. It still is. Of all the emotional vampires, Antisocials are the most likely to be involved in illegal behavior.

As we'll see in the following chapters, illegal behavior is only a small part of the picture, especially in the Antisocial vampires you see on a daily basis. Personality disorders exist along a continuum. At one end are criminals. At the other are exciting, adventurous, grown-up teenagers who are still heavily into sex, drugs, and rock 'n' roll.

The other problem with the name is that the colloquial meaning of *antisocial* suggests people who don't like parties. This is definitely not true of Antisocials. They like being around people, and they love parties for all the opportunities they present. Wherever there's fun, you'll find Antisocials.

In another sense, however, Antisocials are loners. They have a hard time making any sort of commitment because they don't really trust anybody. Antisocials are convinced that the only human motivation is self-interest. They are predators to the core, and proud of it. They are perfectly comfortable with self-ishness because they don't think there's any other form of motivation.

Antisocials are often damnably attractive and a hell of a lot of fun. Imagine taking a regular person, doubling the energy level, tripling the love of excitement, then switching off the circuitry for worry.

Everybody has felt like that once or twice. Remember prom night, when you were dressed to kill and the air tingled with the scent of carnations and contraband beer. What if every day were filled with those kinds of possibilities? What if there were no little voice inside your head spoiling your fun by reminding you of the terrible things that could happen if you let yourself get *too* wild? Compared with a life of prom nights, it would be pretty hard to get excited about your day job.

THE FERRARI-TOYOTA DILEMMA

Many social interactions are like job interviews for various positions in your life—friend, lover, colleague, employee, or perhaps even nemesis. If you were placing an advertisement for people to hire into your life enterprise, what would it look like? I put together a composite of employment ads that I believe sums up many people's fantasy of the ideal employee:

> High-energy, enthusiastic self-starter wanted. We're looking for an independent person who doesn't need to be told what to do every minute of the day, someone with an entrepreneurial spirit who creates his or her own security by being quick, decisive, flexible, and able to think outside the box. Good social skills and political savvy a must. Apply only if you can turn setbacks into opportunities, and are willing to handle a little risk in return for big rewards. No whiners.

If in your mind you can see this applicant standing there with a big smile, a firm handshake, and a two-stroke handicap, what you're looking at is an Antisocial vampire—a Ferrari in a world of Toyotas.

Toyotas are safe and practical, but not much fun. Ferraris are danger-ously powerful, fabulously expensive, and in the shop more than they are on the road. Still, they're what we dream about when we buy Toyotas.

After a few months on the job, the person hired from the previous ad might get a performance review that looks like this:

> Unreliable and at times even dishonest. Does not accept being told what to do! Convinced that most rules are silly, confining, and made

to be broken. Easily bored with day-to-day routine to the point that he or she often cuts corners and leaves important tasks undone. Takes advantage of others and often throws tantrums to get his or her way. Little ability to plan ahead or learn from mistakes. On the personal side, is going through a divorce, has financial difficulties, and is rumored to have problems with alcohol and drugs.

The most important thing to remember about Antisocials is that the ad and the evaluation represent two parts of the same personality. Vampires' traits, both positive and negative, hang together in identifiable clusters. This book is full of descriptions, examples, and checklists that will teach you more than you ever wanted to know about which traits go with which personality type.

It may not make any difference. Impractical as Ferraris are, people want them. Those who own Ferraris love them enough to pretend that they're sensible. Aficionados may talk themselves into believing that the Ferrari-Toyota dilemma doesn't really exist, or that it is the result of an anomaly that can easily be corrected by a skillful enough mechanic. I know this is true because, during my 40 years of work as a therapist and business consultant, people have brought me countless human Ferraris to repair. They think I can somehow get rid of the bad parts and keep the good. I tell them it isn't possible, but most of the time they don't believe me.

In making your own existential choices between Ferraris and Toyotas, it doesn't matter so much which one you pick, only that you know the difference. The people who are most damaged by emotional vampires are those who believe that they can have the speed and exhilaration of a Ferrari with the safety and reliability of a Toyota.

HOW TO RECOGNIZE AN ANTISOCIAL VAMPIRE

Now we come to our first vampire identification checklist. I'll be the first to admit that the test is crude in that it relies more on opinions, impressions, and value judgments than on objective facts. The purpose of the checklists is not to make a medical diagnosis, but to help you recognize emotionally draining people before they suck you dry. Your first line of defense is always your own subjective impression that something is amiss. If you're in doubt, check out your intuitions with other people. This is a good idea even if you are absolutely certain.

Remember the rule from Chapter 2: *nobody is all or none.* Nobody fits a category completely or not at all. Everybody is made up of a set of

THE ANTISOCIAL EMOTIONAL VAMPIRE CHECKLIST: LISTENING TO THE CALL OF THE WILD

True or False   Score one point for each *true* answer.

1. This person believes that rules were made to be broken.   T F
2. This person is adept at using excuses to avoid doing what he or she doesn't want to do.   T F
3. This person has had legal problems.   T F
4. This person regularly engages in dangerous activities for their thrill value.   T F
5. This person can turn on brilliant bursts of charm to get his or her way.   T F
6. This person is not very good at managing his or her finances.   T F
7. This person smokes without apology.   T F
8. This person has one or more other addictions.   T F
9. This person has had more sex partners than most people.   T F
10. This person seldom worries.   T F
11. This person actually believes that some problems can be settled with a fistfight.   T F
12. This person sees no problem with lying to achieve a goal.   T F
13. This person justifies doing bad things to people because others would do them too if they had the chance.   T F
14. This person can consciously throw a tantrum to get his or her way.   T F
15. This person doesn't understand the concept of looking before you leap.   T F
16. This person believes in having fun first and doing the work later.   T F
17. This person has been fired from a job or has quit impulsively.   T F
18. This person refuses to comply with any sort of dress code.   T F
19. This person regularly makes promises that he or she doesn't keep.   T F
20. Despite all these faults, this person is still one of the most exciting people I have ever met.   T F

Scoring   Five or more true answers qualify the person as an Antisocial emotional vampire, although not necessarily for a diagnosis of antisocial personality disorder. If the person scores higher than 10, hold on to your wallet, and your heart.

characteristics that make him or her unique, and some of those unique people are considerably more emotionally draining than others.

WHAT THE QUESTIONS MEASURE

The specific behaviors covered in the checklist relate to several underlying personality characteristics that define an Antisocial emotional vampire.

High Need for Stimulation

At the core of the Antisocial's personality is a lust for stimulation of all sorts. All the other characteristics seem to arise from that central drive for excitement. At any crossroads, Antisocials will usually choose the path that leads to the most excitement in the least time. They themselves may be completely unaware of this dynamic, yet it explains a good deal of their behavior.

On the positive side, Antisocials are not held back by doubt and worry. They embrace risks and challenges that terrify ordinary people. Most of history's great deeds of exploration, financial daring, and physical courage have been performed by people who would meet the criteria set down here for Antisocial vampires. From the beginning of time, we have loved these people, thrilled to their exploits, and built monuments to honor their names. We just can't live with them. Heroes are often as dangerous to their friends as they are to the enemy.

The same drive that leads to courage on battlefields, in sports arenas, and on trading floors leads to boredom with everyday life. The landscape of the Antisocials' world is made up of scattered peaks of pulse-pounding exhilaration with wide deserts of mind-numbing boredom in between. Throughout those long hours when socialized people content themselves with delaying gratification in order to live up to their obligations, Antisocials are pacing like trapped beasts looking for any way to escape. The day-to-day rules that provide structure and meaning in our lives are merely the bars of their cages. Antisocials don't see themselves as looking for trouble, only for the chance to be free. Freedom for them, however, means trouble for everybody else.

In their search for constant stimulation, Antisocials are drawn to all things addictive the way lemmings are to cliffs. Sex and drugs are always popular, as are gambling, credit cards, and risky investments with other people's money. The drug of choice may vary, but the purpose is the same. Under the skin, all addictions are alike in that they provide the rapid change in neurochemistry that is the central goal that Antisocials are striving for.

Impulsiveness

Antisocials seldom reflect on why they do the things they do; they just do them. To them, planning or consideration of alternatives is unnecessary and boring. On battlefields and playing fields, they are more beautiful than any of us could hope to be because they are free of the worry and doubt that slow us down.

Only over time does it become apparent that most of the decisions that Antisocials make are simply a roll of the dice. From the inside, Antisocials don't see themselves as making decisions at all. To them, life is a series of inevitable reactions to whatever is happening at the moment. Give them what they want, and they're cheerful. Frustrate them, and they throw a tantrum. Put them in a boring situation, and they stir up a fuss. They truly believe that their actions are caused by what happens to them. This belief frees them from responsibility and guilt, but it also robs them of the perception of control over their own lives—a view that is one of the essentials for mental health. Worry and doubt may slow us down, but they also provide meaning and continuity to our lives.

Charm

Despite their faults, Antisocial vampires are lovable. You'd think that such predatory people would be hated and shunned, but that is far from being the case. Immaturity is the wellspring of attraction and the source of all charm. Vampires make their emotional living by using other people. To survive, they have to be very good at convincing you that they have exactly what you want. In fact, they *do* have what you want, but seldom for as long as you want it.

Our own immaturity can persuade us that a Ferrari is every bit as practical as a Toyota. Funny how it's usually the most messed-up part of our personalities that makes the most important decisions.

5 Vampire Daredevils

Sexy, Thrilling, and Definitely Bad for Your Health

If you like excitement and fun, you'll love this manifestation of the Antisocial vampire. Be careful that you don't love Daredevils too much—they can be addictive.

The most salient characteristic of Daredevils is their own addiction to excitement, which, as we have just seen, is the central dynamic of all Antisocials. The other two Antisocial types are partial to darker thrills: Used Car Salesmen to deception, and Bullies to aggression. Daredevils like excitement for its own sake, a trait that makes them the most socially acceptable of the Antisocials. At least they're not actively trying to hurt you or take advantage of you.

THE PHYSIOLOGY OF EXCITEMENT

In a physiological sense, excitement is nothing more than rapid changes in brain and body chemistry; these can be achieved by jumping out of an airplane, having wild sex, playing the stock market, drinking a martini, or buying stuff on the Home Shopping Network. We're talking drugs here, even though the substances in question are hormones, endorphins, and neurotransmitters. Daredevils also have strong proclivities for drugs that are manufactured outside the body. Whatever the source, the overriding goal of most Daredevil behavior is to get the biggest jolt in the shortest amount of time.

Daredevils do very little worrying. They have far more important things to think about than deadlines, obligations, or how you'll feel if they break a promise. Daredevils regularly lose jobs, spend money they don't have, and break the hearts of the people who care about them. Everyday reality is no match for the heart-pounding, gut-wrenching thrill of living a fantasy.

Drugs, whether bought from a dealer or squeezed out of the endocrine system by risky behavior, cause a second problem as well. Over time, *tolerance* develops; it takes more and more of a drug to do less and less. The huge jolts that Daredevils love so much inevitably deplete their brains of the smaller amounts of chemicals required to maintain day-to-day equilibrium. In the wide, dry spaces between thrills, Antisocials of all types feel depressed, irritable, and empty.

When they feel bored and depressed, Daredevils want something that will make the bad feelings go away immediately. When they feel good, they want something that will make them feel better. Antisocials, more than any other type of vampire, are prone to substance abuse. However, Daredevils are not likely to sit at home and drink in front of the TV. When they are intoxicated, they want to go out and do something. That something is usually ill considered, self-destructive, and very expensive. Over time, as their tolerance goes up, the mess they make of their lives gets bigger and bigger.

This is where you come in. In addition to playmates, Daredevils usually need somebody to take care of them, clean up after them, and get them back on track. They will offer the world for these services, and pay nothing. There is no surer way to get drained than believing that your love and compassion can cause a Daredevil to change out of sheer gratitude. Codependents don't get gratitude, and their ministrations usually make Daredevils worse. The most self-destructive place a normal person can be is between someone with a personality disorder and the consequences of his or her own behavior. You might as well dance in the middle of the freeway, because you will surely get run over.

Still, when Daredevils are up and running, the ride is awfully sweet. Now that you know what's under the hood, you still have to choose: Ferrari or Toyota?

DAREDEVIL HYPNOSIS

Chemical or behavioral, at whatever level you think about their style, Daredevils offer a wild ride that pulls you out of your workaday world and into their alternative reality of fun and adventure. Without even trying, they are superb hypnotists. The alternative reality they offer is enticing—all fun and no responsibility. It always starts small.

> *"Yo, Vijay. Vampire Brian here with the ski report. Twenty-one new inches of powder last night, with more falling as we speak. If we drive up tonight, we can beat the crowds to the lifts in the morning."*

"Brian, tomorrow's Friday. I'm working. How did you manage to get the day off?"

Suddenly, Brian's voice sounds weak and raspy, as if he had to struggle to draw a breath. "I've got that flu that's going around. It's really hit me hard. I tried to get out of bed this morning, but I just can't seem to . . ." Brian's voice fades into a weak cough.

"Jeez, you really do sound sick. How are you doing that?"

Brian answers in the same faltering voice. "It's simple; just lie down and blow most of the air out of your lungs. It makes you sound like you're about to die. Try it."

Vijay leans back in his chair and ties to imitate Brian's sickly voice. "I have a bad case of the flu—"

"Really lame, Vijay."

"How's this? Do I sound sick enough now?" Vijay chokes out the words.

"Right on the money." Brian's laughter turns into a fit of ersatz coughing that ends in a wheezing gasp.

Daredevils are great at spotting people who could use a little fun, especially fun that involves rebellion against authority. As hypnotists, they speak to the teenager inside us and describe all the wonderful possibilities that life holds if we're just willing to take a risk. The bind they put us in is a dare, simple and effective: do it, or kiss the opportunity goodbye and admit that you didn't have the guts.

There's nothing wrong with calling in sick to go skiing if you do it only once in a while. The problem with Daredevils is that they don't know when to stop. They have a real gift for pulling other people along further than they wanted to go.

FEMALE DAREDEVILS

I have already mentioned that Antisocials, Daredevils in particular, behave like stereotypical male teenagers. There are female Daredevils also, but they act pretty much like the males. You'll find them riding motorcycles, playing guitars, cruising bars, and getting DUIs just like the guys.

There is, however, a feminine version of the Daredevil with a particularly distinguished provenance—the courtesan. Courtesans are far more than mere prostitutes. Since time immemorial, they have collected powerful and creative males, messed with their minds, and inspired them to actions they might not have considered on their own. What would history, art, music, and literature be without mistresses and muses like Nell Gwyn, Madame de Pompadour, Lou Andreas-Salomé, Ruby Tuesday, and a thousand other unnamed groupies?

HOW VAMPIRES KEEP YOU COMING BACK FOR MORE

Until now, we've talked about how vampires use hypnotic techniques to influence a single decision, like hiring, investing, or calling in sick for a day of skiing. In the real world, vampires prey on people by becoming a part of their lives and influencing them to make one questionable decision after another. Nowhere are the mechanics of this process more visible than in a romantic relationship.

Speaking of romance, do you remember Vampire Alec, the smooth operator in Chapter 4, who swept slightly klutzy Brenda off her feet by seeing her as a dancer?

For a while, they were quite a thing. That is, until . . . Well, maybe I'm getting ahead of myself. Let's go back to the moment the affair really began. They'd seen each other a couple of times but hadn't slept together. At first, Alec was attentive, but in the last day or so he'd become almost cool. That night was the kicker. Brenda was sure they'd made plans to see a movie, but Alec never showed.

> *The intercom buzzes, long and loud in the darkness. Brenda looks at the clock: 2 a.m. "Who is it?" she shouts, as she pads through the bedroom door.*
>
> *"Alec." His voice sounds tinny in the ancient speaker. Like somebody from an old radio show.*
>
> *"Alec?"*
>
> *"I'm sorry, Brenda. I . . . Can I come up just for a minute?"*
>
> *"Alec, it's two o'clock."*
>
> *"Brenda, I'm so sorry. I was, like, I don't know, scared or something. It was just that . . . Damn it, if I don't tell you now, I'll never have the courage again."*
>
> *"Tell me what?"*
>
> *"That I . . . Do I have to say it standing down here?"*
>
> *His words are cut short by the buzz and click of the lobby door.*
>
> *This is definitely not like me, Brenda thinks, as she listens to Alec bounding up the stairs.*

The dark force that caused sensible Brenda to open her door to a guy who'd just stood her up sets the pattern for the rest of the relationship. That dark force is, at least partly, hard wired into her own brain, and into yours. To understand why Daredevils and other Emotional Vampires keep people coming back for more, we have to look at the biology and psychology of attraction. Can science explain why the most difficult people seem to be the most attractive, and why, when we are involved with them and know their faults it is still so hard to let go of them?

10 WAYS TO PROTECT YOURSELF FROM DAREDEVILS

Dealing with Daredevils takes a little willpower, and you need to consciously engage your higher brain centers. To protect yourself from emotional vampires, you have to think, not just feel.

1. Know Them, Know Their History, and Know Your Goal

Your best defense against vampires is to understand the hungers that move them. Daredevils are in the game for excitement, not financial gain or everlasting love. That part of them will probably not change. If it did, they'd be different and far less interesting people. The way to enjoy them is to live for the moment and the good times you share. The way to get drained is to believe that these moments will last.

As with any emotional vampire, it's not possible to know what Daredevils are likely to do without knowing their history. The best predictor of what people will do in the future is what they have done in the past. Don't expect vampires to do something different unless there is some vast change in the situation, like they've suffered an enormous loss as a result of their actions, or they've been clean and sober for a year or more. Even then, don't push your luck. Antisocials like themselves the way they are and seldom learn from their mistakes.

Being clear with yourself about your own goals will help prevent you from making mistakes that you will have to learn from. The number one way in which Daredevils drain other people emotionally is not really the poor vampires' fault at all. Their victims drive themselves crazy trying to get Daredevils to keep their charm, but be more reliable at the same time. Don't even think of it. You can't make a Toyota out of a Ferrari.

Your safest bet is to use Daredevils for what they're best at: fun, and jobs that scare the hell out of everybody else. Daredevils excel at hazardous duty, whether the hazards are physical or emotional. They don't get hurt easily, and when they are hurt, they bounce back quickly. If by chance you are fighting a war, they're the best people to send.

If you aren't fighting a war, it's still a good idea to learn from the military, which from time immemorial has been the most successful employer of Daredevils. The reason can be summed up in one word: structure. Have rules and procedures for everything, especially safety. Make Daredevils follow the chain of command, and have strict sanctions for noncompliance. When the shooting starts, however, step out of the way and let them do their stuff. They'll handle the situation better than you will.

Daredevils also make some of the world's best salespeople. They are motivated by challenge, they don't get deflated by being told no, and their innate charm makes customers like them and trust them. Unlike Used Car Salesmen, who may sell more in the short run by using out-and-out deception, Daredevils keep their customers coming back for more.

2. Get Outside Verification

Among vampires, Antisocials in particular often lie through their teeth. Daredevils usually won't try to deceive you for the fun of it, as Used Car Salesmen will. Daredevils will tell you a version of events that you (or they) would like to hear, rather than the way things are. This is especially true when they talk about sex, drugs, money, what they've done in the past, and what they intend to do in the future. If you can help it, never take their word for anything without some sort of external corroboration.

3. Do What They Don't

Daredevils don't worry. If you are going to hang out with them, you'll need to anticipate problems, because they won't. Worry about yourself, not about them. Protecting Daredevils from themselves is a full-time job with no pay and no results.

4. Pay Attention to Actions, Not Words

Give vampires full credit for doing what you ask them to do, even if they're doing it only to get you off their case. This rule works the other way around as well. Give credit only for performance, never for excuses or explanations. This is especially important when you'd rather believe the excuses.

Hold Antisocials accountable for specific deliverables at specified times. Forget about improving their attitude.

5. Identify Hypnotic Strategies

Daredevils can hypnotize you without breaking a sweat. Just saying "cluck, cluck"—implying that you're cowardly—is one of the shortest and most effective hypnotic inductions known to science. Add devil-may-care charm and an alternative reality that's all fun and excitement with nobody having to pay the bills, and you'll know why Daredevils can have you hooked faster than you can say "adolescent fantasy." Speaking of adolescents, the Daredevil's favorite prey are people who have some doubts about how cool they are, the kinds of people who are especially sensitive to dares.

If there's a Daredevil in your life, make sure you recognize the warning signs of hypnosis: instant rapport, deviating from standard procedure, thinking in superlatives, discounting objective information, and confusion. I will repeat these signs so often throughout the book that I'm tempted to make up a catchy acronym. I'll spare us both the indignity, if you'll promise to remember.

6. Pick Your Battles

With Daredevils, the battle you need to win is the one with substances. Their own brain chemistry is already intoxicating enough to impair their judgment. Under the influence of alcohol or drugs, they can become a real menace. They'll do absolutely anything, and they seldom have even the vaguest notion about when to stop. If you are going to draw any lines in the sand with a Daredevil, they should be around substance abuse.

Before you hire a Daredevil for any position in your life, know where he or she stands with addictions. The big ones are chemicals, gambling, spending, and sex. At least one, and possibly all, of these has been or remains a problem for most Daredevils. Know how a Daredevil has dealt with his or her addiction problems. There is a vast difference in the amount of harm Daredevils can do depending on whether they're actively engaged in abusing substances or are actively involved in efforts (preferably some sort of structured program) to control their abuse.

Never believe that making Daredevils, or any Antisocials, feel guilty will have any sort of positive effect. They are who they are, and they are not ashamed of it. Neither will you be able to "teach them a lesson" by doing the same thing to them that they do to you. They'll see such attacks as an invitation to a free-for-all, which they will win.

7. Let Contingencies Do the Work

If you want to know why the emotional vampires in your life do what they do, and if you have any intention of getting them to do something different, you must understand and use contingencies.

A contingency is an *if-then* situation. *If* someone does a particular thing, *then* certain consequences will follow. Contingencies are important because they are the basis of learning; consequences, rather than words, teach people how to behave.

To a psychologist, learning is not just someone telling you something and you remembering it. It is the pervasive process, whether conscious or unconscious, by which virtually all our thoughts, feelings, and actions come into being. Whether you recognize contingencies or not, you are using them, and they are being used on you. If you want to be effective in dealing with the vampires in your life, you need to know the rules by which these contingencies operate.

The first and most important rule is: *whatever is rewarded will happen more often.* The rewards in our lives are less often objects and more often specific reactions from other people. Emotional vampires are very good at using contingencies. Almost everything they say and do is directed toward getting something. They will do whatever it takes to get what they want. The vampires in your life will flatter you, make promises or threats, throw tantrums, send you on guilt trips, or do anything else their devious little minds dream up. If you give them their way, you are teaching them that manipulating you pays off.

Here is a simple, but powerful example of the kinds of contingencies you may encounter:

> *You finally stand up for yourself and tell a vampire no.*
> *"Why not?" he asks.*
> *Being a fair-minded person, you explain your reasons.*
> *The vampire shakes his head. "Those reasons don't make any sense."*
> *Patiently, you explain again in more detail, hoping that this time he will understand. It is only much later that you realize that he has completely forgotten the fact that you said no.*
> *After an hour, you give in just to get a little peace.*

This example contains most of what you need to understand about contingencies. Pay close attention, because contingencies are one of the most useful and most misunderstood concepts in all of psychology.

In the example, it's easy to see how, by giving in, you reward the vampire for pestering you, thereby teaching him that if he wants something from you, he should keep hammering away until he gets it. There is more to this example than that, because there are many other contingencies in operation.

Let's say that instead of teaching the vampire to badger you, you want to teach him not to. To get the opposite reaction, you have to use the opposite of reward. If, like most people, you think the opposite of reward is punishment, think again. The opposite of reward is no reward. In most situations, punishment is a totally ineffective strategy because it causes unintended side effects. Despite its uselessness, people believe in punishment and keep expecting it to change things for the better:

You've had all you can take. You start yelling: "Why do you always try to manipulate me like this? Can't you just leave me alone?"

The vampire keeps manipulating you because it works. You might think that having someone yell at you and accuse you of manipulation would make you feel guilty enough to stop. (It probably wouldn't, but that's another story.) To a vampire, who lacks the empathy needed to feel guilty, having you get angry shows him that your patience is wearing thin, and that all he has to do is keep at it a little longer and he'll get what he wants. What you think of as punishment, he sees as a reward.

The simplest and most elegant solution in this common situation is not rewarding manipulation. *If you say no, and someone asks you why not, don't answer.* I guarantee that this will work, but most people would never consider using it as a strategy because of yet another kind of contingency.

Getting out of a painful situation is a huge reward. We give in to get a little peace right now, even when we know that giving in ensures that the same thing will happen again. Another rule of contingencies is: *the most immediate reward is always the strongest.* This applies to you, the vampires in your life, and everyone else.

If this is the case, you might rightly wonder, how is anyone ever able to delay gratification? The answer involves something you can do that vampires usually can't: develop internal contingencies.

If I were to ask you why you don't steal, you'd probably tell me that it's because you don't want to go to jail, but that's not the reason. Even if you were absolutely sure that you would not get caught, you still wouldn't steal, because stealing is bad, and you'd feel guilty if you did it. This is an internal contingency. Internal contingencies are what enable mature people to do things that they don't want to do because they are rewarded only in the long run. There is still an immediate reward, but it is a little voice in your head telling you to do the right thing, or warning you that there will be dire consequences if you don't. You use internal contingencies all the time; vampires don't. If you don't exploit this fact, they will.

Let's go back to the example once more to look at the internal contingencies.

Over the years, you have learned the rules of politeness. By following them, you hope to avoid unpleasant consequences like hurting people's feelings or having them get mad at you. One of those rules is, *if somebody asks you a question, answer it.* Most of us follow this rule automatically, without thinking about it. To be effective in dealing with vampires, you have to think. By this I mean that you have to create another internal contingency, a voice in your head that says something like, *Even though it's uncomfortable, I have to do what works.* When you are fighting vampires, there is no place for politeness.

Emotional vampires often make choices that are self-destructive, and then charm people into rescuing them from the consequences. If you're ever tempted to rescue a vampire, think about the contingencies you are setting up and what you're teaching him or her about how the game of life is played.

Throughout this book, you'll learn how to set up effective contingencies with the various types of emotional vampires. You'll also learn how to stick by those contingencies long enough to let them work.

Contingencies with Daredevils need to be external. Daredevils are usually not mature enough to have developed the internal contingencies that determine your behaviors.

Don't threaten to leave the relationship unless you're absolutely sure that's what you want to do. If you aren't, Daredevils will always push you to see how far you'll go. Brinkmanship is the Daredevil's all-time favorite game.

The more automatic the contingency, the better. Then you don't have to be the bad guy. The vampires have to choose whether to follow the rule or face the consequence. A good model is: We are leaving at 6:30. If you're not there, we'll go without you.

The only way Daredevils ever learn anything is by facing the natural consequences of their actions. Never stand in the way of consequences, no matter how good the excuse. You'll only be providing advanced training in how to get around the rules.

8. Choose Your Words as Carefully as You Pick Your Battles

First and foremost, don't attempt to explain the concept of responsibility to a Daredevil. Believe me, it's been tried, and it doesn't work. As soon as you're gone, any Antisocial worth his or her salt will be mimicking your attempts at inspiration behind your back.

What you do need to say to Daredevils is *no* when you mean it. Do not expect a Daredevil to pick up on the subtle nuances of *maybe.*

If you want Antisocials to do something, ask them directly and let them know what you'll do if they don't. Never bluff; they're way better at it than you are. Ditto using deception of any kind. They'll see through it immediately.

Don't bother asking Antisocials to feel what you want them to feel, or to read your mind. Never discuss your relationship; they'll tune you out in less than 15 seconds. If you want Daredevils to listen to you, avoid saying anything that isn't entertaining.

9. Ignore Tantrums

When vampires don't get their way, they throw tantrums. They can explode into all sorts of emotional outbursts whose only purpose is to get you to give in. Don't.

Obviously, this is more easily said than done. Many of the reasons for this have already been discussed in the section on contingencies, but there are still more.

Everybody knows that the way you get people to stop throwing tantrums is to ignore them. This is often difficult because of a misperception of how contingencies operate. When you try to extinguish a tantrum by ignoring it, the first response you always get is called an *extinction burst*. People will do whatever it is you are trying to ignore louder, longer, and more enthusiastically. This might make you believe that ignoring them isn't working, but what it actually means is that it is.

When you are ignoring tantrums, you have to stick with it, or you will teach vampires to be more persistent. Behaviors that are rewarded inconsistently will continue indefinitely. This is why people keep playing slot machines. To deal with vampire tantrums effectively, you have to set up an internal contingency that reminds you not to be a slot machine. As we will see throughout this book, vampires use inconsistency to their advantage, so you will also have to remind yourself not to play slot machines.

As we will see, every type of vampire has its own favorite kinds of tantrums. They yell, they cry, they pout, they lecture, they give you the cold shoulder, or they induce guilt even more skillfully than your mother. Many vampire performances deserve Oscars, or at least Emmys. Regardless of their form, there are two important things to remember about vampire tantrums:

First, *the very fact that vampires are throwing tantrums means that you're winning*. If what you are doing had no effect, they wouldn't need to throw tantrums to get you to stop doing it.

The second thing to remember is to *hang in there, no matter what*. If you give in after the tantrum starts, you'll only teach vampires to be persistent. Every chapter will offer specific suggestions on how to hold out against even world-class performances.

10. Know Your Own Limits

Daredevils don't know where to stop. If there are any limits to be set, you will have to set them. Eventually, no matter what you do, Daredevils will leave. Prepare in your heart to let them drift away like the snows of yesteryear.

If by some chance they stay, congratulations. I guess.

6 Daredevils in Your Life

Daredevil Lovers and Spouses

The biggest problem you will face if you love a Daredevil is that you love a Daredevil. They do what they do so well that you are tempted to believe they can do anything. You are not alone in this belief; it is a cultural myth.

THE ACTION HERO

Hollywood loves Daredevils, too. The films they make about them may lead you to believe they can do the impossible. I don't mean single-handedly foiling plots for world domination. Daredevils *can* do that. What's impossible for them to do is settle down to a day-to-day normal life. Ferraris can't transform themselves into Toyotas when it's time to drive the kids to school.

Daredevils excel in jobs that require stamina, bravery, and thinking quickly on your feet. As cops, firefighters, and soldiers, they protect our society. We give them medals; we read about their adventures and watch them on the big screen. We just don't stay married to them very long.

So, what do you do if you are in love with a Daredevil and want to keep him? Here are some suggestions.

First and Foremost, Know What to Expect   Let's face it, you fell in love with a Daredevil because he was fun and exciting, not because he was good at household chores. Daredevils are vital and exciting because they are perpetual teenagers. You will not be able to make them grow up until they are good and ready. This does not mean you just have to let them do whatever they want.

Don't give up hope. You may not be able to change what Daredevils *are*, but with some effort and perspicacity, you can change what they *do*. This is what this section, and indeed this whole book, is about. You bought a Ferrari. You either have to do the maintenance or trade him in for a Toyota.

Don't Expect Mind Reading   The easiest way to be drained by the Daredevil you love is by believing that his sensitivity to your needs is a direct measure of how much he loves you. This is kind of like believing that dogs who really care about their owners will learn to talk.

No matter how much they care, Daredevils, unless they are actively seducing you, will never be able to figure out what you need and do it without your having to ask. This is at least partly genetic, because most Daredevils are male.

Women are socialized to recognize what needs to be done and to do it without being asked. Lower-order creatures, like men, children, pets, and emotional vampires, cannot be trained to be this perceptive. They must be given specific instructions.

If a woman sees a sock on the floor, she will pick it up and put it where it belongs. If a man sees a sock on the floor, he will assume it is there for a reason and step over it.

Any stereotypical statement you might make about men applies to Antisocials, especially Daredevils. They are masculinity made flesh. As we will see shortly, Histrionics are the walking, talking personifications of feminine stereotypes.

Like every other person who ever loved a Daredevil, as you read this, you are probably thinking: "He's a grown man; do I have to tell him everything?"

Yes, you do, and there is even more to it than that.

Ask, Don't Tell   You can't tell him; you'll have to ask.

It is an understatement to say that Daredevils don't like to be told what to do. If there is one in your life, even if you are far more responsible and conscientious, and even if you are right, he will still never allow you to give him orders.

If you want anything done, you will have to negotiate. Emotional vampires always want something. Don't give it to them unless they give you something you want. To you, saying, "If you want sex tonight, wash the dishes and sweep the floor," may sound like crass manipulation. To a Daredevil, it sounds like a good deal.

Unless you actually have more stars on your collar, a Daredevil will never let you outrank him. The reason I bring this up is that dominance battles in a relationship are not usually about who is the actual boss; they are about who is right and who is wrong. The content is often ridiculous. From 40 years of doing marital therapy, I can tell you that after sex, money, and child discipline, the next most frequent thing that couples argue about is how to load the dishwasher. Everyone, it seems, believes that there is a right way and a wrong way to do this.

Life offers a cruel choice: you can be right or happy. Not both. This is true regardless of whom you may be involved with, but it is especially true if there is an emotional vampire in your life. For you to be right, someone has to be wrong for you. All you really win is resentment, and the certainty of another argument.

Structure, Structure, Structure   As I have said before, if there is a Daredevil in your life, take a tip from the organizations in which they are most successful—police and fire departments and the military. All these organizations have rules and regulations, and extensive training in how to follow them. They also have assigned tasks and duty rosters that clearly specify who is responsible for what and when. If you love a Daredevil, you will need duty rosters as well.

Unlike in the military, the duty rosters at home are not handed down by someone of higher rank; they are created by negotiation, like between labor and management, except it's never clear which is which.

Whatever the task, discuss it, decide what actions are necessary, and negotiate a roster specifying who is to do what and when.

This works whether you're talking about taking out the garbage or raising children. Always know who is responsible for what.

If you are a new family, having a parent on duty schedule is essential for survival. Never go to bed without agreeing whose turn it is to get up in the night. The last thing you want is to argue about this at three in the morning.

Whether the duty is that of parent, dishwasher, or garbage taker-outer, all jobs must have authority as well as responsibility. The person on duty's decisions are final. No matter how bad they are, they cannot be changed without a court-martial.

Ignore Grumbling   All men grumble, and all men fart. You should treat both in pretty much the same way. Do not reward them with your attention.

Give him full credit for getting the job done. Pay no attention to attitude. The issue is doing, not doing for the right reason.

When a Daredevil starts grumbling, before you make up soap operas in your mind, look at the contingencies involved. If someone can get out of unpleasant tasks by getting a little surly, what do you think he's going to do, regardless of how much he loves you? What are you teaching him? If you happen to be a woman, you were socialized to pay attention to other people's needs. This is an admirable skill. Don't let vampires use it against you.

Send Him on Missions Daredevils are at their best when they are fixing cars, fighting bad guys, killing animals to stock the family larder, or partying after a successful hunt. At the drop of a hint, they will drop whatever they're doing to deal with an emergency, real or contrived. Use your imagination to keep them busy with fixing, hunting, rescuing, and other manly tasks. If you're smart, you can make doing the laundry sound manly. If Daredevils have too much time on their hands, they will create missions of their own. You will probably not like these missions.

Keep Doing Exciting Things What wins a Daredevil's heart is a playmate who likes the same things he does. Whatever the activity—sports, hiking, climbing, camping, surfing, hunting, fishing, guerrilla sex, or jumping out of airplanes—once you start, you will have to continue participating as long as you want the relationship to last.

If you poop out or get too busy with more important things, your Daredevil will eventually find another playmate. I am not defending this practice, only pointing out that doing stimulating things together is the lifeblood of a relationship with a Daredevil. More boring tasks will have to be scheduled around the fun stuff. Or else.

Never pretend to like what a daredevil likes in hopes of reeling him in, expecting that you can stop doing whatever it is once you have caught him. If you want a long-term commitment, you will have to make one also.

Don't Be His Drinking Buddy The one activity you should not keep doing together is substance abuse. Snowboarding does not destroy lives; drinking does. If his activity of choice is partying, don't assume that he will cut down on it when he has more responsibilities. Stop now in favor of a healthier and more active lifestyle. If he doesn't stop with you, know what to expect. If you can't stop, either don't start or get help now. If there is a Daredevil in your life, the one battle you must win is with substance abuse. We will discuss addiction more extensively in a few pages.

If you are in love with a Daredevil, you have a tiger by the tail. If you don't love riding roller coasters with tigers, go find an accountant. Your life will be less exciting, but it will be safer and more predictable.

THE LIAR

Speaking of myths, one that you will have to confront is that truth and lies are black and white, and that anyone who deviates from the truth is a pathological liar who can't be trusted about anything.

Pathological liars do exist, but they are rarer than you think. They will be discussed in the chapters on Used Car salesman. All emotional vampires lie, but they lie in different ways and for different reasons. Different kinds of lies require different strategies. Daredevils lie to get out of very immediate consequences. They rarely think deeply enough to consider concepts like truth and honesty. Their lies are generally of the dog-ate-my-homework variety.

THE UNFAITHFUL LOVER

Daredevils usually love sex. They may cheat if the opportunity presents itself. You will have to decide if that is a deal-breaker in your relationship.

> *Cathy picks up Kevin's cell phone looking for contact information on a mutual friend. As the phone comes to life, a picture of a woman appears. She's holding an umbrella drink.*
>
> *"Who is this?" Cathy asks, showing the picture to Kevin.*
>
> *"Oh," Kevin says. "She was at the conference I went to last month. She wanted me to take her picture."*

Before we go any further into Kevin's explanation about who the woman in the picture is, we need to discuss a concept from philosophy. The rule is called "*Ockham's Razor*" which, when boiled down, suggests: The simplest explanation is usually the correct one.

If there is a Daredevil in your life, you may find yourself in the same position as Cathy. What should you do?

First, Ask for Time to Think   Close down the discussion right there. Do not say what you think or what you are going to do, because you don't know. The last thing you need is to appear to accept a cock-and-bull story, or to be maneuvered into an irrelevant discussion of trust, love, or your shortcomings as a partner. All the clients I have seen in this situation have wished that they had not lost control when the first evidence showed up. Give yourself that chance. Withdraw from the discussion and think it through before you freak out.

Aside from giving you a chance to get your thoughts in order, this approach will have a much more profound effect on your errant partner than anything else you might say or do. His behavior remains the problem, rather than being supplanted by your emotional response.

Evaluate the Evidence   In the time of silence and self-examination that you ask for, you have to decide whether there is real evidence or only your own insecurity. Hard data, like pictures on a phone or text messages, are very different from flirting at a party or being gone too long on an errand. Evaluate the facts and know yourself.

If you do not score high on the Paranoid vampire checklist in Chapter 25, you are probably not making this up. It is possible that Cathy could be wrong, that Kevin's explanations are true. If they are, there will be other evidence, and he will produce it.

If this is the first time something like this has happened, it is conceivable that it is a stupid mistake that can be rectified. If there have been previous affairs, don't fool yourself.

Focus on Infidelity, Not Lying   Don't imagine that the situation would be any different if your partner came to you and said, "Honey, I'm having an affair."

Decide What Infidelity Means to You   Is it so unthinkable that it means that the relationship is over? If so, it's time to consult an attorney. If you don't know, consult a therapist. The question at this point is about your deepest feelings, not whether you should dump the Daredevil or stay with him. There will be many people who will offer an opinion on that question should you ask. Don't ask. Your decision should be based on what you feel and why you feel it. A therapist can help you sort this out better than a friend can.

Now You Are Ready to Talk   Set a time to discuss the issue. Ask your partner what he or she thinks should be done. If you get more cock-and-bull stories without hard evidence, just get up and walk away. Try it one more time before you make your final decision.

If You Plan to Stay Together, Get Professional Help Sooner Rather than Later   There are so many issues involved in infidelity. You will need help to sort them out and deal with them one at a time. Get it.

DAREDEVIL EX-HUSBAND

Many women grow out of the Daredevils they married when they were in their twenties. They finally get tired of all the things they have to put up with to maintain that Ferrari. If you are one of them, you know what I'm talking about. Your friends and family have been telling you for years to get rid of the guy. When you finally decide to do it, it's much harder than you expect.

Shelly has finally had it with Dylan. She can no longer take the lies, the partying, the irresponsibility, and the cold distance, not to mention that woman. Shelly figures a divorce will be a relief to both of them. She consults with a lawyer and tells Dylan to move out.

All of a sudden, to her great surprise, she becomes the most important thing in Dylan's life. For years, all she has wanted was a little consideration, affection, and emotional support, like when they were dating. There was nothing.

Now, after the papers have been served, here he is on her doorstep late at night with tears, promises, and a bouquet, that handsome devil who so many years ago stole her heart. Maybe after all this time he is finally changing. That's what he says. Can she believe him?

Well, one more night together can't hurt anything.

Anything is possible, but it is not likely that imminent divorce has caused Dylan to grow up—especially since he is still acting exactly like a Daredevil. The relationship is now more exciting and worth pursuing because he can't have it any more. He will say and do anything to get it back. Then what?

I would not be so presumptuous as to tell Shelly what to do with Dylan there on her doorstep. I might tell her that nothing has really changed, but in her heart she knows that already. I will tell her that almost everyone who has ever tried to divorce a Daredevil has found herself in the same position, and that almost everyone invites him in and later feels that she can't tell her friends and family because they wouldn't understand. Vampires thrive in the shadows of dark secrets.

If you, like Shelly, are trying to divorce a Daredevil, or any other kind of emotional vampire, I do have a few suggestions.

Don't Keep Secrets If you admit your mixed emotions and erratic behavior, you may discover that all your friends, and maybe even your mother (and maybe your father, too), has invited a vampire ex back to bed. If you don't, you may feel like you are the only person in the world who has ever been that stupid. Believe me, you aren't. Deciding whether to proceed with a divorce is painful, difficult, and confusing. Don't try to do it alone or, worse, with the vampire himself as your only confidant. You need to be able to think clearly and talk openly to decide what is best for you.

Give It Time If you are considering taking a vampire back, don't do it right away. Give it enough time to see if the changes he promises actually persist. The most important thing he has to prove to you is that he now has patience, and can tolerate not getting what he wants right when he wants it. Sending you 30 texts a day might be different and even flattering, but it is more likely to indicate impatience than a real change in motivation.

If you decide to go ahead with the divorce, here are some things to consider.

Stop Talking to Him You may hope that things will be reasonable and amicable, but don't count on it. Spurned Daredevils sometimes just wander away, or they might get vicious. Or both. If you continue to talk to him, he will try every hypnotic technique he knows.

Line up friends and family to be like sponsors in AA to help you get over your vampire addiction. If you are thinking about talking to him, call them instead.

If he wants to talk to someone, have it be your lawyer.

Get a Good Lawyer Don't even think of a DIY divorce. You will need a lawyer to keep you grounded in reality.

Picking a good lawyer is difficult because the legal profession is itself full of vampires. Talk to friends and interview a few attorneys before you make your choice.

Good lawyers should:

- *Return calls promptly.* I'm surprised at how many lawyers don't. I'm talking about calls during office hours. Never accept an attorney who doesn't get back to you for days, unless someone from the office contacts you to explain why. Even then, be skeptical. How long does a phone call take?
- *Be more decisive than you are.* Good lawyers should be polite, but not necessarily nice. The last thing you want is a lawyer who is too conflict-avoidant to deal effectively with the asshole that your ex will hire. You want your lawyer to be stronger and more decisive than you are, not less.
- *Be proactive.* You do not want a lawyer who counsels you to wait to see what someone else does. The battle goes to whoever gets there first with the most. This is particularly true in matters of custody and visitation. Always ask an attorney what the overall plan is. If there is no overall plan, you have no attorney.

Once the Divorce Is Final, Never Ever Deviate from the Letter of the Decree You've heard the one about what happens if you let a camel put his nose in your tent. Always remember that your ex is that camel.

Vampires don't play by the rules. If you are divorced from one, the best time to make a big deal about this is at the first infraction. This applies to making payments, adhering to visitation schedules, or anything else. Don't let the little things go, because they will become big things. It is for these later issues more than for the divorce itself that you need a lawyer who is more proactive and aggressive than you are.

DAREDEVIL DADS

A side effect of marriage is having children. Daredevils seem to have a lot of them, but they are often scattered about in various different families. For this reason, we will need to look at the Daredevil dad from several different perspectives.

If a Daredevil Is the Father of Your Children

Let's go back a few years before Shelly and Dylan got divorced:

> When it comes to having fun, Dylan has always been a great dad. It's just that when the fun stops, so does he. Shelly keeps trying to explain that being a dad means doing things that are necessary but not fun, like changing diapers, helping with homework, taking kids to the doctor, going to boring school programs, and the biggie, enforcing rules consistently. Dylan's approach to rules is to either ignore them or fly off the handle at tiny infractions that make his life more difficult.

Could Shelly have done things so differently that it would have affected how things came out in the end? There's no saying. If you are trying to parent with a Daredevil, I do have a few suggestions.

Structure, Structure, Structure   Remember this?

With children and emotional vampires, it's absolutely essential that you deal with one thing at a time. Many of the day-to-day tasks of parenting are predictable. Whether it's changing diapers or setting curfews, each one needs to be discussed, and some agreement needs to be reached about how they are to be done, who does them, and when. It will help to have things written down in a manual that can be consulted later.

This approach may seem tedious and unnecessary to someone who already knows how to do things and believes that everyone else should also. There will always be other, more immediate demands on your time, but believe me, setting structure in advance is not a wasted effort. The last thing you want is to be arguing about how things should have been done when they have already been done poorly or not done at all.

Stick with the Parent on Duty Roster Parent on duty is a concept that continues to be useful long after your children have grown out of midnight feedings and changes. There are two reasons for this. The first, the importance of clarity and structure, we have already discussed. The second is more subtle. If you want a partner to stay involved with child rearing, he will need to do it his own way, even if you think his way is wrong. Aside from basic safety issues, there are no right and wrong ways to parent, only opinions.

The reward for taking care of parent-on-duty responsibilities is absolute control. I bring this up because in dealing with irresponsible behavior in a spouse, many people become overly responsible to the point of rigidity.

A clue that this might be happening is being asked, "Why should I do anything when everything I do is wrong?" If you are ever asked this question, it would do you well to remember that it is about contingencies, rather than about who is right or wrong.

If Dad Is Your Daredevil Ex

Shelly tried hard, but nothing worked.

> *Now that the divorce is final, things have gotten worse. Shelly could write a book about how unreliable Dylan is with money, with schedules, with everything. She can't even count how many times he has let the kids down, and when he does take them, it's almost impossible to get them back into a routine after he lets them run wild. The thing that really gets to her is that even with all his faults and broken promises, the kids still think their dad is the greatest thing since sliced bread.*
>
> *It's not that she's jealous, but why does she have to do all the work of child rearing when he gets all the fun?*
>
> *Okay, so she is jealous.*

Daredevils are the original good-time dads. This invariably does more damage to the ex-spouse than it does to the kids. If you are in this situation, here are some suggestions.

Pick Your Battles Remember, Daredevils don't like to be told what to do. The more battles you try to fight over your children's needs, the less effective you will be. It does not matter that you're right; with a vampire, the number of battles you can win is very limited. Make sure they are the important ones.

Children are incredibly resilient. They can handle a lot of shoddy parenting and still come out fine. A good rule of thumb is restricting yourself to safety issues and situations in which your child actually asks you to intervene. Even then, it will work better if the child speaks for him- or herself.

By the way, Daredevil authority issues can be exploited. Should you want one to stay away, all you have to do is tell him he needs to spend more time with his children.

Understand Your Own Motivation   Before you bring up parenting issues to a Daredevil Dad, look into your own heart. How much of your desire to intervene is based on your child's need, and how much is motivated by your own anger and jealousy. Vampires, who are much better at deception than you'll ever be, will immediately know if you're sniping at them from behind your children.

Worse than that, your children will know, and feel that to be loyal to you, they have to be against their dad. Needless to say, this is not a situation you want to foster.

Communicate Directly   Difficult as it may be to talk to him, never send messages to Dad through the kids. The chances of confusion and misinterpretation are boundless. By communicating indirectly, you can create just the kind of environment in which vampires flourish.

Lighten Up   Know always that at some level your kids understand and appreciate the love, effort and structure that you provide that their dad doesn't. Unfortunately, they probably won't say anything about it until they become parents themselves. If you want your kids to think you're an awesome mom sooner, lighten up and have more fun with them, even if you think that there are more important things to be done.

If Your Dad Is a Daredevil

Daredevil dads are fun one minute, but they let you down in the next. Whether you are 10 or 60, it's up to you to figure out how you're going to live with that.

> *Dylan's son Jake loves baseball. At least part of the reason was that his dad loved it, too. When he was younger, before the divorce, they used to play catch all the time. Now, they never do. It's too bad, because Jake has gotten really good. He's a starter this year. His dad keeps promising to come to games, but he always has an excuse for not showing up.*

Here are some suggestions that might help Jake or anybody else whose vampire dad is a no-show, either literally or figuratively.

Understand That It's Him, Not You Responsibility is supposed to flow from parent to child. It's not your job to make attending to your needs easy and fun.

Your dad isn't there for you because there is something lacking in him, not in you. The more you try to get his attention and approval, the more of yourself you will lose. This is very sad, but there isn't much you can do about it.

Get out there and play ball because you want to. Someone will notice.

Speak for Yourself If you don't like the way your dad treats you, tell him how you feel and what you want. Don't let anyone else speak for you. Your words are more likely to affect him than anyone else's, but they may not. Improve your chances by saying exactly what you mean; don't hint and expect him to get it. Tell him how you feel and what you want, not that he's acting like a jerk.

Let Go of Your Resentment It's easy to blame all the bad things in your life on lousy parents. The sooner you stop doing so, however, the more energy you will have to devote to yourself, and the happier and more successful you will be. If you listen to this advice now, it will save you a few years of therapy later.

When He Needs You, Give Yourself Permission to Say No Sooner or later, your Daredevil dad will need you. He'll be bored, broke, lonely, or too old to take care of himself. It is your right to say no. This is one of the hardest things you'll ever do if you are a responsible person. The only thing harder is being the next in line to take care of a person who has never had to take care of himself. Once you start, he won't let you stop. Or you won't let yourself.

Help him if you feel you must, but understand that it is okay to say no. Remember the direction in which responsibility is supposed to flow.

DAREDEVIL ADULT CHILDREN

As he takes out his checkbook, Dylan's father sighs. He looks at his son, and, with all the gravitas he can muster, says, "Okay, I'll pay this month's rent, but this is the very last time."

Both of them know it won't be.

If your adult child is an emotional vampire, you will have to make hard choices for the rest of your life. You will know that you shouldn't intervene, but the alternative will always be unthinkable. You just won't be able to let him go to jail, live on the street, or have no relationship with his children.

Being a father myself, I know that love always triumphs over good sense. I will not insult you by telling you to leave him to his fate. What I will tell you is that there is no more thankless place to be than standing between an emotional vampire and the consequences of his own actions. Of course, you know that already.

I will also tell you a few other things that might prove useful if your adult child is a Daredevil, or any other kind of emotional vampire.

Always Make a Vampire Ask Directly

The usual way vampires get their parents to bail them out is by telling a tale of woe. They seem so upset and hopeless that you feel you have to step in to save the day. We have all done this with our children, and we should all stop. Right now.

If a vampire wants something, he or she should always have to ask. That way, you can maintain some control over the transaction. You can say yes or no, or specify what you want in return.

Give Up the Pretext of Loans

Let's get real here. Daredevils always need money, and if you have it, you will always give it to them. Don't even pretend that the money is a loan, because we all know you will never be paid back.

As with everything you do with emotional vampires, think of the contingencies involved before you act. Loans involve giving the reward first, then hoping that the other person will live up to his or her part of the bargain. This is a lousy business practice. It is the reason that banks require collateral and credit cards charge usurious interest rates, but as we well know, those strategies don't work with emotional vampires. I am always surprised at how long they can go without consequences for failing to make payments.

If banks can't make Daredevils pay their debts, you certainly can't. You're not going to repossess their collateral, so forget about even pretending that the money you give them is a loan.

Set Contingencies You Can Stick With

At the very least, put your wayward child on a salary—however many dollars you can afford on the first of the month. Try and limit it to that.

Better yet, make it a real salary. Get your vampire to do something *before* you give him any money. That something can be for you, like mowing your lawn or washing your car. This will usually involve ridiculous overpayment for a symbolic gesture.

A more creative strategy would be to make what you pay for something that will benefit your vampire or his family. Make money contingent on his finishing his résumé, doing his taxes, passing a class, or volunteering at his kids' school. Whatever it is, demand hard evidence before you hand over any money.

Whatever contingency you set, remember: a deal's a deal.

Put It in Writing

With an emotional vampire, a verbal contract isn't worth the paper it's written on. Whatever agreements you make should be written and signed by all parties involved. Remember, vampires thrive on confusion and misunderstanding.

Pay the Bill, Don't Give the Money

Whenever possible, see that any money you give goes directly to the bank, the landlord, or the power company. Cash given to a vampire has a way of disappearing before it gets where it's supposed to go.

Whatever You Give, Set Limits Before You Start

Whether it's money, babysitting, or letting your child move in, if you give anything to a vampire, always specify how much, how long, and what will happen if he or she goes over the limit. Needless to say, you will have to stick to whatever limits you set. This will always be easier if the limits are set in advance.

Do the Best You Can

Nobody can follow all the suggestions I have offered about how to handle Daredevil adult children. Children of whatever age can soften our hearts and our resolve like no one else can. Good luck. All you can do is your best.

Daredevils are the emotional vampires you will encounter most frequently. As I said earlier in this chapter, they are the basic model. The suggestions I make about how to deal with them effectively apply to most other types of vampires as well.

In the next few chapters, we will be discussing other types of Antisocial vampires who are darker and more dangerous.

7 Antisocial Used Car Salesmen

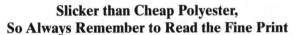

**Slicker than Cheap Polyester,
So Always Remember to Read the Fine Print**

It is not my intention to impugn the dignity of men and women who actually sell used cars for a living. I'm sure most of them are upstanding citizens. The used car salesmen that lend their name to the vampires in this section are those archetypal personifications of verbal chicanery who, clad in white shoes, pinky rings, and plaid polyester jackets, tinker with odometers and claim that their warranties cover *everything* (except anything that breaks).

All emotional vampires lie. Daredevils lie because it's the easiest thing to do at the time, Histrionics lie to you because they believe the lies they tell themselves, Narcissists lie because it's expedient, Obsessive-Compulsives lie because they can't possibly be wrong, and Paranoids lie when the facts don't support their beliefs. Used Car Salesmen lie because they like it.

Antisocials of all kinds love excitement. Used Car Salesmen are partial to the shadowy thrills of deceit. It is not so much that they get off on lying for its own sake; it's more that they want the things they want so much that they don't mind lying to get them. To their prey, the distinction is immaterial. You have it, they want it, and they'll happily lie, cheat, or steal to get it.

Used Car Salesmen have the terrifying ability to imitate human warmth without feeling anything but desire for something you have. If you think that the worst they can do is trick you into paying a lot of money for a piece of junk, you may be in serious danger.

Heidi met Jeff on a Christian singles website. She was hesitant about using an online service, but one of her friends had met her husband there, so she thought she'd give it a try. Jeff seems really nice. Good looking, too. He's an engineer who consults at construction sites, so he travels quite a bit. This is not a problem for Heidi. She's been on her own so long that she appreciates having some space.

Jeff is an old-fashioned gentleman; he actually brings flowers and opens doors for her. He insists on paying for everything. She feels like she's living in a romance novel.

Heidi's friends are dying to meet Jeff, but he keeps putting it off. He's actually kind of shy. Heidi finds this endearing. A man who's so successful and outwardly confident being shy kind of makes him seem like a little boy. She wonders how, after all these years, she could be so lucky.

Heidi's friend Jeanne has her doubts.

"Heidi, what do you actually know about him? Where does he live?"

"Over on the Westside."

"Have you been there?"

"No, it's just a small condo. He doesn't need much; he travels a lot on business."

"Who does he work for?"

"Some engineering consulting firm."

"Let's Google him."

"I already have, but Jeff Wilson is such a common name. There were thousands of them."

"Heidi," Jeanne says, "I don't like this. I hate to say it, but you're pretty well off . . ."

"He's not after my money. He has plenty of his own."

"How do you know?"

Heidi turns bright red. "It's kind of personal."

"Well, we were down at the beach. On the spur of the moment, he asked me if I'd like to stay over. We got a room at a really nice B&B, but when we were checking in, he couldn't find his wallet. I used my credit card. I said it was okay, that I didn't mind paying for it. But the very next day, he paid me back. An envelope of money with a rose on top."

It turned out that "Jeff" was a confidence man, and he ended up bilking Heidi out of a considerable sum of money. She discovered later that he had used that same lost wallet trick on several other women.

What hurt Heidi even more than her broken heart was the fact that she had been so thoroughly taken in.

"How could I be so stupid?"

That is an important and relevant question, but it should be asked not the way Heidi did, for self-castigation, but for information. How do Antisocial Used Car Salesmen persuade us to make decisions that in retrospect seem so stupid? The best way to protect ourselves is to know their techniques and recognize them before the fog of hypnotic confusion settles in upon our brain.

The first and most important thing to remember is something we've all heard before but seem to forget in the heat of the moment: *if a deal seems too good to be true, it is.*

The funny thing is that one of the best ways to make us act stupidly is by making us believe that we are being really smart.

How could you be so stupid? The answer is the same as for everyone else who has been drawn in and drained by an emotional vampire. You were hypnotized.

USED CAR HYPNOSIS

As you can imagine, Used Car Salesmen are masters of using hypnosis for their own personal gain. Their interpersonal world is one sales pitch after another. In their element, they twist and twirl, as graceful as figure skaters and as venomous as snakes.

It's not all that easy to recognize a sales pitch. The best ones go by so quickly that the ink on the contract is dry and the paper is safely filed away before you know you've bought anything. Most sales pitches are based on built-in polite responses—the vampire gives you something, and before you know it you're offering a bite of your neck, just to be nice.

My discussion of various kinds of sales pitches is strongly influenced by the work of Robert Cialdini,* a social psychologist who has made a career of understanding the ways in which people influence one another. He points out that there are only a limited number of possible sales pitches, but an infinite variety of ways in which each may be used. All the patterns rely on people choosing the automatic, socially acceptable response, rather than thinking closely about what they're being asked to do.

Vampire sales pitches usually follow one of seven basic patterns.

Do It Because You Like Me

It's easy to like a vampire. In that short period of time when there is some doubt as to whether you are going to give them what they want, Used Car

---

*Robert B. Cialdini, *Influence: The Psychology of Persuasion*, 5th ed. (New York: Prentice-Hall, 2008).

Salesmen can sparkle with wit and glow with synthetic kindness. The display usually ends three seconds after you give in, but while it lasts, it smells as sweet as cherry blossoms on a warm spring day. No one else on the face of the earth is half as charming as a vampire who wants something. Ask Heidi about the hundreds of endearing little things Jeff did to draw her in.

Research shows that the best way to get people to like you is to show an interest in them. Emotional vampires don't need to read the research; they do what they do instinctively.

From the very beginning, they seem so interested in you, your kids, your hobbies, or whatever else they can get you to talk about. Emotional vampires are the most charming people you'll ever meet. Do bear in mind that the original meaning of the word *charming* was "casting a magic spell."

It's not just intuitive charm that makes you like Used Car Salesmen; it's technique. People tend to like people that they perceive to be similar to themselves. Used Car Salesmen usually begin their pitch by establishing a perception of similarity. They watch you closely. They ask questions about who you are, what you like, and what you think, then profess to like and believe in the same sorts of things. Unless you're paying attention, their probes and ploys can seem like innocuous chitchat.

When actual salespeople start doing this, you can easily steer the conversation back to the product. When other people begin asking a lot of questions about you, ask yourself if they might be trying to sell you something, and what it might be. Of course, they might just be friendly, but then again, friendliness is the most common technique used to elicit information.

One way to recognize the "like me" sales pitch for sure is to identify a repeating theme. Over a period of time, a vampire might unconsciously attempt to establish similarity in a number of different areas. If casual conversations keep drifting back to how much you're alike, it's either an amazing coincidence or a Used Car Salesman who's softening you up for the kill.

Another, more subtle way in which Used Car Salesmen use the perception of similarity to take advantage of people is to identify themselves as members of the same religion or as having the same political leanings. This approach is becoming much more common. How many ads have you seen that have a fish logo or an American flag? It may be reasonable to want to give your business to someone who believes what you believe, but is it relevant? Ask yourself why someone would do a better job of fixing your clogged drain because he is a Christian or a right-leaning patriot. Or a vegan, for that matter.

One of the unspoken assumptions that vampires take advantage of is that both of you are part of an oppressed minority who are against the same things. Unfortunately, being similar in what you hate seems to form a stronger bond more quickly than being similar in what you love, so watch out and check qualifications rather than politics or religion.

At work, Chris and his buddies love to listen to conservative talk radio. A couple of them would be card-carrying Tea Party members if Tea Party members carried cards. Anyway, it was these guys who told Chris about Darla, a bookkeeper who knows way more about taxes than most accountants. She can help little guys exploit the same loopholes in the tax code that big corporations use.

Chris goes to see Darla. Her office is decorated with flags and eagles. More important than that, what she says makes sense. "You know Wall Street and Washington work hand in hand. The tax laws are full of all kinds of giveaways that the IRS doesn't want you to know about."

Her fees are pretty steep, but she assures Chris that he will probably more than make it up in the size of his refund.

As it turns out, she's right. With dollar signs in his eyes, Chris files his return. He's not much good with numbers, so he doesn't check it too closely. Anyway, Darla knows what she's doing.

Unfortunately, when he gets the audit notice, Darla is nowhere to be found. She didn't sign her name as a third-party preparer. She said that was one of those red flags that the IRS looks for.

Chris ended up paying back his refund and more in penalties.

Please don't assume from what I've written so far that conservatives have a monopoly on financial chicanery. Liberals can be just as sleazy.

Naomi is trying to be a vegetarian. She hopes to be a vegan someday like her friend Sierra, who is also heavily, and judgmentally, into animal rights and anything else that is good for the planet.

One day Sierra approaches Naomi with a proposition. "You've never heard of Super Green? It's rated as the most environmentally responsible company in the country. Its vitamins are the purest available. All its products are made from natural substances with no animal testing. The great thing is, its products work even better than all that chemical garbage you get at the grocery store."

After trying some free samples, Naomi has to agree that the stuff works. It smells great, too. So what if it is more expensive? It's way better for the planet, and it just about sells itself.

Naomi gets talked into getting in on the ground floor as a distributor, which requires investing about a thousand dollars in samples, stock, and glossy brochures.

One of Naomi's first sales calls is to her sister, whose husband teaches high school chemistry. "Chemicals are chemicals, Naomi. Petroleum is a natural ingredient. I don't think this stuff is any different from what you'd get at the store."

"But they're rated as the most environmentally responsible company in America."

"By whom?"

Naomi looks at the brochure. "It doesn't say."

Selling was hard enough for Naomi as it was. Now she has lost her faith in the product, and she just can't bring herself to make more sales calls or to throw a party. She's afraid that Sierra will be upset, so she avoids her.

It's not totally clear in this example who is being conned and who is doing the conning. Sierra was undoubtedly convinced by the person who sold the product to her, who herself was probably convinced by the Super Green company. However, being convinced is one thing. Selling distributorships to a friend who has a hard time saying no and is probably too timid to sell is another. Of course, if you want to make money, you have to move product and distributorships.

Needless to say, these days everybody claims to be green and gluten-free. Very few of these claims are actually checked because nobody has the authority or the inclination to do so, especially when the claims are made by a small start-up company that sells its products out of people's homes.

To protect yourself from charming Used Car Salesmen, remember that just because you like certain people, have a similar background, or have the same friends or enemies, it doesn't mean that you have to buy whatever story they are selling.

Do It to Reciprocate

Used Car Salesmen would have you believe that because they gave you something, you owe them something back. In their view, small favors are like the free samples those motherly types hand out in grocery stores. The purpose is not to nourish you, but to get you to buy.

Protect yourself by understanding that a gift or a favor is not a contract unless you make it into one. When someone offers to do something for you or give you something, ask yourself if there are obvious strings attached. If you feel obligated, you can reciprocate quickly with something of equal value, before you are asked for something larger later on. Remember, even if there are strings attached, they bind you only if you let them.

Do It Because Everybody Else Is Doing It

Used Car Salesmen are great at creating a bandwagon for you to jump on. Before you do, remember what your mother said: "If all your friends jump off a cliff, does that mean you should, too?"

This Offer Good for a Limited Time Only

Vampires know that anything that is scarce takes on a value far beyond its intrinsic worth. Call it the Tickle Me Elmo effect.

Do It to Be Consistent

Cognitive dissonance, that amazing force that bends reality to conform to the choices we have already made, is what Emerson would call foolish consistency. Used Car Salesmen call it a gold mine. They're all too ready to sic the hobgoblin of small minds on you until you do what they want.

Foolish consistency is the psychological principle that makes grooming possible. People try to maintain an internal sense of consistency between their actions and their beliefs. This is hard enough to do with careful thought. It's almost impossible when a vampire is trying to confuse your perceptions about who you are and what you believe by making you cross one little line after another.

> *Sierra, in her group of friends, is the arbiter of morality. If you are not green enough, or politically correct enough, or generous enough to the right charity, she will tell you—and everybody else.*
>
> *Sierra's favorite charity is herself. In return for her approval, her friends are expected to pick up tabs, help her with her projects, donate items to her yard sales, and buy whatever she is selling.*
>
> *Over a period of years, her friends have come to realize that their relationship with Sierra has a high price tag, but they are in so deeply that if they tried to get out, they would lose not only Sierra's approval, but that of the rest of the group. Every time they get an e-mail with yet another request, her friends secretly sigh, then do whatever she wants.*

You can protect yourself from the hobgoblin of small minds by never agreeing to a request right away. Always ask for time to think about it. This will give you a chance to decide about each request separately. If you say no, you can offer to do something else instead, and thereby at least partially avoid the charge of disloyalty. Buy one bottle of cleaner rather than a distributorship.

Do It or Else

Mark's boss looks over the spreadsheet and shakes his head. "I can't believe these numbers. Do you realize what this could do to our share price—not to mention our jobs? Look over this spreadsheet really carefully. I'm sure there is a mistake somewhere."

Nobody ever specifically orders anyone to cook the books. It always happens in a situation like this, with a vague request backed up by an implied threat.

If a vampire should put you in this position, you will have to decide what your integrity is worth.

Your best defense in a situation like this is to be completely literal, ignoring the underlying message. Look over the spreadsheet, and if there is no mistake, say so. Vampires will rarely give you a direct order to do something illegal. They will try to preserve their deniability. There will be consequences, but probably not something that could get you indicted.

You Can Believe Me—I'm an Authority

Vampires know that people are likely to do what authority figures tell them. Regardless.

In the most chilling social psychology experiment of all time, Stanley Milgram,* who was trying to understand why relatively normal people participated in the Holocaust, demonstrated that average people would administer what they believed were potentially lethal electric shocks because someone in a white coat told them it was okay. Unquestioning belief can create mass murderers and suicide bombers.

On the other hand, all societies are built around trust in authority. Most of the time, that trust is justified. Everyone can cite exceptions to this general rule, but the fact remains that people who have some knowledge of what they're talking about usually give you better advice than, say, your brother-in-law.

A very dangerous trend in the world today is confusing someone who believes what you believe with someone who knows what he or she is talk-

---

*Stanley Milgram, *Obedience to Authority* (New York: Harper & Row, 1974).

ing about. Everyone does this to a certain extent, but more and more it is becoming the official doctrine of whatever religious or political group people belong to. Dogma is superseding fact, because everywhere, every day people are being told by the most nefarious vampires imaginable that anything that people with different beliefs tell them cannot be a fact.

The scientific method used to be the bastion against superstition, but sadly, to me at least, superstition seems to be winning, as it seems that the preponderance of the evidence can be negated by producing one scientist who disagrees.

In my wildest paranoid fantasies, I imagine that somewhere there is an institute staffed by vampire scientists who will say that cigarettes don't cause cancer, that greenhouse gases don't affect the climate, or that evolution is a myth because God planted fossils as a test of faith.

To protect yourself, search for your own hard evidence before you believe what any vampire authority figure tells you.

IS HONESTY REALLY THE BEST POLICY?

It depends on what you mean by *best*. If you mean does honesty yield the most internal rewards, then the answer is yes. Absolutely.

If you mean is honesty the best way to make money or amass power—well, no.

This is probably why there are so many successful Used Car Salesmen. So watch out.

8 Vampire Bullies

**Big, Scary, Powerful, and Stupid as the Guys
Who Used to Take Lunch Money**

There are few experiences that are more emotionally draining than being yelled at. If you've met a vampire Bully, you know. You also know that the draining comes not just from the yelling itself, but from constantly walking on eggshells because you might be yelled at, or constantly replaying the yelling in your mind, thinking of all the things you should have said. Welcome to the world of the Antisocial Bully.

Like the rest of the Antisocial types, Bullies are hooked on excitement. Their drug of choice is anger. Rage transports them into a simple and bloody alternative reality in which only the strong survive. In their own minds, they are the strong. In reality, their anger may be the source of their strength, but it's also their greatest weakness.

Vampire Bullies like power, but they don't understand it. They aren't interested in the sedate, gray-flannel ways of real power, in which strength is measured by what you *might* do. For Bullies, the excitement comes from actually doing it. No amount of real power can match the raw thrill of confrontation and the sweet, feral scent of fear.

Vampire Bullies are animals. Well, we all are, but Bullies are more in touch with their animal nature than most people. They use that primitive power to manipulate the animal in you.

THE INSTINCT FOR AGGRESSION

By animal nature, I mean the older parts of the brain that have come down to us virtually unchanged from the time of the dinosaurs. The patterns for anger and fear are hardwired into our souls.

"F—-ing garbage!" Vampire Richard snarls, throwing the brief down on the glass top of his desk. "A first-year law student with half a brain could do a better job than this. And I thought you were supposed to be some big-time genius from Harvard. What do you have to say for yourself?"

Ethan's heart flutters like a butterfly impaled on a pin. "Uh . . ."

Richard shakes his head in disgust. "Let me tell you something, Mr. Harvard hot shot," he says, leaning forward and pointing his finger. "If you ever hand me another piece of dreck like this, I'm gonna shove it right down your throat."

Now Ethan feels himself getting mad. Stand up to the bastard, damn it! he shouts to himself, inside his head. Richard's nothing but an old man. You can take him.

Then Ethan imagines what would happen if he actually started a fight with a senior partner. Shock at his own impulse hits him like a blow to the gut. Ethan's mind won't work; still he forces himself to answer. "What's wrong with the brief?" he finally gasps. He wants to say more, but seems to have run out of air.

Richard stands up, rising to his full five-and-a-half feet. Ethan involuntarily shrinks down in his chair. "If you don't know," Richard says, "there's no point in telling you."

It's called the fight or flight response. Our ancestors needed it as a way to shift into overdrive in response to physical threats. Without it, they wouldn't have lived long enough to become our ancestors. The rules were simpler back then. If the danger is smaller than you, kill it and eat it. If it's bigger, run away before it eats you.

Richard's attack neatly transported Ethan to an alternative reality that looked a lot like Jurassic Park. In that world, Richard was completely at home, and Ethan was little more than a babe in the woods, Harvard Law notwithstanding. Even though law school is no place for the squeamish, the aggression there is a bit more subtle.

Richard's simple and transparent actions didn't fool Ethan for a second, but they did fool his brain. The crude attack on his ego was misread as a physical threat, and presto, Ethan's physiology was ready for a race or a fistfight, a state hardly conducive to intellectual riposte.

Never in a million years would Ethan actually throw a punch, but in that one instant, he considered it. Then everything went blank.

Ethan's own brain betrayed him. By the time he figured things out, Richard was already thumping his chest in victory.

VAMPIRE BULLY HYPNOSIS

Bully hypnosis is crude, but extremely effective. Bullies just attack and let your own nervous system do the rest. A Bully assault can bypass the rational part of your brain and set you down in a prehistoric alternate reality where there are only three choices: fight back, run away, or stand still and be eaten. It's the perfect bind; no matter which one you choose, you lose. The newer, smarter parts of your brain may realize what's happening, but they're so awash in chemicals and primitive impulses that they can do nothing but watch in horror as the grim drama unfolds.

A common experience when Bullies attack is not being able to think and not knowing what to say. This happens because the parts of your brain that control thinking and language have been short-circuited. There is no greater isolation than being separated from your own mind.

A Bully's anger elicits dumb, brutish fear. Like all hypnotists, Bullies know exactly what they want, and what they have to do to get it.

Fear leads to avoidance. After a couple of attacks, Bullies usually don't have to do anything to maintain their hypnotic control except snarl once in a while. People let them do whatever they want, because it's easier than confronting them.

Bullies are angry people who have discovered, to their delight, that anger—which they would engage in anyway for its thrill value—also gets them power and control, at least in the short run. In the long run, Bullies' anger destroys them. So what? Knowing that the vampire who's browbeating you right now will eventually get his or her comeuppance offers little comfort and no protection.

The hypnotic relationship between anger and fear has stood the test of time, and it will continue until you do something about it. But what?

WHAT TO DO ABOUT BULLIES

Lots of people have given you advice on how to deal with Bullies.

Your mom probably said to ignore them and they'd go away, but you couldn't and they didn't. They'd walk along beside you, poking, prodding, and teasing you until you felt like you'd explode or, worse, cry. "Sticks and stones can break your bones, but words can never hurt you," your mom said. As each new taunt burned its way into your psyche, you wondered what planet your mother grew up on.

Maybe your dad told you to fight back. If you followed his advice, you learned what abject terror feels like. You and the Bully, circling on the playground, your adversary enjoying the sport, you frightening yourself even more by imagining worst-case scenarios.

The assistant principal, also something of a Bully, made it perfectly clear that fighting would not be tolerated on *this* playground. If you fight, you get expelled. Should anybody hit you, take no action on your own. Report to the office for further instructions.

As an adult, you've probably scanned the self-help shelves in bookstores, looking for some more useful answers. Stand up for yourself, the books say. Don't take a Bully's anger personally. Be assertive, but not aggressive. It may be good advice, but it's harder to follow than the instructions for resetting the margins in Word.

Everybody tells you something different. How do you decide what to do?

The things you've heard are both right and wrong. Any of the strategies might work, depending on the situation. They also might not.

Rather than looking for specific advice, remember one rule only: *the place to defeat a Bully is not in the dust of the playground, but in your own mind.* If you stay in contact with the part of your brain that thinks, even though you're scared to death, you win. The important thing is what happens inside your head. All that's required externally is that you disrupt the ancient hypnotic pattern by doing the unexpected.

> *"I don't know if I can handle working with him any more," Ethan says. His voice trembles as he tells Kathy and Ramon about his encounter in Richard's office.*
>
> *"You can't take it personally," Kathy says. "He does it to everybody."*
>
> *"You got it," Ramon says. "I don't know why they let that SOB get away with verbal harassment like that. A lot of associates have quit."*
>
> *"Maybe you should talk to somebody," Kathy suggests.*
>
> *"Who would I talk to?" Ethan asks. "Richard's a senior partner. The only person who outranks him is God."*
>
> *"There's got to be somebody," Ramon says. "I've heard a few rumors that he's on the way out."*
>
> *"Those rumors have been going around since I was an associate." The three of them look up to see Lorna, the head of the litigation department, standing in the doorway. She turns to Ethan. "I heard about what happened with the brief. I thought I'd come by to see how you're doing."*

"How do you think he's doing?" Kathy says. "Richard just kicked the crap out of him. Why do you guys let him get away with it?"

"Good question," Lorna says. "I think it has something to do with male psychology." She smiles at Kathy. "In case you haven't noticed, there are a number of attorneys in this firm who make very little distinction between the law and Marine boot camp. They think that a successful legal career depends more on how tough you are than on what you know. A lot of people, especially in the old guard, think Richard's temper is a good way to toughen up tender little associates."

"Give me a break," Kathy says.

"I know," Lorna says. "I didn't say that I agreed. I think his behavior is hurting us more than some people realize, but those people are convinced only by the bottom line, which in Richard's case is still pretty respectable."

"So, what you're saying is that nobody is going to do anything."

"Well, you could look at it that way, but I think you'd be missing something important. Not about Richard, but about yourself. What he does works only if you play along."

"What are you talking about?" Kathy asks.

"You said it yourself. I heard you as I came in. 'You can't take it personally. He does it to everybody.'"

Ramon leans forward in his chair. "Easy for you to say."

Lorna shakes her head. "No, it's not easy. It wasn't easy at all."

HOW TO DO THE UNEXPECTED

For a change, let's look at the situation from the vampire's point of view.

First and foremost, Bullies are angry people. If you asked them, they'd say they hate their anger. They know that, like an addiction, it can give them heart attacks, destroy their careers, and drive away the people close to them.

Anger *is* an addiction with vampire Bullies. They don't stop because they're always getting caught up in the rush of chemicals to their brains. Bullies don't know that anger is something they're doing; they think it's being done to them. They think that they're just trying to go about their business, but then some idiot does something stupid that messes up their day. From that point on, the rest is automatic. Bullies experience the adrenaline rush of the fight or flight response just as you do, but they choose to fight.

Bullies say that they're not looking for an altercation; it's just that they can't allow other people to push them around. Actually, when they're angry, which is most of the time, they don't see other people as people at all, but as obstacles or, worse, threats to their dignity. Throughout history, the worst aggression has been committed in the name of defending a reputation.

As you can imagine, with a worldview like this, Bullies get involved in a lot of fights. Eventually they get good at them. When regular people get angry, they distrust their own feelings and hold themselves back. Not Bullies. They lean into their anger and swing it hard to achieve the maximum impact. Later they may be sorry, but in the heat of the moment, they give themselves over to the primitive excitement of battle.

Not only do Bullies give themselves over to the excitement, but they actively court it, whether they know it or not. If you look at Bullies' lives, you'll see that time and again, they go out of their way to get into fights. Many of them abuse substances, which lowers their threshold for anger. Invariably, they will say that they're getting high to relax.

Always remember that Bullies are fighting to achieve an altered state of consciousness, rather than to get you to *do* anything in particular. Any of the three responses dictated by the primitive brain centers is perfectly acceptable. Bullies will be equally happy if you fight back, run away, or cringe in fear. The way to win is to do something unexpected that will jolt Bullies out of their familiar, primitive pattern and make them think about what's going on. They hate that, because it spoils their high.

Of course, in order to do the unexpected, you have to be able to think in the midst of an adrenaline rush. That's what all the advice is about, whether it comes from your mother, the assistant principal, or this book. You can follow any of it, so long as it keeps you in the thinking part of your brain.

I received a letter from a woman who attended one of my seminars. She said it had saved her life. On the way home from my talk, she was accosted in a parking garage by a man with a knife and a ski mask. Instead of panicking, she asked herself, "What would Dr. Bernstein do in this situation?" She decided to scream at the top of her lungs and run toward a group of people at the other end of the garage. This was not a technique I had taught in the seminar. What saved her, she said, was thinking about what to do instead of descending into the fight or flight response. Responsible or not, I was happy to take credit for her newfound bravery.

What do you do if you meet a Bully on the road and you can't fight back, run away, or freeze in terror? The first thing you do is question your assumptions. Who says you have only three choices?

Richard comes storming down the hall, red-eyed and wild. Kathy's stomach begins to quiver. Since she was little, she has always been able to tell when someone was about to yell at her.

"Who the hell set up for a deposition in the big conference room?" Richard bellows.

Kathy tries to keep her voice calm. "I signed up for it two weeks ago. Is there a problem?"

Richard extends his hands toward heaven in mock supplication. "A problem, she says! Yes, there's a goddamn problem! I've got six heavy hitters from Yoshitomo coming over in 10 minutes for a contract review. You know how those guys are. Unless they get the big conference room, they're insulted; it's like they lose face or something. So, if all you're going to do is a take a piddly little deposition, you need to get your stuff out of there and into one of the smaller rooms down the hall. Right now!"

Kathy's muscles clench so tightly she fears her bones may break. Needles of ice jab at her spine. By sheer force of will she pushes a breath past the band of iron around her chest.

What to do next?

The primitive part of your own brain tells you that angry people are big, powerful, and dangerous. They may be, but they're also really stupid. This is true no matter how smart they are in other areas of their lives. If you use the thinking part of your brain and they're operating on primitive instinct, you'll have an advantage of about 50 IQ points. If you can't win with an advantage like that, you ought not to play.

Thinking, however, isn't all that easy when a bully attacks.

In that one awful second, everything Kathy has been and done in 32 years comes rushing down on her in a torrent of conflicting emotions.

It's not fair! I signed up for the room! *Objection overruled by the darker law that says whoever is biggest, strongest, and maddest gets his way.*

Be nice, dear. Do what he wants. *Her mother's all-purpose smile shines out like a beacon, luring her to the false safety of shallow water.*

Don't take it personally. *Advice she's heard a thousand times plays in the background like a song in another language. Just a string of words.*

Hide and it will all go away. *A sad little voice wails just as talons of shame drag her out from under the bed.*

WHAT HE DOES TO YOU IF YOU SAY SOMETHING WILL BE NOTHING COMPARED WITH WHAT I'LL DO IF YOU DON'T.

But can I afford to make an enemy of a senior partner?

DO SOMETHING, NOW.

Don't take it personally. *Yeah, right.*

Maybe I could work at a smaller firm where it's less stressful.

DON'T LET THAT MAN ABUSE YOU! THIS IS ABOUT WHO YOU ARE!

No, it isn't.

Slowly, creaking like a rusty hinge on a seldom-used gate, Kathy's mind swings open. It's not about who I am. It's about him.

As her focus moves from herself to Richard, she sees a pitiful old man who is making a scene because his carelessness might blow his image with a big client. His bullying has nothing to do with her. Unless she completely loses it, her reputation isn't at stake here. His is.

Don't take it personally.

Suddenly, the words have meaning. Kathy feels them tingling and fizzing in her body, like giggles.

For some silly reason, she remembers a verse from Dr. Seuss: What happened then?

"Well, in Whoville they say the Grinch's small heart grew three sizes that day."

Giggles are the sound a heart makes when it's growing, Kathy knows. Richard's piddly little tantrum is no longer a problem.

She smiles in the face of wrath. "I think I hear you asking for a favor, counselor, but I'm not sure. Maybe you could rephrase?"

Here, in one small vignette, is the whole reason that there are therapists and books full of helpful advice. It's not what we tell you to do—you've probably heard the same advice a thousand times before. It's the knowing you can do it.

The purpose of all the explanations and examples is to help you understand difficult situations well enough to recognize other possibilities. Your heart grows when you step out of an old pattern and do something new and unexpected, even if it's scary and difficult.

Especially when it's scary and difficult. If you don't believe me, ask Kathy.

To defeat Bullies, you have to stay cool and keep your wits about you. Here's some advice that may help.

Ask for Time to Think

Only in the primitive jungle do you have to respond to attacks immediately. That's where the Bully wants to send you, but there's no law saying that you have to go.

Normal people don't get angrier at you if you ask for a minute to think things over. By your actions, you are communicating that you take the situation seriously and want to handle it well. Vampires may try some other device to get you to respond in an immediate, emotional manner. They want a fight, not a rational discussion. They may mistake your silence for freezing up with terror, which you may be, but you don't have to let them know it.

Whatever you're feeling, just asking for a couple of minutes to think things over is usually so unexpected that you may be able to end the confrontation right there. No matter what, take your time and think before you respond.

Think About What You Want to Have Happen

While you're taking your minute to think, consider the possible outcomes. Immediately discard any that involve making the Bully back down and admit that you're right. You cannot be right and effective at the same time. Don't even try.

Get the Bully to Stop Yelling

Actually, this is easier than you might think. Just keeping your own voice soft may do the trick. Bullies expect you to yell back; don't oblige them. If either of you is yelling, nothing reasonable will be said.

Another unexpected way to get a Bully to stop yelling is by saying, "Please speak more slowly. I'd like to understand." Often people will comply with this request without thinking about it. Reducing the speed will also reduce the volume. Have you ever tried to yell slowly? This strategy works particularly well on the phone.

On the phone, also remember the "uh-huh" rule. We usually respond with "uh-huh" when the other person takes a breath. If you go three breaths without saying "uh-huh," the other person will stop and ask, "Are you there?" Using this technique will allow you to interrupt without saying a word.

Whatever You Do, Don't Explain

If you are ever attacked by a vampire Bully, you may feel a powerful urge to explain the whys and wherefores of your own actions. Don't do it! Explanations are the way in which primitive responses sneak down from your reptile brain and out your mouth. Explanations are usually a disguised form of fighting back or running away. The typical explanation boils down to, "If you know all the facts, you will see that I am right and you are wrong," or, "It wasn't my fault; you should be mad at somebody else." Never mind that your explanations seem true and reasonable to you. Bullies always recognize the primitive patterns for dealing with aggression. They will see your explanation as an invitation to go for the jugular.

Ask, "What Would You Like Me to Do?"

Nothing stops a vampire attack dead in its tracks like this simple little unexpected question. Angry people either do not know or will not admit what they want you to do. Bullies just want you to stand there while they yell at you, but it sounds awfully silly if they have to ask for it.

When you ask angry people what they want you to do, they'll have to stop and think. This may be enough to move them into the more rational part of their brain, which can only help you. If Bullies are trying to conceal their real motivation, they'll have to ask you for something more acceptable than what they really want. Give it to them and vanish into the night, unscathed.

Don't Take Criticism Personally

This is the hard one. To follow this advice, you have to understand what it means to take things personally.

All of us have external things—our children, our pets, our favorite sports teams, our opinions, and our creations at work—that we experience as if they were parts of our bodies. Psychologically, we make little distinction between verbal disparagement of these things and physical attacks on our vital organs. That doesn't mean that we have to respond to every criticism with an instinctive kill-or-be-killed counterattack.

If you're attacked by a Bully, it's time to employ the vampire fighter's number one strategy—*use your confusion as a cue to stop and think about what's actually going on.* With vampires, how it feels is seldom what it is. Bully attacks are *not* personal. Bullies yell at everybody. If you think about it, the attacks actually say more about who and what Bullies are than they do about you. To keep from taking an attack personally, you have to look beyond your initial emotional response to see the pattern, then step out of it.

Learn from Criticism

Every criticism contains useful information as well as an attack. If you don't hear anything useful at first, keep listening until you do. Not everyone who criticizes you is a Bully. Be especially alert when you hear the same thing from several sources. My grandfather used to say, "If three people call you a horse, buy a saddle."

If you make it a practice to wait 24 hours before you answer criticisms, it will drive vampires crazy. Other people will be impressed by your maturity and reasonableness. You may even learn something.

Reverse these roles if you have to criticize someone who has a penchant for taking things too personally. Structure the situation so that the other person doesn't have to admit wrongdoing by accepting what you have to say. Always offer a face-saving option. Make it clear in your comments that you understand how a reasonable and honorable person might do what he or she did. Direct your advice toward improving the situation rather than pointing out mistakes. *Focus on what you want to have happen rather than on what's wrong with what has already happened.* As we'll see in later chapters, this technique will prove invaluable if you want to criticize vampires in a way that they can hear and accept.

9 Antisocial Used Car Salesmen and Bullies in Your Life

If there is a Used Car Salesman in your life, whether it is a spouse, a friend, or an adult child, the hardest thing to deal with is the lies. How do you know what to believe? Isn't honesty a part of love? How can someone close to you keep lying to you while swearing to tell the truth?

LIVING WITH A LIAR

All emotional vampires lie. They lie differently and for different reasons.

Honest people are more damaged by lies than they need to be because they have little or no experience with lying themselves. They make one huge mistake that clouds their minds and often breaks their hearts: they believe that doing something wrong means the same thing to an emotional vampire as it does to them.

For honest people, right and wrong are connected to powerful internal contingencies. You feel bad when you do something you think is wrong. To a vampire, doing wrong refers to an external contingency; the only bad thing about doing something wrong is getting caught.

To protect yourself from Used Car Salesmen and other vampire liars, you have to learn more about lying than you probably want to know.

The Truth About Lies

Most likely, what you *want* to know is how to tell whether somebody is lying. What you *need* to know is not so much how to differentiate a lie from the truth, but how to protect yourself from the damage that lies can do to you.

The first step is understanding that there are different kinds of lies told by different people for different reasons. They require different strategies to protect yourself. Here are a few examples, arranged roughly according to potential for harm, from little and white to big and black.

- *The little white lie.* This is the kind of lie someone might tell you when the truth might hurt your feelings, like saying that your new jeans don't make your butt look big. The way to protect yourself is by not asking a question when you really don't want to hear the answer, or by giving the people you ask permission to be honest even when the answer might hurt. Be sure you are being honest about this yourself.
- *The dog ate my homework lie.* This is the quintessential adolescent lie, often used by Daredevils and, as we will see later, by Obsessive-Compulsives who realize that they have made a mistake. This kind of lie is little more than a lame attempt to avoid immediate, negative consequences. The way to protect yourself is to forget the dog and whether or not the person is telling the truth. Ask to see the homework.
- *The frilly pink lie.* This is a stereotypical feminine lie beloved by Histrionics. These lies are usually told by people-pleasers to avoid the conflict and unpleasantness that might arise if they said no. "I'd love to go, but my fibromyalgia is acting up." To protect yourself, recognize that anything other than an enthusiastic yes means no.
- *The macho lie.* This type of lie is often told by male Antisocials and Narcissists as a way of presenting themselves as cooler and tougher than they actually are. "If somebody did that to me, I'd beat the crap out of them." No protection is required. Just grunt assent.

    If the person speaking is a Bully, this may not be a lie at all.
- *The rose-colored lie.* This is the kind of lie you tell yourself about yourself. A good example is, "I never lie."
- *The neon lie.* Everybody exaggerates by making the details of his or her life bigger than life. The purposes vary. If it's for entertainment, sit back and enjoy it. If the purpose is persuasion, take it with a grain of salt.
- *The only-when-his-lips-are-moving lie.* This is the kind of lie that is told by people whose professions require a certain amount of prevarication, like lawyers and politicians. When you disagree, they are despicable. When you agree, they are the truth. The only protection is having your own lawyer, or having enough research skills to check the facts independently.
- *The red, white, and blue lie.* This is a lie that is told for very good reasons, like national security or to keep the family on the right track.

Some examples are, "We do not use torture," or, "No, your father and I never smoked pot." Often the very good reason is to prevent the people in charge from being embarrassed. The only protection is recognizing that some subjects simply will not be discussed.

- *The gray pinstripe lie.* This is a typical, predictable corporate lie, often presented by Narcissists as PowerPoints or between the glossy covers of a prospectus or annual report. To get the facts about a business, do what hedge fund managers do: ask the people who do business with that business.

- *The lie carved in stone.* This kind of lie, beloved by Obsessive-Compulsives and Paranoids, appears in countless forms. It boils down to asserting that everything in the world fits into one of two categories: right or wrong, good or evil, black or white. To protect yourself, don't look at the carving; look at the stone itself. Like most of human experience, it is gray.

- *The big black lie.* This is an active, conscious, hurtful deception that benefits the liar and harms the person being lied to. "Like the odometer says, this baby has only thirty thousand miles on it."

  This is the most dangerous kind of lie, most often told by Used Car Salesmen and Bullies, and, as we will see later, by Narcissists and Paranoids, the kinds of emotional vampires who may have no problem with hurting other people to achieve their own ends. Unfortunately, there is no sure way to protect yourself from this kind of lie, because the people who tell them are usually quite skillful.

The best defense is understanding the strategies and techniques that liars use, and recognizing them for what they are rather than being hypnotized by them. Your first line of defense should always be to ask yourself: "Why is he or she telling me this?" If you can't answer this question, stop and think about it until you can. Maybe you should go back and read the section "Used Car Hypnosis" again.

The second line of defense is not confusing yourself by lumping less harmful lies with the big black kind.

Once you have done these, you are ready to approach liars on their own ground.

How to Tell If Someone Is Lying

As I have said, there's no sure way to know whether somebody is lying, unless it's about something that can be independently verified. Forget about lie detectors and those little things on phones that flash in different colors.

The theory behind those devices is that people become more physically aroused when they lie. Usually, only small-time liars worry enough to have it change their physiology. Bigger liars can do it in cold blood. The biggest liars don't have to lie at all. They groom somebody else to do it for them.

Nevertheless, if you are willing to tolerate a little uncertainty, there are a few guidelines based on psychological research into the behavior of liars that may come in handy for separating truth from falsehood. Use them with care.

- *Lies are vaguer than the truth.* The fewer specifics, the harder it is to check up. Usually the vagueness increases as you get closer to the center of the issue. Beware of people who don't answer questions directly.
- *Lies are often more complicated than the truth.* Remember Ockham's razor. The simplest explanation is usually correct. Liars may include superfluous peripheral details as a way of skirting the central issues. Sometimes they try too hard. Always remember that just because something is possible doesn't mean that it's likely.
- *Only liars swear that they are telling the truth.* This is not always the case, but think about it this way: it never occurs to people who are telling the truth that you might not believe them, so they don't need to swear.
- *Liars are perfectly capable of looking you in the eye.* The research is absolutely clear on this point. Liars are likely to exploit this widespread misconception by making more eye contact than people who are telling the truth.
- *Liars benefit from their lies.* Why would someone make up a story if there were nothing to be gained from doing so? The more someone will gain from your credence, the more careful you have to be. This is the reason you must always ask yourself why the person is telling you this.
- *Liars are usually repeat offenders.* You know the saying: fool me once, shame on you; fool me twice, shame on me.
- *If it sounds too good to be true, it is.* This is the most reliable method of distinguishing truth from falsehood, but the one least often employed. Liars know that if they tell you what you want to hear, no matter how unlikely it is, you are likely to believe it.

To Protect Yourself from Liars, You Should Know How to Lie

Like most honest people, you probably can't lie your way out of a wet paper bag, and that makes you vulnerable, even when you know all the danger signs.

Used Car Salesmen know how to lie effectively. To protect yourself, you should also. Not that you would use their techniques to deceive people, but knowing how they do it is the last best way to keep them from doing it to you.

These techniques might also come in handy if some day you consider running for office.

The most dangerous liars are, in a word, calculating. They think carefully about what they are doing. They assess the gains versus the risks, and tailor their lies to the goals they are trying to accomplish. No small-time "dog ate my homework" crap from these guys. They are pros. Here's how they do it.

Follow these directions and you too can lie like a pro:

- *Know your goal.* Sometimes liars want to be believed, and sometimes it doesn't matter to them whether you believe them or not. They just want you to hand over the goods.
- *Assess the situation.* Calculating liars know that certain situations are ripe for deception because it will be almost impossible for them to get caught. Unlike you, liars often do not care whether you know that they are lying; they just want to make sure you can't prove it. In the following situations it is relatively easy to get away with lying:
  - *When it's your word against someone else's*
  - *When there is no clear way to check up*
  - *When someone else is lying or trying to cover something up*
- *Tell people what they want to hear.* Liars assume that everyone operates the way they do: totally in their own self-interest. More often than not, they're right. If there is the tiniest scrap of larceny in your heart, liars will find it and use it to their advantage. Your only defense is not lying to yourself.
- *Groom your victims.* Everybody who exploits other people knows that you start slowly and work your way up. Sexual abusers start with just a touch; physical abusers start with a few sharp words. Liars know that if you let their small deceptions get by now, they can get away with whoppers later on. Start small and work your way up.
- *Use your imagination.* The most effective liars use the same techniques as fiction writers. They make up stories, then work out all the details and implications. If their lies are to be accepted, they have to fit into the context of a believable narrative. Once liars have created a story, they stick to it by accepting the basic premises themselves and telling the story as if it were true. They also need to have good memories.

- *Draw a mental curtain around your actions.* Emotional vampires who consciously choose to do things that they know are wrong deal with their consciences by compartmentalizing. They focus on one event at a time and pretend that it exists in total isolation just this one time, and that it has no relation to anything or anyone else in their lives. Liars are also good at persuading themselves that the end justifies the means.
- *Repeat your lies as often as possible.* The more often people hear something, the more likely they are to believe it.
- *If you're caught, change the subject.* Even the most skilled liars sometimes get caught. When they do, they use all sorts of techniques to distract the people who catch them. Here are some favorites:
  - *Get angry.*
  - *Never, ever admit to a lie.* Call it something else, like poor judgment. Whatever you do, stick to your story.
  - *Give your reasons as if they justify your actions.*
  - *Accuse your accuser.* Caught liars will try to convince you that two wrongs make them right.
  - *Claim executive privilege.*

This is how liars do it. If you don't have the stomach to use these techniques, you'd better stick to the truth. If you want to protect yourself from the lies the Used Car Salesmen and other emotional vampires may tell you, your best defense is a deeper understanding of deception.

Only you can decide how much deception you are willing to take.

BULLIES IN YOUR LIFE

Bullies are highly explosive. To keep from being blown up, you'll have to learn about anger—what it is, how it works, and what to do about it.

LIVING IN A MINEFIELD

If you are married to a Bully, you know what it's like to live in a minefield. The slightest misstep can cause an explosion. The anger may be directed at you, at your children, or at an inanimate object.

"There's something wrong with this stupid toaster," Scott says, yanking the plug from the wall and beginning to fumble with the lever. "This thing is stuck."

"Maybe you should work on it later when you have more time," Bethany suggests, knowing that he won't listen.

Scott's movements become more rapid and jerky. His conversation turns to four-letter words muttered under his breath.

Bethany clears out of the kitchen, knowing what's coming next. Just as she closes the door, she hears the crash of the toaster hitting the floor.

If scenes like this have played out in your life, you know how draining it is to walk everywhere on tiptoe, never knowing when the next mine will go off.

Actually, if you stop and think about it, you do know. The way to deal with living in a minefield is recognizing that a minefield is exactly what you're living in.

If you pay attention, you will notice that the explosions are not random. They cluster around particular topics. Vampires set mines to keep people from bringing up these topics. Over time, everyone in the family learns, consciously or unconsciously, to avoid these minefields, thus rewarding Bullies for outbursts of anger or other kinds of emotional vampires for whatever kinds of tantrums they throw.

The minefield technique is the most common way for all vampires to exert control over the people around them. You learn to avoid asking them to do anything they don't want to do, or mentioning anything they don't want to talk about. For that reason, we will examine the minefield technique in some detail using a Bully as our example, because Bullies are less subtle than other vampire types.

The minefield technique has been successfully used by hundreds of thousands of male Bullies to get out of doing housework.

Bethany looks at the clock and leaps up from the table. "I've got to change right now or I'm going to be late. This is Bunko night."

Scott's face signals a storm warning. "Well, who's going to do these dishes and give the kids their baths?"

"I thought you . . ."

"You thought! Did you ever think of asking if I had plans for tonight? You said you wanted me to change the spark plugs on your car."

"You can do that tomorrow night. You know the first Wednesday of the month is Bunko. I have it marked on the calendar."

"Like I can even see the calendar with all the stuff you have written all over it."

"All that stuff is there so we'll know where we have to go and what we have to do." Bethany says, inching toward the bedroom.

> *Scott gets up and starts moving dishes from the table like a bull-dozer clearing a construction site. Amid the clatter, he mutters loudly enough to be heard in the bedroom. "There's no way to win here. You work 10 hours a day, and then come home and work some more so her highness can go out drinking and gambling with her friends."*
>
> *Finally, his persistent pushing of her hot button about her efforts not being as valuable as his gets to Bethany. She rushes from the bedroom, still buttoning her blouse. "You think I don't work? I have a job just like you."*
>
> *"Oh, sorry," Scott says, "but I couldn't tell from the size of your paycheck. What did you make last month? Was it $800?"*
>
> *"Scott, you know the girls were sick, and I was out almost a whole week."*

Scott's strategy is simple, although it is probably not conscious. When asked to do something he doesn't want to do, he lashes out in as many directions as possible, hoping to engage Bethany in an argument. In about two minutes, he has brought up every contentious issue he can think of. The overall strategy is to make it so unpleasant for her to ask him to do anything that eventually she won't bother. Over time, it will be easier for her to just skip Bunko and avoid asking him for help around the house.

How Angry People Think

Though Scott's strategy is transparent, as I have said, it is probably not conscious. Angry people are usually not aware that they use their anger to manipulate people. They don't even think of anger as something they do, but as a natural reaction to other people's annoying behavior.

Their internal dialogue is an almost constant repetition of grievances. "Do I have a right to be angry? Damn straight I do!" Then the playlist of injustices starts rolling.

Angry people see their outbursts as explosions that come out of nowhere and are over almost as soon as they begin. This is convenient, but it is totally incorrect. Angry people may be aware of the actions that detonate blasts, but they don't realize that their minds are arsenals full of explosive devices.

When Scott's plan for an undisturbed evening of tinkering and TV is threatened, he feels a rush of adrenaline, and immediately the whole playlist in his head starts rolling, repeating every annoying thing Bethany has ever done. All he has to do is turn on the external speaker, and he has a prerecorded argument, full of tried-and-true hooks to pull her in. He doesn't have to think about any of it.

What Scott is doing is blatantly unfair and manipulative, but it works. If Bethany points out how unfair and manipulative it is, it will work even better, because he will have one more thing to add to his playlist: "Coming at me with more of that psychological crap."

Please be aware that the two most useless sentences in the English language are "You're being manipulative" and "You're in denial" because both processes are, by definition, unconscious. There is no first-person form of the verb *to manipulate*.

If an angry person has laid minefields in your life, it's time to develop some strategies of your own. Here are some ideas.

Make Your Plan Before the Argument Starts   Once the shrapnel is flying, it will be hard to communicate with your neocortex, so do some thinking in advance.

Map Out the Minefield   What actions and issues bring on explosions? In Scott's case, the mines are thickest around any suggestion that he should help with housework. You can spot a danger zone by asking yourself what subject you're most afraid to bring up. Most marital minefields are laid around spending money, sex versus affection, the uses of free time, and—the all-time favorite—one partner's perception that the other is trying to be the boss. Once an argument gets going, all of these issues are usually hauled in like ammunition to the front. In the smoky din of battle, it's easy to get confused about what you're fighting for.

Pick Your Battles, and Fight Only One at a Time   Think about what you want to have happen, and stay focused on that. Objectives should be phrased in terms of what you want the angry person to *do*, not what you want them to *not do*. Bethany will have far more success at getting Scott to do housework than at having him stop getting so angry whenever she brings it up.

Positive goals imply that you need to take some action to achieve them. Negative goals are often merely a wish that you can continue doing what you've always done, but the other person's response will, miraculously, be different.

The Best Defense Is a Good Offense   Once you know your objective, you can choose how and when to ask for it. Make sure there is sufficient time and space to maneuver; you can't negotiate with a cornered animal. Don't bring up important issues when the other person is going out the door, and *never,*

ever, discuss inflammatory issues in the car or in bed! If there is an angry person in your life, negotiate to have these areas declared demilitarized zones.

The most effective way to get someone like Scott to do housework is to ask him in advance and bargain for specific tasks at specific times. It has been my experience that women have a hard time doing this. For women, household tasks are an ongoing process, without beginning or end. They see something that needs doing and they do it, then they move on to the next thing. No one tells them to wash dishes, vacuum the carpet, or put in a load of laundry. They see the task and do it with little separation between the two, almost like Zen.

Men are generally unable to achieve this level of awareness. They can be taught to do housework; however, they need to be told what, where, and when, *but never how.* Remember the *on duty* strategy. The goal you will not be able to achieve, at least all at once, is for men to do household tasks as well as you would. This is a completely separate objective. You must get them to do these tasks before you have a prayer of getting them to do them correctly. Remember, one battle at a time.

> *"Scott," Bethany says, "I need about 15 minutes to talk over an important issue. Is this a good time?"*
>
> *Scott's face is already beginning to grow red. "What is it?"*
>
> *She smiles. "If this is a good time, I'd be happy to tell you, but I don't want to start if you're getting ready to do something else."*
>
> *"What kind of manipulative game are you playing?" he says. "Just tell me what you want to talk about."*

Notice how Bethany has neatly closed at least one of the back doors to discussion. By asking her to tell him what she wants to talk about, Scott is conceding that he has time to listen. Even angry people will usually play by these conversational rules. The other thing to note is that in dealing with an angry person, every word seems to move the situation in one direction or another. To be effective, you have to be deliberate, paying close attention to what is actually being said and choosing your responses carefully.

Don't Let Aggressive Hooks Pull You Off Course   The favorite strategy of angry people is getting you angry, too. They're much more experienced at fighting than you are, so they're more likely to win. Bethany did well to ignore Scott's facial display and accusation of manipulation. They were merely feints, and they had nothing to do with her objective. As she gets closer, the flak will get heavier. If things get too hot, she may decide to withdraw and live to fight another day.

Ask Questions, Don't Make Statements   In a battle, you need to take the high ground as quickly as possible. In discussions with angry people, there are several forms of high ground to go for. Be careful; most of them will not be useful in achieving your goal. If you go for the moral high ground ("I am good and you are bad, so you should do as I say"), you'll never hold it. You will have set up a situation in which an angry person must, by doing what you ask, admit to being wrong.

It is much more useful and far less noticeable to take the conversational high ground by being the one who asks the questions. If you ask a question, it is almost a law that the other person must answer before going on. If you keep asking thought-provoking questions, you can keep control of the conversation and perhaps encourage the angry person to think. This cannot hurt.

Questions can also help by making unconscious assumptions conscious. When spoken these assumptions are often far less defensible than when they are merely acted upon. Scott's actions say that he shouldn't be responsible for any work around the house, but he can't say this aloud, or he will sound like a male chauvinist pig even to himself.

Asking questions is a simple and effective tactic, but you will find it surprisingly difficult the first few times you try it. You'll discover that every angry person on earth already knows and uses it.

> *"Scott," Bethany says tentatively, "we seem to be getting into a lot of arguments about housework. I think we need to make some ground rules about who does what."*
>
> *"And why do we need to do that?"*
>
> *"Well, to keep from getting into arguments."*
>
> *"We could keep from getting into arguments if you stopped nagging me about taking out the garbage right in the middle of the playoffs."*

Oops.

To keep control of the conversation, you need to start by asking the first question, and resisting your own reflexive answering. Another caution: a favorite tactic of dominant people everywhere is to ask you why you feel something or want something. Never answer a *why* question! You will suddenly discover that the discussion has changed to a critique and defense of your reasons, and your original statement has suddenly changed to a tentative proposition that you will be allowed to keep only if your reasons are good enough. When this happens, you will feel, correctly, as if your words are being pulled out of context and twisted around. The purpose of a *why* question is *never* to understand your reasoning, it is to elicit words that can be twisted. If you don't give them, there'll be nothing to twist. Remember, the answer to a *why* question is an explanation, and explaining always makes angry situations worse.

It may take a number of attempts to clear a minefield. If you step on a mine, don't stay to argue irrelevant issues. Withdraw and fight your own battle another day.

> *Bethany holds up her hands and smiles as she backs away. "I can see this isn't a good time to talk about this. We'll try again another time."*
>
> *"And why* isn't *this a good time?"*
>
> *Bethany shakes her head, still smiling. "Do you really need to ask?"*

The person who asks is in control. Why do you think therapists are so fond of answering questions with questions? I can assure you that it isn't because we don't have all the answers.

> *It's another day.*
>
> *"Honey, what do you think is a reasonable amount of housework for you to do?"*
>
> *Scott exhales loudly enough to be heard across the cul-de-sac. "I already do a lot around here. I take care of the yard. I fix things. I take out the garbage."*
>
> *"Yes, you do. But, what percentage of the total amount of weekly work do you think that is?"*
>
> *Scott exhales again. "I don't know; why don't you just tell me?"*
>
> *"Come on, I asked first. I really want to know what you think."*
>
> *Scott thinks for a few seconds. "About a quarter, I guess. Why are you asking?"*
>
> *"How much work in terms of hours per week do you think it takes to run this house?"*
>
> *"What is all this housework crap? What are you trying to do?"*
>
> *Bethany smiles and turns on the PowerPoint projector. "This chart shows a list of household tasks and the average amount of time they take. Please look at them and tell me if you agree that these tasks need to be done, and that the time estimates are reasonable."*

Do Your Homework   Okay, so you don't have a PowerPoint projector in your living room. Use paper. The point is that taking mined territory back from an angry person requires as much poise and preparation as a presentation to the board of directors. You can't just speak off the cuff. Everything you say and do must be directed toward achieving your goal.

Here's a final question to see how well you understand what that goal is and how you can best move toward it. To answer correctly, you need to take into account everything you've learned about anger up to this point.

Should the time estimates on Bethany's slides be:
a. *Overstated?*
b. *Accurate?*
c. *Understated?*
d. *All of the above?*

It's not *d*. This is one of the few questions in this book to which the answer *isn't* "all of the above."

If the figures are overstated even slightly, it will lead to an argument about how the list is ridiculously padded. You'd be surprised at how many people do overestimate because they forget that the purpose of such a list is to get someone else to do more housework, and succumb to the temptation of using the list to demonstrate how hard they work.

If you said that the figures should be accurate, I agree in principle, but I still don't think you chose the best answer. Without independent time-and-motion studies, you can't know what accurate is.

Remember how closely anger, both his and yours, is tied to beliefs about right and wrong. With angry people, you're always in the most danger when you think you're most right. Your estimate could be biased, and even if it isn't, it could seem biased. In order to look correct, the estimates should appear conspicuously low, at least to you.

The answer is *c*. The estimate should be understated, if only to forestall arguments about padding, but there are reasons beyond that. If Scott thinks the time estimate for a task is overstated, his wife can agree to a test. Scott can do the job and time it to make sure the measurement is fair. Regardless of the outcome, she will win something. The most important prize is drawing him into the whole process of estimating task times with a view toward reassignment.

Another reason for understated estimates is that when Scott finally gets to the point of picking one, he'll end up doing more than he bargains for. Or if he goes for a bargain, his wife can make cleaning the bathroom a more attractive option by slightly *overstating* the time involved. If this is what you were thinking when you answered *a*, you get full credit.

If you are thinking that the process I'm describing is manipulative, you're absolutely correct. Everybody manipulates, but not everybody does it consciously and well. Conscious manipulation is called *strategy*.

If you're thinking that you shouldn't have to go through a process like this to get a little help around the house, I'd also agree. Unfortunately, the world is as it is, not as it should be. In dealing effectively with angry people, your own shoulds are your greatest liability.

Make a Contract   The reason for contracts is that people break them. When Scott finally picked his jobs, Bethany demanded that they put it in writing. Of course he asked why, but she just shook her head and smiled. Writing isn't always necessary, but a clear, firm agreement is.

Contracts should specify *who, what, when, where, how often,* and *if not, what happens.* Scott and Bethany each agreed to put up $50 a month to pay at an hourly rate for tasks that were not done within specified limits. Nagging turned into saying things like, "If it isn't done by noon, I get $15 for doing it."

Bethany thinks that the $50 a month she loses is the most useful money she's ever spent.

10 Therapy for Antisocial Vampires

What should you do if you see signs of Antisocial behavior in yourself or in someone you care about? This section provides a thumbnail sketch of the sorts of self-help and professional therapeutic approaches that might be beneficial. The purpose of this section is to help you to help yourself or to understand the treatment that someone else is getting. It is not a how-to-do-it manual. Please remember what we in the trade learned in Psychotherapy 101: attempting to treat someone you know will make you both sicker.

THE GOAL

The basic goal of treatment for Antisocial emotional vampires is overcoming their addiction to excitement (and any other addictions). Socializing Antisocials involves teaching them how to delay gratification, endure boredom, and live by someone else's rules. The way this is done is by helping them to develop internal contingencies that are stronger than the more immediate external ones.

A way to think about internal contingencies is the way they were pictured in old cartoons, with a little devil on one shoulder and an angel on the other. The devils on Antisocials' shoulders are not evil, but impulsive, saying, "Get what you want right now!" The angel is usually mute.

Therapy for Antisocials, and indeed for all personality disorders, involves giving the little angel some convincing arguments to advance. They are not necessarily the same arguments that *your* angel uses, such as, "It's wrong to take advantage of other people." It's almost impossible to teach empathy to an emotional vampire. They can fake it, but they have a hard time feeling it.

Arguments that are convincing to a vampire must always be in that vampire's own language—self-interest. To be heard, angels must say, "You can get more of what you want and/or keep from losing it if you listen to me." Crafting such arguments is the art of psychotherapy. For Antisocials, little subtlety is required, at least at first. "If you do that, you'll get caught" will often suffice.

ANGER CONTROL TREATMENT

Anger control treatment is a joke. If you don't believe me, watch some late night television.

The reason people joke about anger control is that, as it is often practiced, it attempts to teach management techniques to people who, like most of us, feel that anger is something that happens to them rather than something they do.

Bullies believe that they are nice, easygoing guys until some jerk pisses them off. Getting them to grasp the irony in this belief requires considerable finesse, but it is absolutely essential if the teaching technique is to work.

Effective anger control treatment never puts people in a classroom until they are ready to learn.

TREATMENT FOR ADDICTION

The battle that Antisocials must win is with addiction, whether it is to external substances or to their own neurochemistry. All addictions have two components: the substance itself and the thought patterns that lead to abusing any substance. Any treatment must deal with both to be effective.

The longer I practice, the more respect I have for Alcoholics Anonymous. This is a bit uncool in the crowd I hang out with. AA is considered amateurish and unsophisticated compared to what *we* do.

In my opinion, the amateurishness is part of the sophistication. The only people whom Antisocials might remotely consider trusting are other Antisocials, as they share the belief that self-interest is the only viable motivation and that anyone who won't admit to that is hypocritical. Addictions are one of the few exceptions to the general rule that says that a therapist should never treat anybody for what he or she has or is recovering from.

Twelve-step programs and Antisocials were made for each other. Literally. Alcoholics Anonymous was created by Antisocials for Antisocials, and nobody has yet devised a better system for dealing with substance abuse in the thrill-seeking personality. The structure, social stimulation, constant reminders of behavioral consequences, and sponsors who can be called at a moment of weakness are all just what the doctor ordered. Actually, they're better than most things that doctors come up with.

The real genius of AA, however, is in teaching Antisocials how to develop internal contingencies. Those bumper sticker slogans are exactly the arguments that the little angel needs in order to kick the devil's butt when he advocates stinkin' thinkin'. My own favorite is: "If you find yourself in a hole, put down the shovel." Shakespeare could not have said it better.

The thing about AA that turns people off in the beginning is the spiritual part. Many Antisocials are too cool for that, or for following anybody else's rules about anything, which is what they desperately need to learn. AA's pragmatism helps Antisocials learn that spirituality is not dogma, and that Higher Power means anything you want it to mean, so you're not a wuss if you believe in one.

SELF-HELP

If you recognize Antisocial tendencies in yourself, the following exercises will be very difficult for you, but they will make a difference in every area of your life.

Learn to Endure Boredom

This is essential. If you can't stand the long stretches of boredom that come with being a responsible adult, you'll never be one. Don't believe for a minute that shifting your addiction to a more socially acceptable form of excitement will change anything. Addicts usually go back to their drug of choice.

Live by the Letter of the Law

This means every law, not just the ones you agree with. Start with turning in your paperwork on time and driving within the speed limit. Even if other people break a few rules here and there, you can't. If you do, accept the consequences without trying to talk your way out of them. You have to learn to be straighter than the straight people.

Laboriously Consider the Effects of Your Actions

Recognize that you don't live in a vacuum. Every time you break a rule, it hurts someone else. If you can't figure out how, sit there until you can.

AA folks will recognize this as Step 4.

Avoid Name-Calling or Raising Your Voice

Think of it as the duct-tape solution to temper problems. Until you learn to express your anger in a constructive way, don't express it at all.

Keep Promises

Don't make *any* promises to *anyone* unless you're absolutely sure you can keep them.

WHAT WILL HURT

Emotional vampires tend to select approaches to improving themselves that make them worse rather than better. Antisocials should stay away from extensive examination of family-of-origin issues and approaches that emphasize the expression of feelings over learning to control feelings. Antisocials have enough excuses already, and insight into the past seldom affects their behavior in the present. Beware of nice therapists who write letters to get Antisocials out of things because of extenuating circumstances. With Antisocials, there are no extenuating circumstances.

Antisocials *do not* need advocates to help them escape the repercussions of their behavior. If there are Antisocials in your life, the best thing you can do is stand aside and let them face their own consequences.

11 Show Business, Vampire Style

The Histrionic Types

Just as Antisocial vampires like excitement, Histrionics love attention and approval, and they're willing to work hard to get it. Given half a chance, they'll sing and dance their way into your heart. They invented musical comedy. They do more subtle performances, too. Histrionics are virtuosos of polite conversation, so interested that they make you feel interesting. One of their finest inventions is small talk, the miracle glue that holds conversations together. They also invented gossip.

Histrionics have what it takes to get hired into your business or your life. You want good looks? They've got them (or they'll spend hours trying to get them). They bubble with enthusiasm, sparkle with wit, and sometimes tingle with sexual excitement. Be careful. *Histrionic* means dramatic; what you see is all a show, and it's definitely not what you get.

Histrionics are always acting. Mostly, they try to do cheerful sitcoms, but the performance can change before your eyes into a sordid, overacted soap opera with you as a part of the cast. Or into a medical drama. Or a seamy talk show. Or even professional wrestling.

These vampire performers have tendencies toward Histrionic personality disorder. The condition is old, but the name is new, an attempt to replace the less politically correct *hysterical*. Ancient Greek physicians like Galen and Hippocrates thought that the dramatic emotional shifts and vague physical complaints they saw in Histrionics were caused by the migration of a childless womb (*hystericum*) to other parts of the body.

For centuries, a Histrionic personality has been considered primarily a disorder of women. This misperception arises from the fact that the Histrionic types most often seen in clinics are stereotypically feminine.

There are plenty of Histrionic men as well. They tend to seek approval and acceptability more than attention. Their roles are masculine stereotypes—fifties dad, avid sports fan, joke-telling raconteur, or highly motivated businessman. Histrionic men also play at being tough guys; professional wrestlers are a good example. They can sometimes be misdiagnosed as Antisocial, but if you look more closely, you can see that the violence is faked, and that the real goal is trying to put on a good show. In Chapter 14, we'll look more closely at male-pattern Histrionics.

Histrionics were Freud's favorite patients. They gave him the idea that much of human experience occurs outside awareness. If you spend any time with Histrionics, you too will believe in the unconscious.

The internal landscape of Histrionics is foggier than a Transylvanian night. They can get lost in whatever role they happen to be playing. They can forget who they really are and what they really feel. Or think. Or anything. Their true feelings come out in body language, the sound of their voices, and their unintentionally revealing choice of words. Histrionics also invented the Freudian slip.

WHAT IT'S LIKE TO BE HISTRIONIC

Histrionics' desire for attention and approval is so strong that, in their minds, they divide themselves into the parts people like and the parts that aren't there. When Histrionics are forced to confront those unacceptable missing parts, everything falls to pieces.

Imagine walking into a party in a brand-new outfit that you couldn't have worn only 10 pounds ago. You're feeling turned on, toned up, trimmed down, and decked out. You can sense people's eyes following you. For a few minutes, life is exactly the way it's supposed to be. You feel marvelous! Then you pass a full-length mirror and see in excruciating detail what it means to be still 5 pounds from your goal. The evening is ruined. This is the ecstasy and the agony of the Histrionic.

In normal people, there's an internal contingency, a little voice that says: "It's who you are, not what you look like." Histrionics do not hear that voice. Seeing themselves as unacceptable in any way unleashes a storm of emotions that requires hours of reassurance to abate. Reassurance may not be enough. Sometimes they feel compelled to intensify the performance to fever pitch, or to engage in bizarre and destructive actions to regain their sense of equilibrium. Histrionics invented crimes of passion. Ditto anorexia and bulimia.

It's also possible that the emotional storm won't be expressed outwardly, that it will be forced into a dark cupboard in the mind where it will roil and seethe, mixing with other unacceptable impulses until some tiny slight blows the door off the cupboard and unleashes a hurricane.

When it comes to the three elements of psychological health—a sense of control, connection to something larger than oneself, and pursuit of challenge—Histrionics are all over the map. Their beliefs and abilities change with their moods. The world of Histrionics is a mass of contradictions—cheery sunshine one minute, fog and lightning the next. You never know what's going to happen, and neither do they.

One thing is sure: if you're close to a Histrionic, you'll be the one who has to clean up after the storm.

The favorite prey of Histrionics is someone who will rescue them from themselves and from the complexities of everyday life. They hate boring details worse than a stake through the heart. What they offer in return is a really good show and promises they just can't seem to keep.

THE HISTRIONIC DILEMMA

If Antisocials are Ferraris in a world of Toyotas, Histrionics are more like those beautiful little model cars that have all the moving parts, but do nothing except sit there and look good. Actually, they're less like cars and more like rare and beautiful flowers that require an enormous amount of maintenance, but still fade in a day. The dilemma they present is simple, though fiendishly difficult to resolve: either you supply the maintenance or someone else will.

WHAT THE QUESTIONS MEASURE

The specific behaviors covered on the checklist relate to several underlying personality characteristics that define a Histrionic emotional vampire.

Sociability

First and foremost, Histrionic vampires are social creatures. They enjoy other people's company, and most of the time they are enjoyable to be with. They can be cheerful, cordial, witty, sexy, exciting, or anything else you want, except substantial. Without Histrionics, the world would be a less friendly place: all business, and devoid of drama and style.

Need for Attention

Attention is the lifeblood of Histrionics. If they don't get enough of it, they feel themselves start to shrivel up and die. Histrionics always seek out the

THE HISTRIONIC VAMPIRE CHECKLIST: LIVING A SOAP OPERA

True or False   Score one point for each *true* answer.

1. This person usually stands out in a crowd by virtue of his or her looks, dress, or personality.   T F

2. This person is friendly, enthusiastic, entertaining, and absolutely wonderful in social situations.   T F

3. This person treats superficial acquaintances as if they were close friends.   T F

4. This person may become visibly upset when forced to share the spotlight.   T F

5. This person frequently changes his or her style of dress and overall look.   T F

6. This person loves to talk, gossip, and tell stories.   T F

7. This person's stories usually become more exaggerated and dramatic with each retelling.   T F

8. This person has a good fashion sense, but is perhaps a bit too concerned with his or her appearance.   T F

9. This person can become very upset over relatively small social slights.   T F

10. This person seldom admits to being angry, even when his or her anger is quite apparent to other people.   T F

11. This person has very little memory for day-to-day details.   T F

12. This person believes in supernatural entities, like angels, deities, or benevolent spirits, who regularly intervene in everyday life.   T F

13. This person has one or more unusual ailments that come and go according to no discernible pattern.   T F

14. This person has some problems doing regular chores like paperwork, housecleaning, and paying bills.   T F

15. This person has been known to get sick to avoid doing something unpleasant.   T F

16. This person fervently follows several television shows or sports teams.   T F

17. This person's communication, though highly colored, is often indirect and vague.   T F

18. This person requires more maintenance than a rare orchid, but believes that he or she is the easiest person in the world to get along with.   T F

19. This person often seems seductive, although he or she may not admit to it.   T F

20. Despite all the problems, this person is always in demand and more popular than most people could ever hope to be.   T F

Scoring   Five or more true answers qualify the person as a Histrionic emotional vampire, although not necessarily for a diagnosis of Histrionic personality disorder. If the person scores higher than 10, be careful that you don't inadvertently join the cast of his or her soap opera.

most appreciative audience. This tendency can destroy relationships. If anybody flirts with them, Histrionic vampires will usually flirt back, regardless of their intentions.

If you don't give them enough attention, they will always find a way to get more. The more desperate they are, like if someone else has the spotlight, the more destructive their methods.

Need for Approval

Histrionic vampires prefer that all the attention they get be positive. They strive for social acceptability, and they work hard to live up to everyone's expectations—unless those expectations involve taking care of boring day-to-day details.

Histrionic vampires hope everybody thinks they're wonderful. They regard criticism either as meaningless grumpiness that needs to be charmed away or as an affront to natural law. Either way, they will not hear anything but unqualified praise.

If you dare to criticize them, you will be stupefied at how quickly you go from being the most wonderful person in the world to evil incarnate.

Emotionality

Histrionics live in a world of emotions. Their reality is defined by what they feel, rather than by what they think or know. This emotionality can be disconcerting to anyone who tries to reason with them. A butterfly flapping its wings in China is sufficient to change a Histrionic's mood. Even less is required to change his or her mind.

Histrionics are famous for their selective memories. They can tell you how exciting a meeting was, who came, what each person wore, and who was mad at whom, but not what topics were discussed.

Dependency

No matter what role they're playing, beneath the makeup, Histrionics feel incompetent. They are easily overwhelmed by all those little details that they have such a hard time remembering. The whole purpose of their incessant showmanship is to cajole some big, strong, competent person to like them enough to take care of them, and maybe change all those annoying little rules. Usually, the strategy works.

Concern with Appearance

Looks are the stock in trade of Histrionics. They devote a good deal of energy to keeping them up—about as much as you put into your career. On the whole, it's not a bad investment. Physical attractiveness beats everything else hands down when it comes to predicting who will succeed. Needless to say, Histrionics invented aerobics, face-lifts, and liposuction.

Beware: no creature of the night is more desperate than a Histrionic vampire whose looks are beginning to fade.

Suggestibility

Histrionic vampires are such good shape shifters that it almost seems as if they have no permanent form of their own. They automatically start becoming what you want them to be as soon as they sense that you want it. They are superb hypnotists. They don't have to create an alternative reality; they are one. They can easily talk to plants, meditate on their past lives, and see angels. Histrionics invented New Age everything.

Lack of Insight

Histrionics know how to get looked at, but they don't have a clue about how to look at themselves. They often know less about their own history and motivation than about those of their favorite television characters.

Histrionics' selective memories make their lives into a series of vivid but unconnected events, no more related to one another than the programs broadcast on a given night.

Physical Symptoms

Histrionics invented the undiagnosable illness. Their lives are confusions of reality and fantasy, obsession and repression, impulse and inhibition. When they feel bad, they express it with their bodies. Illness is an art form. Histrionic diseases have to be interpreted like poems as well as treated with medicine and surgery. Histrionics get backaches when they can't stand up to somebody. Or constipation when they can't take any more crap.

Just giving them pills is missing the point. We will explore the uses of illness as metaphor in Chapter 13 when we examine Passive-Aggressive vampires.

HOW TO PROTECT YOURSELF FROM HISTRIONIC VAMPIRES

In a sentence, know them better than they know themselves. Enjoy the show, but try not to get written into the script.

12 Vampires Who Ham It Up

Whether It's Sex, Sickness, or Secrets of Success, There's Only One Show Business

Vampire Hams will do absolutely anything for attention. Overdo it, actually.

Histrionic Hams are typically not great artists. Their ploys for getting people to notice them are often crude, transparent, and superficial. To their intended audience, however, they're riveting.

Damon hears Vampire Shandra's laughter in the hallway. He looks away from his computer screen, toward the door. He doesn't notice it, but every other man in the accounting office is looking in the same direction.

Enter Shandra, wearing a slinky red dress that reveals some spectacular cleavage. She smiles, nods, and waves at people as if she were walking into a party. She turns toward Damon. He feels his heart speed up as their eyes meet.

Shandra stops cold, eyes and mouth open in pleasant surprise. "Damon," she says, rushing up to his desk. "Is that really you? You look so different without that old beard."

Shandra's perfume smells like flowers and spice all mixed together. It takes Damon's breath away as she leans over his desk to touch his face. "I didn't know you were so handsome under there!" she says. Her fingertips lightly graze his now smooth cheek.

Damon's face burns. Through sheer force of will, he keeps his eyes from glancing downward. "I, uh, thought it was, like, you know, time for a change," he says.

Shandra tilts her head and smiles as if it were the most interesting thing she'd heard all day. "You look so cute! I bet girls just follow you around the office."

"I wish," Damon says.

Shandra laughs. "Oh, you! You're just trying to be modest." She pokes at him with a long red nail as she lays a stack of folders on his desk. "Mr. Doyle asked me to see if I could get somebody to work up these figures today. Do you think . . . ?"

Damon pushes a deskful of projects aside and pulls the folders toward his heart. "No problemo," he says.

Damon is smitten. Nobody else is fooled for a minute, especially other women.

Later, in the break room, Jen, with a towel stuffed under her sweater, regales Brandy and Elise with her Shandra imitation. "Oh, Damon, you look soooo cute without that icky old beard." Jen speaks in a breathless, Marilyn Monroe voice and a fake southern accent. She leans over in front of Elise as if she were Damon. "See anything you like?" she says, batting her eyelashes.

Elise is laughing so hard she almost falls over.

"You should have seen Damon's face!" Jen says, shaking her head. "He never knew what hit him."

"How can men be so stupid?" Brandy asks.

Good question. How can men be so stupid? Are they so blind from testosterone poisoning that they can't see through phony and manipulative Ham-It-Up Histrionics like Shandra?

It's not just men.

Lest we assume that these sexual caricatures are all female and their dopey victims are all male, let's run the clock back a few months to the weekend that Jen, Elise, Brandy, and some of the other folks from the office spent in Aspen. There was this ski instructor named Wolfgang, tall, blond, and still tanned from his summer of surfing and bodybuilding in Hawaii.

Last winter, Damon was doing Wolfgang imitations in the break room.

If we look closely at these little vignettes, we can begin to see the dark and enigmatic power that Histrionics wield. To begin with, their victims are not the people that they are trying so transparently to manipulate. People like Damon are usually quite willing to be used in return for an enjoyable illusion. *It is the people watching the process who are most annoyed, and in the end they are the ones that the vampire is draining.*

Remember that Hams are trying to get the most attention possible, and they don't care whether it's positive or negative. For people who spend most of their lives trying to look good, it takes no effort at all to get people of the opposite sex to drool over them. Their real audience is much larger. The attention that seductive vampire Hams crave is from everyone, especially the people they are competing with for attention, and beating hands down. Whether you love these drama queens or hate them, you *will* notice them.

Getting noticed is a competitive sport, and Hams are the real pros. Boy toys, drag queens, death rockers, outrageous athletes, foul-mouthed deejays, and all the unsung small-time seducers like Shandra and Wolfgang have discovered that if you're flagrant enough, you can get twice as much attention from the people who hate you as you get from your adoring fans.

Unless the people with whom they play their sexual games are very naive, seductive Hams present very little danger to them. Like prostitutes, these vampires offer a simple business transaction—I put on a show to make you feel attractive and sexy; you pay me with attention and little favors. The real problem these vampires cause is the disruption of the social order. Histrionic Hams invented sexual harassment, both doing it and suing for it. One theatrical vampire can turn an entire office into a battlefield.

Other people competing for the same attention and favors using less effective tools, like brains, talent, and hard work, resent the fact that Histrionics get special treatment because they're obnoxiously sexy or just plain obnoxious. It isn't fair!

No, it isn't. It *is* show business.

HAM-IT-UP HYPNOSIS

Histrionic Hams are the kinds of hypnotists who get people to cluck like chickens and enjoy doing it. Hypnosis is a show, and these vampires have an instinctive ability to work an audience.

The alternative reality that Histrionic Hams offer is themselves. They already live in the magical world of show business, where everything is bigger and better than life, but simpler and easier to understand. Boy meets girl; good guys fight bad guys; knights in shining armor rescue maidens—we all know the stories, and we love them. Histrionic hypnotists offer the chance to live them.

Ham-It-Up Histrionics invite you to go on stage and live out their fantasy with them. You can be a good guy and play along or a spoilsport bad guy, full of criticism and negative vibes. Either way, you're part of the show.

Histrionic vampires spend most of their lives in a hypnotic trance. When they're around, it's almost impossible not to be hypnotized. To understand them, and to protect yourself, you must pay close attention to those danger signs.

Deviating from Standard Procedures

Ham-It-Up Histrionics hope you'll be so enthralled by their performances that you'll relieve them of their tedious day-to-day responsibilities. Their most common strategy is to hypnotize you into believing they are too ditzy to take care of things themselves. Histrionics unconsciously structure the situation so that it seems much easier for you to do things for them than it is to get them to do things for themselves. If you find yourself running around madly, trying to get someone out of the preposterous messes he or she has stumbled into, that person is either your child or a Histrionic vampire. Or both.

Thinking in Superlatives

Histrionics prefer brightly colored emotional impressions to thought. Their world is made up mostly of superlatives and hyperbole, so it is no wonder that they elicit the same from you. You either love them or hate them, but you just can't ignore them.

The superlatives go in the other direction as well. If there is a Histrionic in your life, you know how quickly you can go from being the most wonderful person in the world to being the most terrible.

Instant Rapport

Histrionics invented love at first sight. If they don't get you with their first impression, they probably won't get you at all.

Seeing the Person or Situation as Special

Histrionics offer a devious and dirty deal. Here they are: attractive, exciting, and needy. It's easy to imagine that if you take care of a few trifling details for them, they will be *so* grateful that they will continue to shower you with attention and love. You might even believe that you can pick up a relationship with a really attractive person at a bargain price, just by being a little nicer than all those other meanies.

Dream on. Ham-It-Up Histrionics may be a lot of things, but they are never a bargain. Like all skilled hypnotists, they use your own hidden needs to control you. If you find yourself engaging in pleasant fantasies of rescue and eternal gratitude, wake up and rescue yourself.

Lack of Concern with Objective Information

If people you used to trust tell you that you are being played for a fool, and you think they're just jealous, you'd better hope that God will have mercy on your soul, because the vampire won't.

Confusion

With Histrionics, the play's the thing, and you can't *not* play. Sometimes it's easy to see that you're being manipulated, but devilishly difficult to figure out what to do about it. Theater is the secret of Histrionics' power and vulnerability. If you have to deal with a Ham-It-Up Histrionic, your best defense is to write a role for yourself that keeps you at a safe distance. The only way to fight show business is with more show business.

WRITING A SAFE ROLE FOR YOURSELF

The closer you get to Histrionic Hams, the more dangerous they are.

If you become their main audience, you'll discover that the price for their performances is extremely high—your complete attention and taking care of their every need. If you let them down even slightly, the script will shift from light comedy to horror. Unappreciated Histrionics instantly explode into rage, sadness, or whatever it takes to regain the center of attention. You'll never know what got into them or what hit you.

Your best defense is not to get taken in by their performance in the first place. The way to do that is by writing a simple, easily understood role for yourself that puts you outside the sweep of Histrionic drama.

ILLNESS AS THEATER

Histrionics have a limited amount of energy. The downside of their enthusiasm is a vague feeling of lassitude and general malaise when life gets too complicated. Trust their vivid imaginations and instinctive flair for the dramatic to turn not feeling like performing into a performance. Burned-out Ham-It-Up vampires can change their life scripts to medical dramas when they discover how much attention they get for being sick. You can bet that their maladies will be as draining to you as they are to them. We will examine Histrionic illness in more detail in Chapter 13.

CELEBRITIES, FANS, AND WANNABES

If, as you read about Histrionic Hams, you think you recognize them from the racks of tabloids at checkout counters, you are correct. They are also the people who are buying the tabloids and the people on the street who are dressed up as their favorite characters when it isn't Halloween.

Most of us develop an identity that is fairly well fixed sometime between the ages of 20 and 30. We come to know who we are in our careers and our relationships. We may not like the person we are, and if we don't, it may motivate us to make an effort to change and grow.

For Histrionics, no effort is involved; they just pretend. They are all actors and actresses. Many of them confuse their identities with the roles that they play. Some lose their identities altogether.

You can see this clearly in the lives of real performers. If they play lovers with someone, chances are that you will read that they've dumped their present spouse and are planning a lavish wedding with their costar du jour.

When Histrionics become celebrities, they lose themselves in that role. The show never stops because there is always an audience. Even if celebrities are miserable, their lives are more interesting than ours. We love to watch them, and as long as we do, they will put on a show for us. Most of them say they hate having no privacy. The only thing they seem to hate worse is when no one pays attention to them. That's when they start doing reality TV.

Fading celebrities are not the only ones doing reality TV. Every other Histrionic Ham in the world has his or her own show, whether it's on broadcast, cable, YouTube, or right in your own neighborhood. Histrionic Hams desperately want to be someone that people will pay attention to. Some can actually act or play music; most merely act like their favorite actors and musicians. It is as if dressing like a celebrity or knowing the details of their lives somehow imbues Histrionics with some celeb identity as well. It used to be that only teenagers acted like this. Now there seems to be no age limit on playing dress-up or air guitar.

Histrionic Hams, whether actual celebs, fans, or wannabes, often do not know who they are, but they always know who they'd like to be.

We the audience, don't know whether to pity them or envy them. We only know that we cannot look away.

NINE WAYS TO PROTECT YOURSELF FROM HISTRIONIC HAMS

Step out of Ham-It-Up Histrionics' never-ending drama with a new script.

1. Know Them, Know Their History, and Know Your Goal

Histrionic Hams are usually ridiculously easy to spot. They're right at the center of attention. Look for sexual stereotypes; listen for jokes, juicy gossip, mindless effervescence, motivational talks, or maybe even heart-rending sobs.

If you ask other people about Histrionics, you'll hear many different and contradictory stories. This is because Histrionics are, each of them, many different and contradictory people.

Your goal with Histrionic Hams is to keep from being drawn into their drama. This is difficult. At first, they'll treat you as if you are the most wonderful person on earth. They may compare you with other people who have been mean, cruel, unappreciative, unloving, or whatever. Let the fact that their world is filled with good guys and bad guys alert you before you step into their fantasy. If you let them down, you can easily be transferred from one group to the other.

If you pass up the flattery, you can avoid emotional turmoil later on. Your best bet is to write yourself a role that allows you to stand on the sidelines and just watch the show. Avoid the impulse to become a critic, because sooner or later, that will turn the spotlight on you—as the villain.

Histrionic Hams are outrageous. If you allow yourself to be outraged, you will be the one who gets drained.

If you are involved with a Histrionic Ham, expect to provide a great deal of maintenance in exchange for an occasional great performance. If you expect consistency or reciprocity, you will get only a headache, either in the vampire's head or in yours. The effects will be pretty much the same.

Histrionics of both sexes invite sexual harassment and sexual harassment suits. Think long and hard before you embark on either of these paths. Ham-It-Up Histrionics sometimes give their greatest performances on the witness stand.

2. Get Outside Verification

Histrionics prefer to give their emotional impressions of events rather than facts. Their stories are interesting and entertaining, but very short on accurate information, and often quite biased. They expect you to believe them, and will regard it as a slight if you don't. Risk their displeasure by asking someone else's opinion. You'll be glad you did. Remember the rule about not letting a vampire be your source of information.

3. Do What They Don't

Be boring. Be consistent. Plan ahead. Let the facts rather than your emotions determine your response. Learn to keep your mind open and your mouth shut.

4. Pay Attention to Their Actions, Not Their Words

As with all vampires, you have to hold Histrionics responsible for what they do rather than what they say. With Histrionic Hams, the do and say distinction begins with listening to the actual content of their words. Histrionics seldom lie, but they seldom tell the whole truth, except when it slips out between the lines.

Pay attention to detail. Ask questions to determine the who, what, when, where, and why of situations before assuming you know what's going on.

5. Pick Your Battles

Always remember that the battle you need to win with Histrionic Hams is to avoid being cast as the person whose emotions are drained. Hams can drain you by wearing you out with their endless dependency or, just as surely, by making you angry at them.

You have to decide when Hams' erratic and sometimes obnoxious dramatics cross the line and require retaliatory action. If you are going to fight back, be sure that you've got your own act together.

Never take action when you're angry. Histrionics will perform far better in the heat of any moment than you will. Plan carefully, and check out your ideas with other people before you say something that you'll regret.

The most thankless task you can possibly take on is trying to explain Histrionics to themselves. Histrionic Hams are quite unaware of their own motivations even when everybody else sees them clearly. You'll be astounded at how much they can ignore. You won't believe that they can't see how obvious their manipulations are. Spare yourself an enormous amount of trouble by remembering Histrionics really are *unaware of what they are doing and why they are doing it*. They invented denial.

Not only do Histrionics not understand themselves, they don't have a clue why anyone does anything. Their understanding of psychology and physics is often tinged with magic. They may believe that things happen because of the alignment of stars, the vibrations of crystals, or the intervention of guardian angels. If you suggest otherwise, they'll just think you're crazy.

Speaking of crazy, the last thing you want to do is engage a Histrionic in a battle over how he or she dresses.

6. Let Contingencies Do the Work

The best kinds of behavior control programs for Histrionic Hams are the same ones that work for obstreperous children. Be as clear as possible about the exact behaviors you want to see, and structure all contingencies so that Hams get more attention for doing things right than they do for doing them wrong.

Histrionics have chronic problems with day-to-day tasks. They forget to pay bills, run errands, or do enough advance planning to get anywhere on time. There is no record of a Ham-It-Up Histrionic ever having balanced a checkbook. It will seem easier to do for them rather than making them do for themselves. Indeed, the implicit deal they try to make is that performing should exempt them from all other duties.

To get Histrionics to do anything they find unpleasant, you'll have to set strict limits and stick by them in the face of all manner of dramatic distractions. Never let performances of any sort get Histrionics out of their responsibilities.

That's the theory, anyway. In practice, being consistent with Histrionic Hams is almost impossible. Sometimes they'll just wear you out. They can put on a two-hour performance to get out of a five-minute task.

All contingencies should revolve around things that Histrionics are supposed to do, rather than how they're supposed to act around other people. You won't get very far with rules about flirting, off-color jokes, or other annoying behaviors because Ham-It-Up Histrionics are constitutionally unable to see their own behavior as anything but charming and appropriate. That's why educational seminars on sexual harassment and cultural sensitivity seldom work on the worst offenders.

You'll get further by using Histrionics' acting ability to direct them toward more productive roles. If you give them a sexual harassment lecture, they may ask, "What do you want me to do, act like some kind of saint or something?"

Say, "Yes, exactly."

The very best contingency with Histrionics is to sneak up on them when they're being good and praise the hell out of them.

7. Choose Your Words as Carefully as You Pick Your Battles

This one is simple. If you want to get anywhere with Ham-It-Up Histrionics, use praise and flattery in sugared doses that would put a normal person into a diabetic coma. Regular praise for even the smallest of accomplishments is the only thing that keeps Histrionics anywhere near copacetic.

Don't waste your breath on criticism of any sort. Histrionics will always believe that the problem is with your perception rather than their behavior.

Anyway, if you remember the praise, you can pretty much forget about everything else.

8. Ignore Tantrums

If you criticize or forget the praise, there will be tantrums. Their forms will be as wild and various as the vampires who throw them. Ham-It-Up Histrionics use emotional outbursts in the same way Afghan rebels use Kalashnikovs: as weapons and threats, or simply as expressions of general exuberance.

Tears, however, are the Histrionic's specialty.

For a civilized human being, another person's pain requires action. It is almost impossible to watch other people cry and do nothing to make them feel better—even when you know they're using tears to get around the rules.

To handle manipulative crying, use an old therapist's trick: don't let the tears or the reason they're falling become the subject for discussion. When Histrionics cry, hand them a tissue and go on with whatever you were talking about. This technique takes practice, but it works.

9. Know Your Own Limits

However much attention you have to give, Histrionics will need it all. They will draw it out of you at first with flattery. They put you in a special category all by yourself. Usually, the last thing you hear before Histrionics start draining away your life force is, "You're the only person I can talk to." We will discuss this more fully in Chapter 14, "Histrionics in Your Life."

Ham-It-Up Histrionics do have useful talents and abilities. They can be good and entertaining friends and productive workers, especially when the job requires being dramatic and engaging. Histrionics can blossom, but they require as much care as a rare and beautiful orchid. Only you can decide how much such a flower is worth.

13 Passive-Aggressive Vampires

Deliver Us from Ghoulies and Ghosties
and People Who Are Only Trying to Help

Please do not confuse Passive-Aggressive Histrionics with the old diagnosis of *passive-aggressive personality disorder*, which was removed from the *Diagnostic Manual* because the criteria were hopelessly unclear. Some people are consciously passive-aggressive, negativistic, and resistant to authority. They are not the people we are discussing here. Passive-Aggressive Histrionics are not aware of their own aggressive actions. They may fool themselves, but the people around them are seldom taken in.

Passive-Aggressive Histrionics hunger for approval. If you ask them, they're always doing what they're supposed to do, thinking what they're supposed to think, and feeling what they're supposed to feel. They're relentlessly obedient, cheerful, thrifty, brave, clean, and reverent—at least in their own estimation. You may wonder how such nice people could create problems for anyone. The answer, stated simply, is: what *they* don't know can hurt *you*.

What these aggressively nice vampires don't know is how real people operate. Like all Histrionics, Passive-Aggressives create a role for themselves and then become lost in it. Unlike their flamboyant Ham-It-Up cousins, the role these vampires create is more internal than external. In their minds, they are good children—innocent, happy, eager to please, and always willing to do more than their share.

Real people are complex, full of base motivations and unacceptable desires as well as the stuff of angels. Passive-Aggressive Histrionics have the frightening capacity to deny any but the most superficial and attractive thoughts. They blithely ignore the ugly stuff, even if it's plainly visible to everyone else. Histrionics are not perfectionists; they're more like perfectionist wannabes. Even then, they don't necessarily want to *be* perfect; they just want to *look* perfect. It is as if they are trying to be Barbie and Ken, without realizing that their role models are nothing but plastic dolls.

Since the role they're trying to play is impossible, no wonder they keep stepping out of character.

> *Vampire Meredith moves up to the counter to order her coffee. She eyes the double-fudge brownies in the case, but virtuously passes them up in favor of a container of yogurt. She makes quite a show of checking the nutritional labels. "Oh, look," she says. "This one is only 120 calories!"*
>
> *"Come on, Meredith, live a little," Erin says. "Get one of these brownies. They're great!"*
>
> *"Yeah, right," Meredith says. "If I even like smell one of those, it goes right to my hips." She pats her rather ample derriere.*
>
> *As Meredith sits down with her yogurt and nonfat latte, Erin shakes her head. "You've got more willpower than I do. I'd die without my daily chocolate fix."*
>
> *Meredith shrugs. "It's like so not hard once you get used to it. I haven't had chocolate in such a long time, I hardly even remember what it tastes like."*
>
> *"You're incredible," Erin says as she takes another bite of her brownie.*
>
> *On the way home, Erin passes the coffee shop. Inside, she sees Meredith pointing at the double-fudge brownies in the case. The counter guy takes out four, bags them up, and hands them to her.*
>
> *Erin, excited about catching her friend in the act of being human, hurries in and sneaks up behind Meredith. "If you give me one of those brownies, I won't tell anybody I saw you here," she says, giggling.*
>
> *Meredith turns slowly. Her eyes seem unfocused. She looks at Erin for a second or two before appearing to recognize her. "Hi," she says. "I was just getting some brownies for my niece."*
>
> *"Oh, okay," Erin says, feeling embarrassed. As she hurries out to catch her bus, she seems to remember Meredith saying that her niece lived in Chicago.*

Erin thought she saw a regular person succumbing to the urge for a little illicit chocolate. To her, there was nothing unusual about it. She occasionally binges on brownies herself and jokes about it later. What Erin actually saw was a Histrionic stepping out of her perfect role while hypnotizing herself into believing that she was still in it.

Meredith is operating as two people at the same time: a person of exemplary willpower who always follows her diet, and a regular person who occasionally binges on brownies. The one with willpower is the one she sees as herself. The other one she hardly sees at all.

This kind of splitting of the personality is the hallmark of Passive-Aggressive Histrionics. Please don't call them "schizophrenic." Schizophrenia is a biochemical psychotic disorder in which the splitting is from reality. Histrionics are the people who divide their personalities into acceptable and unacceptable parts, then do their best to ignore the unacceptable. If you want a name for it, *dissociation* comes closest.

The real problem is not with brownies and diets. Had Erin pressed, Meredith would probably have admitted that the chocolate was for her. There are other things that Meredith would be far less likely to recognize. At the top of the list are the aggressive impulses that such a confrontation would evoke.

To a psychologist, *aggression* refers to a continuum of thoughts and actions that have to do with imposing your own will on the world. At one end is angry, assaultive behavior; at the other are simple attempts to act in your own self-interest and get your own way. Histrionics, who accept only the loving and giving in themselves, reject the whole continuum. They prefer to believe that they live their lives for others and never put themselves first. Many of them have problems acknowledging their sexual impulses as well.

The problem is that all people, Histrionics included, are biologically hardwired for sex and aggression. We all want things for ourselves that may be embarrassing or inappropriate. Normal people recognize that they can't act on their impulses. Passive-Aggressive Histrionics try to believe that they have no inappropriate impulses to act on. This is what makes them dangerous.

Back to Meredith and Erin. At work, most people like Meredith, but they see her as a bit ding-y. They call her "Little Miss Perfect," knowing full well that she is neither little nor perfect. To Erin, catching Meredith *in flagrante delicto* with a bag of brownies is wonderful material to share at coffee break. In a day or two, the brownie story is all over the office. In a week, it's forgotten—by everyone but Meredith.

Inside, Meredith feels hurt, misunderstood, betrayed, and angry, but she can't acknowledge these feelings even to herself, much less to Erin.

Not being aware of her anger doesn't stop Meredith from acting on it. Suddenly, she begins to realize that Erin is not really such a nice person. Meredith likes her and all that, but she is a bit hypercritical and, well, bitchy. *Everybody* says so—especially a few disgruntled employees in Erin's department with whom Meredith finds herself spending more and more time.

Eventually, Meredith tries to help Erin by telling her in a very nice way that a lot of people really don't like her. Not only does Erin not listen, she actually gets mad!

Meredith is frantic. The only person she can go to is Jane, the department manager.

"Knock, knock." Meredith taps tentatively on the fabric of Jane's cubicle. "Do you have a minute? I really need to ask you a question."

"Sure, come on in," Jane says.

Meredith sits down and opens her planner so that she can take notes. "I need some ideas about how to work with Erin. I'm absolutely at my wit's end."

Jane waits a minute to see if there's more to the question. Apparently not. "Did something specific happen to make you feel that way?"

"It's just, well, everything. Since she came here, there's always been something. I mean, I really like her as a person and all, but she's just so totally unpredictable. You never know when she's going to bite your head off for some little comment."

"Did you get into an argument with her?"

"I don't know if you could call it an argument. I mean, she was the one yelling. I was just standing there with my mouth hanging open." Meredith demonstrates the astonished expression she wore at the time.

"Was there something in particular that Erin was upset about?"

"She said I was trying to undermine her authority." Meredith does her astonished face again. "Can you believe that? It is so not like me to try to undermine anybody. I was only trying to help."

"How were you trying to help?"

"I just told her that some of the people in her department were going on stress leave because they can't take her management style."

"Really? Who's going on stress leave?"

"Well, nobody right now, but a lot of people are thinking about it. They come to me because they're afraid to talk to her. I just told Erin about it so she could maybe talk to them or something, but instead she went completely ballistic.*"*

Under the guise of being helpful and standing up for the poor underdogs who are too frightened to speak for themselves, Meredith mounts a Passive-Aggressive assault on Erin. There's a good possibility that everyone in the unit may be hurt as a result of a stupid bag of brownies.

GIVING UNTIL IT HURTS

Passive-Aggressive Histrionics love giving. Most of it is truly sincere, but some crosses the line into manipulation. They believe that the Golden Rule is a binding contract: if they do unto others, others are supposed to do back.

Everybody takes. Some people ask you for what they want. Passive-Aggressive Histrionics are more apt to give and give until you finally get the idea they want something. If you don't get the message, they'll keep on until they make themselves sick and make you sick of them. But, in their own minds at least, their accounts payable look great. Everybody wants something, and everybody gets angry at not getting it. This is a law of nature, but Passive-Aggressives keep thinking they can break it.

Many Histrionics also believe that the more you deny yourself, the better you are as a person. Viewed in this context, anorexia is the height of nobility.

Histrionics are also frustrated and angry. Not that they would admit it. They will, however, point out the well-documented fact that they do for everybody else, but nobody even listens to them. All they can do is keep giving, suffer in silence, and throw more fuel on the subterranean fires that keep them burning with resentment.

This pattern of pathological giving, though not specific to women by any means, does correspond to what has been expected of females throughout thousands of years of male domination. Pathological giving may also be the result of the mind-warping influences of a dysfunctional family. As always, however, knowing where a problem comes from is not the same as solving it.

It is possible to consider Passive-Aggressives as being victims of forces beyond their control. That's probably how they see themselves, and that in itself is a big part of the problem. Another law of nature is that victims victimize.

ILLNESS AS COMMUNICATION

Jason comes home from his fishing trip late at night to find Danielle sitting up in the living room. Her eyes are closed, but she's not asleep. She has a heating pad on her stomach.

"What's wrong, honey?" Jason asks.

"Just a little tummyache," she says. At the same time, she winces and draws in a sharp breath.

"Do you want me to get you your medicine?"

"I already took some, but it doesn't seem to help."

Jason puts his hand on her forehead to see if she has a fever. She puts her hand on top of his. It's ice cold.

"How long . . ."

His question is cut short by a moan of pain.

"We need to get you to the Emergency Room," Jason says as he calls Danielle's mother to ask her to come over to stay with the kids.

This is not the first time this has happened. Danielle and Jason have spent several previous nights in the ER when she was having attacks. She's been to several specialists. All the tests have been inconclusive. Nobody can figure out what's wrong.

Jason hates himself for being suspicious, but it seems to him that the attacks all seem to happen when he has gone fishing or hunting. Could the problem be in her head? Before he left, he broached the subject with Danielle, but very cautiously.

"Maybe it's too stressful for you when I go away—I mean with the kids and the house and everything."

"No, I can handle it, except for this stupid tummy stuff."

"Do you want me to stay home?"

"No, no. You work hard. You need your relaxation."

Jason is in a bind. On the one hand, he thinks that Danielle's attacks are related to his trips with the guys, but she keeps telling him that he needs to go. What is he to do?

Early the next morning at the ER, after all the scans have come up negative, the gastroenterologist shakes his head. "The only thing left is exploratory surgery."

The chances are good that Danielle's surgery will discover nothing unequivocal. The sickness in her body is, at least partly, an expression of the tumult of unacknowledged aggression in her mind. Her psychological state is hard to grasp for people who have never been there, and almost impossible for people who have. Think of it this way: the little angel on her shoulder is saying that Jason needs his trips (and all the other forms of recreation he always seems to be involved with), and that she should be able to take care of her job, the kids, the house, the dogs, her mother, and everything else. The little devil says . . . what little devil? If there is one there, Danielle is not aware of her. Nevertheless, the resentment the little devil might have spoken about still plays out in Danielle's body.

Let me make this perfectly clear: *Histrionics' ailments may be stress-related, but they are definitely not all in their heads.* No self-respecting Passive-

Aggressive Histrionic would *ever* fake an illness. They really are sick. What causes their sickness and what you can do to get them well is the part that's confusing.

Here's how stress-related disorders work.

Back in Chapter 8, on Bullies, I brought up the fight or flight response, which almost everyone has heard of and experienced. Few people understand just how complex and pervasive that response is. Virtually every physiological system is affected when huge doses of hormones shift the body into overdrive. Every bit of energy is diverted to the organs involved in fighting or running. The heart and lungs speed up, muscles engorge with blood, the brain goes on the alert for sources of danger, and the digestive process shuts down. If there is any food in the system, the body tries to dump it from whichever end is closest. Needless to say, this process is hard on the physiology, especially if the stressors causing the fight or flight response are chronic.

We tend to think of stress as coming from outside—rambunctious kids, critical parents, money problems, a demanding job, or whatever. Actually, most people can handle external stressors pretty well. The most damaging stress comes from inside, when you're being pulled in two different directions at the same time—loving your parents, but hating to be around them; having a job that drives you crazy, but that pays more than anything else you could get; or not being able to stomach the conflict and negative feelings that would arise if you asked your husband to stop taking so many damned fishing trips.

Passive-Aggressive Histrionics like Danielle are often too nice to ask for anything for themselves, like a little help once in a while. Sometimes, their bodies have to ask for them.

In addition to being medical phenomena, Histrionic illnesses are a form of self-expression. They are metaphors for what Histrionics feel about themselves and their world. These vampires feel confused and overwhelmed; therefore, their disorders are confusing and overwhelming to the Histrionics themselves, and to the people who have to treat them. Living with a sick Histrionic is confusing and overwhelming as well. You are always wondering what you should do and what you should be feeling.

Jason has gone to Danielle's appointments with her. On the one hand, he worries that some terrible undiagnosed disorder is causing her pain. He pushes the doctors to do more tests, consult more specialists, do whatever it takes to find out what's wrong.

On the other hand, he agrees with her primary-care doctor, who long ago said that it could be stress. Jason knows Danielle thinks this means that medical science has given up on her, so he doesn't talk about it. He just stops going on fishing trips and takes on more and more of the household chores.

If you're thinking, "Good for him!" think again. Even if he is absolutely correct and should be around more and helping out more, doing it this way will make the situation worse, not better. Jason is rewarding Danielle for being sick instead of asking for what she wants. He is merely shifting the load of unexpressed resentment to himself.

Resentment does not just evaporate, as Histrionics so devoutly wish; it merely comes out in some other form. Jason will get grumpier and more withdrawn, and Danielle, in response, will get sicker. The battle can continue for years without anyone ever raising his or her voice.

The problem with stress-related or psychosomatic disorders like this is not the stress itself but the passive avoidance of conflict. Dealing directly with the stress by eliminating it or medicating its symptoms away with antidepressants or, worse, with benzodiazepines or alcohol merely perpetuates the problem or creates a new one, substance abuse.

The most effective cure is getting the dynamics of the situation out in the open. To break the cycle, Danielle needs to recognize what she wants and ask for it. This is probably not something that Jason and Danielle can discuss themselves. It usually requires a skilled therapist who can guide them around the possible misinterpretations, so that Danielle doesn't think she's being told that the stomach pain is in her head, or that she is selfish for wanting some time off of her own.

Many Histrionics will resist therapy because they are sure the problem is medical and not adequately diagnosed. Sometimes they are correct. For some doctors, *stress-related* is a synonym for *I don't know.*

To a psychologist, psychosomatic disorders follow patterns just as physical disorders do. They occur in particular personality types, and there is almost always an element of internal conflict and external confusion.

The most effective thing Jason can do is help Danielle to find a doctor she trusts and insist that she follow up with whatever treatment is recommended.

If he is serious about helping, Jason can also look at balance in the relationship. Histrionics almost beg to be taken advantage of. They rarely ask for what they want as directly and effectively as, say, a typical male. It's easy to let things get way out of balance with respect to the most valuable commodity in most relationships: free time without kids.

If Jason willingly sacrifices some of his autonomy by insisting that free time be evenly and scrupulously balanced, there is likely to be more free time for both of them, without all those trips to the doctor or the emergency room. This will not be easy; Danielle will probably say that things are fine the way they are, except when she is having tummyaches. Which, of course, means that they are not fine at all.

The critical difference between this strategy and just not going on fishing trips is that it is communicated directly and explicitly in words rather than symptoms. Danielle gets time off not because she is sick, but because she deserves it as much as Jason does.

The more vehemently a Passive-Aggressive Histrionic like Danielle insists that she doesn't need something, the more you should insist that she take it.

The other thing Jason should look at courageously is his own behavior. Wives of alcoholics who are afraid to tackle drinking head on often express their disapproval by getting sick. If this particular shoe fits, Jason should put it on and walk himself to the doctor's office to have his substance use evaluated.

For their medical metaphors, Passive-Aggressive Histrionics favor vague maladies that are as debilitating as they are hard to diagnose. Allergies are big, as are all forms of gastrointestinal disorder. Also popular are fibromyalgia and chronic fatigue syndrome as well as designer diseases, like hypoglycemia and malevolent yeasts.

Many Histrionic disorders are psychological, ranging from depression and anxiety to delayed posttraumatic stress. The symptoms are usually pervasive, confusing, and frustratingly sporadic. Some of the psychological epidemics of the 1980s, especially recovered memories of sexual abuse and multiple personality, may have been the result of overly protective therapists mistaking Histrionics' metaphors for actual reality. These disorders do exist, but not in the vast numbers diagnosed at the height of the "me" decade.

With all the ambiguity surrounding Histrionics' medical and psychological disorders, there is a temptation to believe that they get sick in order to get out of doing things that they don't want to do. That is not really what is going on. Histrionics do get out of doing things that they don't want to do, but the price they pay for it is ridiculously high. The technical name for this getting out of things is *secondary gain*. The primary gain is escaping conflict, both external and internal. That is what Histrionics are willing to suffer for.

PASSIVE-AGGRESSIVE HYPNOSIS

Passive-Aggressives can cloud minds better than the Shadow in the old radio program. The only trouble is it's their own minds that they cloud. They create an alternate reality in which they are admired and loved by one and all because they never need anything for themselves, and they never, ever do anything bad. The logical contortions they go through to maintain this illusion are enough to make anybody's eyes glaze over.

If you listen closely to them, you'll find yourself entering another dimension, where everything is entertaining, but nothing makes much sense—*Alice in Wonderland* is a fairly realistic portrayal of a Histrionic's world. It is somewhat humorous viewed from the outside, but imagine living there.

People react differently to Passive-Aggressive hypnosis. Some are enchanted enough to want to rescue the poor waifs; others get a pounding headache. Everybody gets drained, especially the poor souls who keep trying to get Histrionics to admit that they really are angry.

THE HIGH-SELF-ESTEEM SYNDROME

Mary Wollstonecraft Shelley wrote a book about a sad and unintentionally dangerous creature sewn together from mismatched bits and pieces. She could have been describing another kind of monster created out of the scraps of late-twentieth-century pop psychology—the person with high self-esteem.

Self-esteem used to be the effect of success, but somehow an insufficient amount of it evolved into the cause of failure. Over the past 40 years, most human problems have been ascribed to the pernicious forces of low self-esteem. Self-esteem is taught in school, and people are advised to repeat affirmations under the assumption that raw good feelings about yourself can be shaped into any sort of achievement.

Self-esteem now seems to be regarded as an end unto itself, the prime mover of the human mind, like motivation in the world of business.

There is a logical flaw in this concept: anything that explains everything also explains nothing. The worst problem, however, is that many approaches to improving self-esteem are unwittingly teaching people to be more like Passive-Aggressive Histrionics.

The basic idea is to improve self-esteem by accentuating the positive and eliminating the negative, which is fine in theory. The only difficulty is that the negative isn't eliminated; it's merely plastered over with affirmations and often projected onto other people. It has become fashionable to see low self-esteem as the result of some form of abuse or mistreatment in one's past. People are supposed to get better by bringing their resentments out into the open. Everybody except abusers is loved and affirmed, and anything that makes good people feel bad is defined as abuse.

What's missing in this popular approach to psychology is the same thing that is missing in all Histrionic creations—namely, an attempt to go below the surface and deal with the self in all its complexity. The human psyche is constantly aswirl with contradictory thoughts and impulses. The great challenge we all face is to understand this roiling mass of instinct and emotion and organize it into moral and productive behavior.

Even if my concerns about popular psychology are prejudiced and unfounded, there are still problems with the idea of making people better and more successful by raising their self-esteem. As we'll see in the later chapters on Narcissistic vampires, high self-esteem itself can be a destructive force.

NINE WAYS TO PROTECT YOURSELF FROM PASSIVE-AGGRESSIVE HISTRIONICS

Don't get mad at Passive-Aggressives; get smart.

1. Know Them, Know Their History, and Know Your Goal

Often, Passive-Aggressives have a history of interpersonal problems that, according to them, come out of nowhere to plague them. Their world is two-dimensional, full of villains and victims. In a job interview, they will usually tell you about personality conflicts in their previous job. On a first date, they might tell you about their last dysfunctional relationship because you're a nice person and will understand. Be warned: Nice person or not, in their next interview or on their next first date, they'll be saying the same things about you.

The more these hapless vampires like, respect, or fear you, the less able they are to say directly, "I'm angry," or, "I don't want to do that." They have to rely on misunderstanding, forgetting, getting sick, or falling apart to do the job for them. That's the way it is; accept it or pay the price. The most frequent cause of headaches is pursuing the one goal that is absolutely unattainable with Histrionics—having them admit to their actual motives.

Even if Passive-Aggressives don't understand their motives, you should. Remember that they hunger for approval, and they cause the most trouble when they aren't getting it.

The most productive goal with these vampires is preventing their Passive-Aggressive outbursts by giving them the approval they want, but making it contingent on specific behaviors. Never let them guess what you want; the consequences are too great if they get it wrong. Tell Passive-Aggressives in explicit detail what it takes to please you, and praise them profusely when they do it. This strategy is simple and almost foolproof, but it is seldom employed. It's hard to praise somebody who gives you headaches. Hard as it is, it's far easier than the alternative.

As long as they are getting explicit direction and plenty of praise for their successes, Passive-Aggressives can perform most social tasks even better than normal people. They'll be caring friends, devoted lovers, and hard-working employees. They're happy to give and give as long as they're getting something back. But then it isn't giving, is it? Never mind. If you try to apply logic to the behavior of Passive-Aggressive Histrionics, you will always end up frustrated and confused. Instead, just love them and praise them. If you can't, stay away from them.

2. Get Outside Verification

Frustrated Passive-Aggressives will come to you with all kinds of stories about who said and did what to whom. It is important to remember that their perceptions are often distorted by their belief that they couldn't possibly do anything wrong. Histrionic tales may be dramatic and convincing, but you should never believe them without getting corroboration.

If Passive-Aggressives tell you that other people are upset with you, it means *they're* upset. The way these vampires ask for anything is by telling you that somebody else wants it.

Dealing with Passive-Aggressives will teach you an important truth about the human condition—you can never know what is really going on, because there is no such thing as an objective source. People will see the same events differently, according to their own needs. In the end, verification is always a judgment call.

3. Do What They Don't

Understand yourself and your own motivations, both acceptable and unacceptable. Always assume you are acting in your own self-interest, and know what you expect to get for what you give.

Be direct. Tell people what you expect to get. Make it very clear what you feel and what you want. If you're angry, say so. Don't try to disguise attacks as constructive criticism. Better yet, wait until you're over your anger before you approach the problems that Passive-Aggressive Histrionics cause. As with all vampires, you should think about what you want to happen rather than about what's wrong with what's already happened. Let your goals determine your actions. Easy to say, hard to do.

4. Pay Attention to Their Actions, Not Their Words

The maddening thing about Passive-Aggressives is that their words are so different from their actions. If you ask them what they want, they'll say they want to make you happy, even as they do things to make you miserable.

On the surface, their actions make no sense, but there is an underlying logic. If you want to understand Histrionics, read their actions as if they were sad, angry adolescent poems about how the expectations of others are a prison from which they can never escape.

If you're involved with Passive-Aggressive Histrionics, you cannot avoid being perceived as the person who is imprisoning them. Don't try to convince them that they are free. Instead, focus on your own behavior, and try to be a compassionate jailer.

5. Pick Your Battles

Forget any attempt to make Passive-Aggressives admit to what they really feel. It'll only make your headache worse. Don't make the mistake of demanding that they talk to you directly about problems. You might as well demand that they speak in rhyming couplets.

With a Passive-Aggressive, there really are no battles you can win. Once the situation turns into a battle, you have already lost.

The battles you can win are all with yourself. Dealing with Passive-Aggressive Histrionics requires you to go beyond your own conceptions of how things ought to be done.

6. Let Contingencies Do the Work

At work or in relationships, Passive-Aggressives want to be rated *excellent* on all performance reviews. You can use their powerful need for approval to teach them how to be less Passive-Aggressive. Here are some suggestions.

Always Pay Attention   If you ignore a creature whose major goal in life is to get your attention, there will be consequences. Remember, you aren't the only one using contingencies. Headaches are powerful tools for modifying your behavior. You'll get them if you forget to notice all the wonderful, helpful things the Passive-Aggressive vampire is doing.

Make Contingencies Explicit   Passive-Aggressives want to please you, and hope that you'll please them in return. If you don't specify clearly what you want, these vampires will give you what they think you ought to want and expect you to shower them with what they want in return. If you value your sanity, never accept this sort of implicit deal, no matter how good it looks on the surface. If you take it, you will pay, believe me. Your life and the vampire's will be much easier if nobody has to guess.

If you live or work with Passive-Aggressive Histrionics, tell them what you want them to do.

Always Give Lots of Positive Feedback Explicit instructions, while absolutely necessary, will not work as well as you think they ought to. Passive-Aggressives deal with the world by misunderstanding and by being misunderstood. The thing they never misunderstand is praise. Use gobs of it.

Avoid Punishment, Because It Never Works Berating Passive-Aggressives will make the situation worse, because they'll have more reason to fear you or get back at you. Criticism of any sort will elicit explanations rather than behavior change. If you try to induce guilt, you'll trigger an equal amount of resentment.

For all passive-aggressive behaviors, prevention is the best strategy. We have been through this before, but it's important enough to mention again. Most passive-aggressive people, vampires or not, feel chronically underappreciated. They need more praise than other people. Figure at least four times what you'd need (more if you're particularly macho).

Be Consistent If the contingencies you set don't apply evenly to everyone, all the time, they don't apply to anyone, any time.

Be Fair Passive-Aggressive Histrionics will almost beg you to take advantage of them. Don't, because you'll regret it. Do unto them as you would have them do unto you.

Be Sensitive If you discover clear evidence of hidden hostility, don't rub a Passive-Aggressive's nose in it. Instead, offer a positive way to resolve the problem. All these vampires really want is your approval.

7. Choose Your Words as Carefully as You Pick Your Battles

Telling Passive-Aggressives what they're doing and why it's wrong always makes the situation worse. Many people will assume that they just haven't explained the situation well enough, so they will go through it again, this time in more detail. Engineers and other left-brain types are particularly likely to persist in this kind of error. Their careful efforts get them nothing but bigger headaches.

Dealing effectively with Passive-Aggressive vampires is often a matter of semantics. Your words must reflect an understanding of their view of the world, rather than demanding that they accept yours. Passive-Aggressives live in an alternate reality where their thoughts are pure, their motives are selfless, and all their mistakes are caused by misinterpretation. That is where you must go to have any meaningful communication with them.

Phrase everything in a way that doesn't assault their view of reality. Instead of criticizing them, acknowledge that Passive-Aggressives were doing their best, then let them know how to do better. Don't even think of talking to them when you're angry. They'll see it as verbal abuse.

They will do better if you phrase instructions as a personal request for their help, and specify what you're willing to do to reciprocate. Forget about explaining; just ask and pay up.

If Passive-Aggressives seem angry and you want to know why, you'll get more information if you approach the situation indirectly. Ask them what other people might be concerned about. Always use emotionally neutral words like *upset* or *concerned* to describe the emotional state. Passive-Aggressives will usually be only too happy to tell you the kinds of things that may be bothering somebody else. If they have a chance to voice their concerns, however indirectly, they may have less need to act out.

8. Ignore Tantrums

Passive-Aggressive Histrionics throw passive tantrums. When they're upset with you, they show it by getting sick, misunderstanding your instructions, or talking about you to somebody else. If you get angry, they'll see you as an abuser and feel justified in taking further retaliatory action. In the short run, it can seem easier not to deal with them at all, but instead just do whatever they were supposed to do yourself. Big mistake. One of the reasons these vampires are so difficult is that most people deal with their passive tantrums passively, by absolving them of their responsibilities. This approach ensures that the next time there is something difficult to be done, Histrionics will again handle it by not being able to handle it.

9. Know Your Own Limits

If you can't control your own temper, you should never even attempt to deal with Passive-Aggressive Histrionics. They'll make you hate them and yourself. If you feel angry at one of these vampires, walk away and cool down before you commit yourself to words or actions that you'll regret.

Passive-Aggressives cause far more trouble than they should. Their dynamics are simple, and they respond well to praise and attention. The problem is that their annoying behavior can distract you into fighting with them when the really important battles are with yourself.

14 Histrionics in Your Life

As you have seen, there are two distinct kinds of Histrionic vampires, the overly dramatic Hams and the Passive-Aggressives. On the surface, they seem so different, but underneath, they are quite similar. Both kinds of Histrionics lose themselves in the roles they play, and both get desperate when the audience is not appreciative enough. Rejections, no matter how slight, are severely punished, usually indirectly. Whether Histrionics are drama queens or adorable waifs, they are about as effective in combat with the people who love them as Navy SEALS are with terrorists.

HISTRIONIC MARTIAL ARTS

Think for a minute of the many subtle ways in which a person close to you can signal that he or she is irritated: sniffing, snorting, sighing, eye rolling, choosing words and phrases that imply criticism, or even saying nothing at all. The list is endless, and Histrionics use everything on it to clobber unsuspecting friends, lovers, and family members. The most common pattern goes something like this:

> *Vampire: (Snorts, sniffs, or whatever.)*
> *Victim: What's wrong?*
> *Vampire: Nothing.*
> *Victim: What do you mean "nothing"? Whenever you make that sound, you're upset about something. So tell me, what's wrong?*
> *Vampire: (Long pause) Nothing.*
> *Victim: (Growing agitated) You always do this. You snort and sniff and make faces, then you say nothing's wrong. I know something is bothering you, so why don't you just tell me what it is?*
> *Vampire: (In a voice tinged with ice) I said nothing is wrong.*
> *Victim: (Shouting) I know something's wrong! I demand that you tell me what it is instead of doing what you always do, just sitting there making faces and saying nothing's wrong!*
> *Vampire: You really need to get control of your temper.*

The only way to parry this sort of attack is to use psychological jujitsu.

Vampire: (Snorts, sniffs, or whatever.)
    Victim: What's wrong?
    Vampire: Nothing.
    Victim: Oh, okay. (Goes to another part of the house.)

A relationship with a Passive-Aggressive vampire can be draining and difficult, a perpetual battle of the inarticulate against the indirect. I hope this chapter will help you to be more adept in fighting—or, preferably, avoiding fights—with the Histrionics in your life.

MY MOTHER, THE DRAMA QUEEN

Carly's mother (please call her Liz, not Mom) wears all the latest styles; however, they're for 18-year-olds and Liz is 52 and a bit beyond pleasingly plump. She also has a stud in her nose, a tramp stamp, and two bright orange streaks in her hair. Liz is loud and exuberant, and often inappropriate. She flirts unmercifully with any man she sees, regardless of age, and runs on and on about the tiniest travails as if they were the labors of Hercules. Still, everyone seems to like her, not as BFF, as Liz would like to believe, but as, well, a curiosity. Carly loves her, but she is so embarrassing.

The few times Carly has tried to say something to Liz about her clothes or her behavior have been disasters. Nobody takes her seriously, but Liz just doesn't get it.

Maybe it's Carly who doesn't get it. If there is a Histrionic Ham in your life, it's easy to be embarrassed and irritated by the sheer transparency of their attention-getting ploys and their utter disregard for being seen as ludicrous. Yes, Liz is outrageous, but that is what she chooses to be. If Carly is outraged, she is the one who will be drained.

The reason Carly is embarrassed is that she imagines how awful it would be if people thought *she* was as clueless as Liz. Just the thought makes Carly cringe and not want to be around her mother in public. She also feels guilty, because Liz is really a nice and generous person who really works hard to get people to love her. She'd give you the tank top off her back.

This is the dilemma you will face if you have a Histrionic Ham in your life. You just can't imagine being seen as a buffoon, and think that deep down, she (or he—we will discuss male Histrionics later in this chapter) doesn't want to be seen that way, either. What you must remember is that for Histrionics, there is no deep down. They are the role they're playing, and that's that. They will do whatever it takes to get attention. You can suffer their embarrassment for them, or, like everyone else, you can sit back and watch the show.

Carly does have another choice, but it is more difficult and much more expensive. She can try to create a new role for Liz by buying her a couple of really chic, age-appropriate outfits and making her an appointment at the best hair salon in town (having first conferred with the stylist about what sorts of cuts to avoid). If Liz thinks her new look is really becoming, she may adopt the behavior that goes along with it like an accessory. Or she may be back in tank tops in a week; there are no guarantees.

If you are going to try this strategy with the Ham in your life, you will also need to take her places where she can be the belle of the ball. If enough people compliment her on how glamorous she looks, she may embrace the new style.

Getting a new look for your Histrionic Ham should never coincide with an event, like your wedding, when *you* want to be the center of attention. Start months before, so that she has time to get comfortable in her new role.

THE QUEEN OF GOSSIP

There are other Histrionics who are not as harmless and lovable as Hams.

> *Vampire Lauren calls Amanda. In the midst of the usual chitchat, Lauren mentions that she's worried about Stephanie. "She's acting so strange lately, like she's depressed or something. Have you noticed anything?"*
>
> *"No, not really," Amanda says. "Well, come to think of it, she seemed a little crabby the other night, but I don't think that means she's depressed."*
>
> *The conversation goes on, and Amanda thinks nothing of it, until two days later she gets a text from Stephanie:*
>
> *I hear ur mad at me. WTF?*
>
> *Before she texts back, Amanda calls Lauren. "I just got this bizarre text from Steph. She thinks I'm mad at her."*
>
> *"I told you she's been acting weird," Lauren says.*

When there is a storm among her friends, Lauren always seems to be in the middle of it, calm and concerned, ready to hear everyone's point of view and to offer helpful advice. It takes Amanda a long time to realize that Lauren embellishes everything that people tell her and passes it on, then lies through her teeth about doing it.

> *"Did you tell Stephanie I said something about her?"*
> *"No. What makes you think that?"*

Amanda, stop! She's doing it again.

Gossips never admit that they told anybody anything, and even in the midst of their denials, they can elicit more information to pass on. If there are rumors flying around your group of friends, you can be sure that there is a Passive-Aggressive at work. You may not be able to tell who she is, and any attempt you make to find out will result in more gossip about you.

There is only one defense against a skilled and devious gossip: *never say anything about one of your friends to another, especially anything that could even vaguely be construed as negative, and never try to get specifics about anything you hear about yourself, no matter how bogus.*

If you follow this strategy, you will be out of the loop, but that's exactly where you want to be.

YOUR DEPRESSED SISTER

Depression comes in many forms. Most typically, depressed people are sad and withdrawn. Not Histrionics. Their depressions often seem like a frantic search for someone, anyone, who can make them feel better. If that someone is you, at first your heart will go out to them, until you discover that trying to make a depressed Histrionic feel better is a full-time job.

> *"I just don't see the point in going on,"* Tanya says, *in her typical monotone.*
>
> *"Come on, Tan,"* you say, *a bit less enthusiastically than you'd hoped. "Don't think that way. You have a good job, you have friends who care about you, and it's a beautiful day for a walk in the park."*
>
> *"I know I should want to,"* Tanya says. *"I know I have no reason to be sad. There are lots of people who are worse off than me. . . . But when I walk in the park, I see lovers hand in hand, and I wonder what's wrong with me that I can't find a relationship. It's probably the way I look."*
>
> *"That's ridiculous; you look fine."*
>
> *"If you like fat."*
>
> *"You're not fat."*

You can't talk depressed Histrionics into feeling better for more than a few minutes. Don't even try. It will only wear you out, and it won't do them a bit of good. Even worse, you will become *The Only Person Who Under-*

stands, thus assuring yourself of many more futile conversations, often in the middle of the night or at some other totally inconvenient time.

> *The phone rings just as you're going out the door. It's Tanya, crying.*
> *"I'm really sorry, Tanya," you say, "but I don't have time to talk now. I've got to get to the bank before it closes."*
> *"It's okay," Tanya says. "I don't mean to be a burden."*

You don't have to be a psychologist to recognize that in a conversation like this, both of you are saying the opposite of what you mean. Your unavailability is *not* okay with Tanya, and, for that matter, you're not particularly sorry that you can't talk with her. Each of you is too worried about the other's feelings to say what you really mean. You may not even know what you really mean. One minute you're irritated at Tanya for being manipulative; the next, you're beating yourself up for having uncharitable thoughts about someone who is obviously in pain. Tanya is undoubtedly doing the same thing. Back and forth your emotions go, between guilt and resentment. Just two short sentences spoken, but they can reverberate inside both your heads for days. One of the dangers of trying to help a Histrionic is that it can make you think and act like one.

To get out of this bind, you have to do what Histrionics are incapable of doing: recognize that guilt and resentment are not separate; they are two sides of the same feeling. One cannot exist without the other. You can't blame yourself without blaming someone else, or vice versa.

You also need to recognize that you can't make a depressed Histrionic like Tanya feel better for more than about ten minutes at a time. What both of you really need is to pay less attention to what she feels and more to what she does. This is the way therapists treat depression. I am not suggesting that you try to be a therapist to the depressed Histrionic in your life, only that you understand how depression is treated so that you don't get drawn into actions that will make things worse for both of you.

The point of psychological treatment is not to make depressed Histrionics feel better, but to make how they feel less of a factor in their day-to-day choices. If depressed people start thinking better and doing better, they will usually feel better as well, but it's merely a positive side effect.

The first thing you should do is make sure Tanya is getting professional help. Stand firm on the point that you are not qualified to treat her depression.

Once she is in treatment, you won't be out of the woods. She will undoubtedly tell you that her treatment is doing her no good. Her therapist is not nice, and the medication she is on doesn't work.

There is no doubt about it, antidepressant medications can work wonders. For some lucky folks, they can even make the whole disorder disappear. Usually, this is not the case for Histrionics, which will lead them to believe that the medication doesn't work at all. The actual purpose of medication is not to cure but to make depressed people feel well enough to do the things that *will* cure them.

If there is a depressed Histrionic in your life and you want to help, your part in this process is to encourage her to keep doing.

One way to look at depression is as a lack of positive reinforcement. For whatever reason, the circuitry in the brain that makes people feel good is not working properly. Depressed people have a broken feel gooder. They don't get much out of doing what they used to enjoy, so they stop. They want to wait until they feel better to do the things that will make them feel better. The problem is that if depressed people do only what they feel like doing, they will become even more depressed. The second step in treating depression is to disrupt the downward spiral by getting people up and moving. They will see any activity as absolutely pointless, so don't try to explain; make them do it to humor you.

They won't like it, but so what? They don't like anything. Their software for liking has crashed, and they need you to help them reboot. Let them mumble and mutter, as long as they're moving. Even when depressed people start feeling better, it will take them a long time to realize it, and even longer to admit it to you. Helping the depressed is a thankless task. Literally. If they thank you, you're probably not helping. Better they should be slightly annoyed with you for pushing them.

> *"Seems like you have a choice," you say to Tanya. "You can sit in here and feel lousy, or you can go out and feel lousy in the fresh air. I don't know about you, but I'm going to the park. Want to come with me?"*
>
> *"I guess one waste of time is as good as another," Tanya says, reaching for her jacket.*

Now that you understand your part in the treatment process, we can go back to those inconvenient phone calls. Here are some suggestions that will help you to be part of the solution rather than perpetuating the problem for both of you:

Take Everything Literally

Ignore the undercurrents, no matter how obvious.

It's pretty clear that Tanya is ticked off because you won't abandon your needs and minister to hers. She's not aware of these hostile feelings; she's just acting on them.

As she cringes at your rejection, Tanya actually believes that you are treating her like a burden because she *is* one, that you're only giving her what she deserves. She feels hostility toward herself, but not toward you—at least, not consciously. Never in a million years would Tanya accuse you of being the sort of person who'd let a friend down. You have to do that to yourself.

There is only one way to keep from being sucked into this neurotic morass: *take her absolutely literally*. Let therapists worry about unconscious meanings. What you want is a relationship with Tanya in which she asks for what she wants, and you are free to say yes or no. Sanity lies in playing by those rules yourself, even if you suspect she isn't.

Think like a psychologist, but never talk like one.

Forget the Word *Manipulate*

The concept of manipulation as we use it today is a relic of the human potential movement. In that simpler world, in which we were not put to live up to other people's expectations, manipulation, whether conscious or unconscious, is bad, so histrionics don't do it. Manipulation, by definition, is unconscious. As I have said, there is no first-person form of the verb *to manipulate*. Manipulation is something *parents* do to us, not something Histrionics do to others.

To avoid senseless arguments, erase the word manipulate from your vocabulary. The way to be effective in the situation formerly known as *being manipulated* is to respond to what people are doing, not trying to explain it to them.

Be Clear About What *You* Feel, What *You* Want, and What *You* Are Willing to Do

There is no way another person can deny *your* feelings. If you have to talk about the emotional bind people like Tanya put you in, do it something like this:

> *"Tanya, when you say you're a burden, I feel stuck. If I go do what I need to do, it's almost as if I'm admitting that you **are** a burden. If I stay and try to convince you that you're not a burden, then I have to cancel my own plans, and **I** get upset.*

> *"I know that none of this is your intention, because you did tell me to go ahead. Still, I end up feeling like the kind of person who lets down a sister in need. But I guess that's my problem, isn't it?"*

There are times when addressing the issue in this way can clear the air between people who are close. Tanya has a face-saving out, and you get to leave without feeling quite as selfish.

Generally, it works better to skirt the issue altogether. Just tell Tanya what you're willing to do, and let the guilt fall where it may.

> *"Tan, I have some errands to run, but I'll be free at 7:30. Call me and we can talk then."*

Schedule Appointments

Take a tip from your friendly neighborhood therapist. We have regularly scheduled times to talk with our clients, and we discourage emergency calls when there is no immediate danger. This is mostly for our own benefit, of course, but it is also the most helpful thing we can do for high-maintenance people like Tanya.

Step back and look at the larger picture. Tanya's emergencies are usually overreactions to day-to-day frustrations. She replays events in her mind, expanding their implications and making herself more depressed with each retelling. Eventually, she feels she can't take it any more, so she picks up the phone and calls you, hoping that you will make her feel better.

If you are always available, you become an emotional landfill where she can go to dump her loads of distress. If you're not there, she must at least figure out how to manage her feelings until you get back.

If you have a friend or family member like Tanya, it will help both of you if you put limits on your availability for discussing emotional issues. I'm not suggesting that you avoid them, but that you set specific times for the beginning and end of your talks about how she feels. At other times, do something else, like going for a walk in the park.

MALE HISTRIONICS

Male Histrionics are not as rare as you might imagine, given that many Histrionic behaviors fit so well with what we think of as the feminine stereotype. Barbie, Madonna, and Cheerful Patient are only a few of the roles Histrionics can play to the hilt.

Male Histrionics play stereotypical male roles, like Pro Wrestler, Ward Cleaver, or Family Comedian (or Pathetic Clown, depending on your point of view).

Pro Wrestlers act like testosterone on steroids, but it's all for show. You don't have to be afraid.

Ward Cleavers go to work, play golf, and sit with pipe and slippers, dispensing aphorisms. And that's pretty much it. Sitcom dads are exempt from conflict and all other emotional engagements, but when they give you the look, you'd better pay attention and shape up.

Family Comedians are not funny. They're like your uncle who tells lame jokes over and over, mistaking polite laughter for guffaws. If you let yourself be annoyed by or embarrassed for them, it is you who will be drained. You might try giving them some better material.

These roles are different on the outside, but similar in that they require more showmanship than thought. Male Histrionics are not deep thinkers. Don't attempt conversations more intimate than "How 'bout them Dodgers?"

The goal of these male Histrionics is less to get attention and approval and more to get peace and quiet after a hard day of work. They are masters at avoiding anything they don't like to do. Don't bother them with unimportant details like your emotional life, especially if there's a game on TV.

Histrionics, male and female, are what they are. You may not like what they are, but you probably can't change them. If you try, you will be drained, and it will somehow end up being all your fault.

The best defense is to know the patterns of the dramas Histrionics create, and use that knowledge to avoid joining the cast as the bad guy.

15 Therapy for Histrionic Vampires

What should you do if you see signs of Histrionic behavior in yourself or someone you care about? This section is a thumbnail sketch of the sorts of self-help and professional therapeutic approaches that might be beneficial. Always remember that attempting psychotherapy on someone you know will make you both sicker.

THE GOAL

The most important goals of treatment for Histrionics are to get them to know themselves well enough to recognize what they want, and to organize their lives so that they can get it. Of the three aspects of maturity discussed in Chapter 2, control, connection, and challenge, Histrionics are most lacking in a sense of control over their lives. It is as if their centers are not inside themselves, but outside with the people whose attention and approval they feel they need if they are to survive. Histrionics must learn to take care of themselves rather than using their charm, devotion, or neediness to get other people to take care of them.

One part of taking care of themselves is learning to ask directly for what they want. The other part is more subtle, as it has to do with self-esteem, which is less about affirmation and more about accomplishment. To feel good about themselves, Histrionics need to set goals for themselves and accomplish them without being diverted by their own emotions or by the needs of others. Whatever goals they set for themselves, they have to stick with them. To do this, they must learn to think instead of feel.

This process I've described here usually requires professional guidance, but Histrionics can accomplish some parts of it on their own.

PROFESSIONAL HELP

Histrionics are more likely to go into therapy than any other kind of emotional vampire. They love treatment, but often get nothing lasting out of it. This is because they see the task as trying to please the therapist. Very quickly, Histrionics learn how to be the "best patients ever" by responding to the therapist's needs rather than their own.

Often, what therapists really want are emotional breakthroughs like we see in the movies, blinding flashes of insight in which patients grasp the whole of their problem and change before our very eyes. Histrionics will do this every week. They are experts at turning themselves into what people want, but it is the very nexus of their problem.

The first step in successful treatment for a Histrionic is selecting a therapist with enough experience not to be fooled.

Histrionics favor New Age approaches that make them feel better without requiring them to change a single thing about their wonderful selves. Therapy of this sort is like going to a day spa—calming, but very temporary.

Histrionics profit most from structured therapeutic approaches that emphasize thinking rather than emoting or aimless recounting of unconnected feelings. More than most patients, Histrionics can benefit from a rigorous examination of their past. The focus should be on recognizing continuity in their own thoughts, feelings, and choices, rather than on cataloging the things that others have done to them. If Histrionics feel that their treatment is boring and difficult, they are probably on the right track.

SELF-HELP

Histrionics are seekers. They really want to feel better, but they don't know how, so they're always looking for someone to teach them. They read books, go to classes, and attend weekend retreats, but they seldom stay with any one thing long enough to get below the surface.

> *Yoga has changed Denise's life. She's been to two classes, and it has already made a huge difference in how she feels. She's thinking of getting an Om tattooed on her shoulder. She's really getting into Ayurvedic cooking, too.*
>
> *On her wrist, Denise is still wearing the red cord from the Kabala she was studying last month. The unread literature from the Course in Miracles gathers dust on the shelf.*

If you recognize Histrionic tendencies in yourself, the following exercises will be very difficult for you, but they will make a difference.

Whatever You Choose, Stick with It

There are many paths to health and enlightenment. None are easy, and none are immediate. Pick one, and follow it even when it gets boring and difficult.

Let Your Thoughts Be Your Guide

First, learn to recognize the difference between what you *think* and what you *feel*. Then, try to make more choices based on thinking. A good way to keep track of this is by journaling. Instead of running on about what happened and what you felt, make your journal a record of the choices you make, the goals you set for yourself, and your progress toward attaining them. Instead of a lovely folio of scented, handmade paper, think of keeping your journal on an Excel spreadsheet.

Banish the Phrase "I Don't Know" from Your Vocabulary

Try not to space out when people ask you tough questions. The things you need most to think about are always the ones that are most difficult.

Do Things for Yourself and by Yourself

Try it. You may come to like your own company.

Listen to the Little Devil

You, like everyone else, have a dark side to your force. You need to recognize it, but you don't have to go over to it.

Ask for What You Want

Everybody takes; it's a law of nature that no amount of good intentions can repeal. It's far better to be aware of what you want and ask other people to give it to you. It's not selfish if you say *please* and *thank you*.

Give Someone Permission to be Honest with You

Find someone you trust, and give that person permission to always tell it like it is, even if it hurts your feelings. When that person tells you something, listen. Don't go shopping for a nicer person.

Openly Disagree with Somebody Every Day

Say it nicely, but say it.

WHAT WILL HURT

Emotional vampires tend to select therapeutic approaches that make them worse rather than better. Histrionics would prefer medical treatment for their aches and pains to any examination of psychological issues that may be causing them. If two doctors say the problem is psychological, check with a psychiatrist or psychologist before looking for further physical remedies.

Many Histrionics have been damaged by "trauma" therapies, especially the kind that list the sorts of symptoms victims *should* experience and the stages that they *must* go through to be healed. Histrionics will happily do whatever is expected of them, even if it destroys them and all their relationships except the one with their therapist.

Histrionics probably shouldn't be treated by therapists who have what they have, even if the therapists purport to be recovering from it.

Fellow sufferers sometimes forget that real recovery means growing out of the need to have people depend on you the way you depended on *your* therapist.

If your therapist hugs you when you cry, you are in the wrong place.

16 Big Egos, Small Everywhere Else

The Narcissistic Types

Narcissistic vampires have a disorder that is both psychological and cosmological. They believe the universe revolves around them. Unlike Antisocials, who are addicted to excitement, or Histrionics, who crave attention, Narcissists just want to live out their fantasies of being the smartest, most talented, and all-around best people in the world.

Some Narcissists turn out to be little more than legends in their own minds, but a surprising number are adept enough to turn some of their grandiose fantasies into reality. There may be narcissism without greatness, but there is no greatness without narcissism. One thing is certain, however: in the eyes of other people, these vampires are never as great as they consider themselves to be.

Considering themselves is what Narcissists do best. The trait they most conspicuously lack is concern for the needs, thoughts, and feelings of other people.

These vampires have tendencies in the direction of a Narcissistic personality disorder. The name is derived from Narcissus, a Greek youth who fell in love with his own reflection. To outsiders, it looks as if Narcissists are in love with themselves because they think they're better than other people. The actual situation is a bit more complex.

More than loving themselves, Narcissists are absorbed with themselves. They feel their own desires so acutely that they can't pay attention to anything else. Imagine their disorder as a pair of binoculars. Narcissists look at their own needs through the magnifying side, and the rest of the cosmos through the side that makes things small to the point of insignificance. It's not so much that Narcissists think they're better than other people as that they hardly think of other people at all—unless they need something from them.

Narcissistic need is tremendous. Just as sharks must continually swim to keep from drowning, Narcissists must constantly demonstrate that they are special, or they will sink like stones into the depths of depression. It may look as if they are trying to demonstrate their worth to other people, but their real audience is themselves.

Narcissists are experts at showing off. Everything they do is calculated to make the right impression. Conspicuous consumption is for them what religion is for other people. Narcissists pursue the symbols of wealth, status, and power with a fervor that is almost spiritual. They can talk for hours about objects they own, the great things they've done or are going to do, and the famous people they hang out with. Often, they exaggerate shamelessly, even when they have plenty of real achievements they could brag about.

Nothing is ever enough for them. That's why Narcissists want you, or at least your adulation. They'll try so hard to impress you that it's easy to believe that you're actually important to them. This can be a fatal mistake; it's not you they want, only your worship. They'll suck that out and throw the rest away.

To Narcissists, the objects, the achievements, and the high regard of other people mean nothing in themselves. They are fuel, like water forced across gills so that oxygen can be extracted. The technical term is *Narcissistic supplies*. If Narcissists don't constantly demonstrate their specialness to themselves, they drown.

WHAT IT'S LIKE TO BE NARCISSISTIC

To know how Narcissists experience life, imagine playing golf, tennis, or some other competitive sport and having the best day of your career. You feel great, but the mental wall between confidence and fear is thin as tissue paper. Everything is riding on the next shot, and then the one after that. For Narcissists, the game encompasses the whole world, and it is never over.

Imagine the pressure should the only meaningful goal in your life be proving that you are something more than human. Narcissists' greatest fear is of being ordinary. They can't feel connected to anything larger than themselves, because in their universe there *is* nothing larger. Beyond their frenetic attempts to prove the unprovable lies only a dark, unexplored void. You might be tempted to think of them as tragic figures if they weren't so petty and obnoxious.

Narcissists are usually talented and intelligent. They are also among the most inconsiderate creatures on earth. You'd think that such smart people would recognize the importance of paying attention to other people. Dream on.

Narcissists are so wrapped up in their own dreams that there is no room for anything else. It is an ironic coincidence that sometimes the realization of Narcissistic dreams benefits all humanity. Narcissists invented art, science, sports, business, and everything else you can compete at. They invented saint-hood, too, for that matter. Our lives are better because of Narcissists' attempts to prove themselves better than we are.

THE NARCISSISTIC DILEMMA

More than any other vampire type, Narcissists evoke mixed feelings. When we view them from a distance, we admire them and even love them. We vote for them, and we contribute to their campaigns. We read their books, listen to their music, and view their artwork in museums. We study their lives in history class and marvel at the monuments they create for themselves. We give them Nobel Prizes.

Up close, Narcissists are the most hated of vampire types, even though other types generally accomplish less and do more damage. Much of what is written about Narcissists in memoirs, on the Internet, and even in clinical texts has overtones of personal loathing. Dangerous Antisocials are often given more sympathetic treatment.

Why the hatred? All emotional vampires use people, but Narcissists do it openly and without apology, firm in the belief that they are better and more deserving than others. This attitude of entitlement stirs in us some of the same judgmental feelings that led the French to cheerfully send their aristocrats to the guillotine.

We resent Narcissists. We deplore the way they ignore our needs, yet unconsciously we respond to the infants inside them that need us so much.

And we need them. Without Narcissists, who would lead us? Or who, for that matter, would think themselves wise enough to say where leadership ends and narcissism begins?

There's no doubt that too much narcissism is a dangerous thing. But how much is too much?

And what is narcissism, anyway? To live at all, we must have some instinct to put our own needs first. Narcissism may be the power behind all motivation. To live as human beings, however, we must balance that power with responsibility. Struggling with the Narcissistic dilemma is what being human is all about.

Emotional vampires are people who have never struggled with the Narcissistic dilemma. Antisocials ignore it because it's no fun. Histrionics pretend that they never act in their own self-interest. Narcissists believe that what's good for them is all that exists. Emotional vampires are forced to prey on other people for the answer that the rest of us must struggle to find within ourselves.

What's the answer? A great teacher summed that up:

Do unto others as you would have them do unto you.

Narcissists break the Golden Rule without so much as a thought. Does this make them evil or just oblivious? Your answer will determine how much damage they do to you.

The easiest way to get drained is to take Narcissists' lack of consideration personally, to get upset over what they must be thinking of you to treat you the way they do. *The most important thing to remember is that Narcissists are not thinking of you at all.*

NARCISSISM AND SELF-ESTEEM

Narcissism is not the same thing as high self-esteem. Self-esteem is a concept that has meaning primarily to people who don't have it. Narcissists don't need a concept to explain why they are special any more than sharks need a concept to explain water.

You might argue that their constant need for Narcissistic supplies to buoy them up is evidence that the whole purpose of their life is to compensate for low self-esteem. This may lead you to the mistaken belief that all it takes to fix Narcissists is to teach them how to feel good about who they are inside, so they can just relax and let themselves be regular people. As we'll see in the next chapter, which covers Narcissistic Legends in Their Own Minds, it's possible to waste your whole life pursuing this futile goal.

WHAT THE QUESTIONS MEASURE

The specific behaviors covered on the checklist relate to several underlying personality characteristics that define a Narcissistic emotional vampire

Well-Advertised Talent and Intelligence

The first thing you'll hear about Narcissists is that they are extremely intelligent and talented. In fact, you'll probably hear this from the Narcissists

THE NARCISSISTIC VAMPIRE CHECKLIST: IDENTIFYING THE SELF-STYLED SMARTEST, MOST TALENTED, ALL-AROUND BEST PEOPLE IN THE WORLD

True or False Score one point for each *true* answer.

1. This person has achieved more than most people his or her age.　　　　　　　　　　　　　　　　　T F

2. This person is firmly convinced that he or she is better, smarter, or more talented than other people.　　　　T F

3. This person loves competition, but is a poor loser.　　T F

4. This person has fantasies of doing something great or being famous, and often expects to be treated as if these fantasies had already come true.　　　　　　　　　T F

5. This person has very little interest in what other people are thinking or feeling, unless he or she wants something from them.　　　　　　　　　　　　　　　　　T F

6. This person is a name-dropper.　　　　　　　　　T F

7. To this person, it is very important to live in the right place and associate with the right people.　　　　　　T F

8. This person takes advantage of other people to achieve his or her own goals.　　　　　　　　　　　　　T F

9. This person usually manages to be in a category by himself or herself.　　　　　　　　　　　　　　　T F

10. This person often feels put upon when asked to take care of his or her responsibilities to family, friends, or coworkers.　T F

11. This person regularly disregards rules or expects them to be changed because he or she is in some way special.　T F

12. This person becomes irritated when other people don't automatically do what he or she wants them to do, even when they have a good reason for not complying.　T F

13. This person reviews sports, art, and literature by telling you what he or she would have done instead.　　　　T F

14. This person thinks that most criticisms of him or her are motivated by jealousy.　　　　　　　　　　　T F

15. This person regards anything short of worship as rejection.　T F

(continued on next page)

16. This person suffers from a congenital inability to recognize his or her own mistakes. On the rare occasions when this person does recognize a mistake, even the slightest error can precipitate a major depression.   T F

17. This person often explains why people who are better known than he or she is are not really all that great.   T F

18. This person often complains of being mistreated or misunderstood.   T F

19. People either love or hate this person.   T F

20. Despite having an overly high opinion of himself or herself, this person is really quite intelligent and talented.   T F

Scoring Five or more true answers qualify the person as a Narcissistic emotional vampire, although not necessarily for a diagnosis of narcissistic personality disorder. If the person scores higher than 10 and is not a member of the royal family, be careful that you aren't mistaken for one of the servants.

directly, since they are not the least bit shy in saying good things about themselves.

A surprising number of Narcissists know their numerical IQ scores and share them with new acquaintances. These numbers are usually inflated. Nobody boasts of an IQ of 130 (the threshold for Mensa membership), although most commonly used tests are not meaningful above that level. If a Narcissist boasts of an IQ of 160, ask: "On what test?" And watch the fun.

In addition to IQ numbers, you may also hear about famous people whom these vampires have met and in some way impressed.

At seminars and meetings, Narcissists often have their hands in the air, but they never ask real questions. They make comments to demonstrate to everyone that they know at least as much and probably more than the person at the front of the room.

The pattern of trying to dazzle you with their talent and intelligence persists with Narcissists long after they make their first impression. They'll keep on until you're no longer visibly awed, then they'll ignore you completely.

Achievement

Most Narcissists have achievements to back up their high opinion of themselves. Unlike other vampire types who are just as happy to pretend, Narcissists are quite willing to work hard to glorify themselves.

In their careers, these vampires are usually focused and goal-directed. Many are workaholics, but unlike Histrionic people pleasers, who'll work themselves half to death for approval and love, Narcissists take on only those tasks that pay off in money, fame, or power.

Grandiosity

Narcissists are absolutely shameless in their fantasies about how great they are and how much everybody admires them, or should.

If you press them, they'll admit that they consider themselves the best in the world at something. Actually, you won't have to press very hard.

Entitlement

Narcissists believe they are so special that the rules don't apply to them. They expect the red carpet to be rolled out for them wherever they go, and if it isn't, they get quite surly.

They don't wait, they don't recycle, they don't pay retail, they don't stand in line, they don't clean up after themselves, they don't let other people get in front of them in traffic, and their income taxes rival great works of fiction. Illness or even death is no excuse for other people not to immediately jump up to meet their needs. They aren't the least bit ashamed of using other people and systems for their own personal gain. They boast about how they take advantage of just about everybody.

Competitiveness

Narcissists love to compete, but only when they win. Usually, they'll do whatever it takes to win, whether it be practice or stacking the deck in their favor.

Narcissists are obsessively concerned with status and power. They'll fight to the death over a corner office, not because they want a nice view, but because they know what a corner office means in the organizational hierarchy. They know what everything means in every hierarchy. What they wear, what they drive, where they live, and who they're seen with are not random choices based on something as silly as what they like. Everything Narcissists do is a move in the great game of self-aggrandizement, which is their main reason for living.

Conspicuous Boredom

Unless the subject of the conversation is how great they are, Narcissists will become visibly bored. One of the main reasons Narcissists wear expensive watches is so they can look at them when someone else is talking.

Besides boredom, Narcissists have only two other emotional states: they're either on top of the world or on the bottom of the garbage heap. The slightest frustration can burst their balloon and send them crashing to the depths.

Lack of Empathy

To a Narcissist, other people are either prospective purveyors of Narcissistic supplies or invisible. More than any other vampire type, Narcissists are incapable of seeing their fellow humans as having wants, needs, talents, and desires of their own. Needless to say, this lack of empathy is the source of untold amounts of pain to the people who love them.

But for their lack of human warmth, there is a lot about these vampires to love. This is unfortunate, and it seems terribly unfair. Many people destroy themselves by believing that it's their fault that Narcissists don't love them back. They will work hard and long, sometimes for their whole lives, without realizing that Narcissists can't give what they don't have.

A particularly scary trait that Narcissists share with Antisocials is the ability to feign empathy when they want something. Narcissists are the best flatterers on the planet. They give great ego massages even as they're draining people dry. Needless to say, this talent makes them great at politics. Even though Antisocials and Histrionics can be sexy, all the best seducers are Narcissists.

Inability to Accept Criticism

Narcissists' greatest fear is of being ordinary. God forbid they should do something as mundane as making a mistake. Even the smallest criticisms feel like stakes through the heart. If you reprimand Narcissists, the least they'll do is explain in great detail why your opinion is wrong. If you're right, the situation will be much worse. They will melt before your eyes into pitiful, dependent infants who need enormous amounts of reassurance and praise just to draw their next breath. You can't win. There's no such thing as a Narcissist being objective about his or her faults.

Ambivalence in Other People

Other people usually feel strongly about Narcissists. They either love them for their talents or hate their guts for their blatant selfishness. Or both. It's hard to say which does the most damage—the selfishness, the hatred, or the love.

Narcissists always know what they want from you, and they won't be the least bit reticent about asking for it or just taking it. To deal effectively with these self-absorbed children of the night, you must be equally certain about what you want from them. Always drive a hard bargain, and always make them pay *before* they get what they want from you. Remember this rule, and there's not much else you need to know.

Well, maybe one more thing: unless you want your heart broken, never make Narcissists choose between you and their first love, themselves.

17 Vampires Who Are Legends in Their Own Minds

With Talent Like Theirs, Who Needs Performance?

Narcissism carries within itself the seeds of both success and failure. Grandiose dreams of being special and unique can be used as goads to get ahead, or as rationalizations for not having to do what success requires.

Many Narcissists push themselves to succeed. They recognize that they can get at least some of the supplies they need just from having an office with their name on the door and making lots of money. Those hapless Narcissists who don't do well in their careers have to scramble harder to get the admiration they feel they deserve.

Narcissists who can't turn their grandiose dreams into reality may turn their reality into dreams. They become Legends in Their Own Minds.

With no objective support whatsoever, Narcissistic Legends see themselves as more talented and intelligent than other people. They are expert in finding small ponds that will let them be big fish, and extorting Narcissistic supplies from people whose need to be needed is as great as their vampiric need to be adored.

> *The house is silent but for the rattling of keys on Vampire Tyler's computer.*
>
> *"Tyler, it's two o'clock. Are you still on the Internet?" Kristin calls from the bedroom.*
>
> *"I'm almost done," Tyler says. "I'll come to bed soon."*
>
> *"Come on, honey, get some rest. The Internet will still be there in the morning."*
>
> *"I know, I know. I'll be there soon. I'm closing a big sale with a guy in Norway."*

Closing a sale! Kristin's heart soars. For the past six months, since Tyler started Netmarket.com, there have been no sales, even though he's been working on it night and day. The project is a great idea. It's a subscription purchasing network for small businesses, through which Tyler can match up customers and suppliers anywhere in the world. The earning potential is enormous. Kristin has seen the projections.

But then again, all Tyler's ideas are great. His creativity is one of the main things Kristin admires about him. Just talking to him makes her see the world differently.

But interesting conversations don't put bread on the table. Kristin hopes against hope that Netmarket will. Tyler says it's only a matter of time until things fall into place.

Kristin can't help worrying that time is running out. Lying in bed listening to the soft clatter of keys, she dares to hope that tonight is the night. It would be so wonderful if Tyler could make his project pay off. They could use the money. Not that she'd put any pressure on him. Since she got promoted at work, they've been able to make it on her salary. Just barely. Mostly, she wants this project to work out for Tyler. He could use a little good luck for a change.

Half an hour later, the keys are still clattering. If this is Tyler's big moment, maybe she should be there to support him. She drags herself out of bed and pads softly into the office to stand by her man.

Tyler is a Narcissistic Legend in His Own Mind. He really does know quite a bit about the art and science of purchasing. Ask him. He won't be the least bit shy about telling you that he knows more than most business school professors, not to mention the heads of the five or six purchasing departments where he's worked and been let go. He'll go to great lengths to explain that his ideas are so radical that a lot of people just don't understand how great they are.

Kristin tries to understand. She loves Tyler, and wants to help him succeed. She knows how hard he works, how much he worries, and how depressed he gets when things don't go right. In Tyler's mind, helping him means relieving him of anything that might distract him from working on his project. That's why Kristin earns the money, does the housework, and takes care of the kids. She feels it will all be worthwhile if it helps Tyler get his business off the ground. More than that, Kristin hopes Tyler will see that her sacrifices for him mean that there's someone who believes in him and cares for him. Maybe that will help him believe in himself and do what he needs to do to pull himself out of this terrible slump. Late at night, she sometimes wonders if what she's doing is actually helping.

It isn't. Kristin's nurturing is no more noticeable to Tyler than the air he breathes. He may need it, but he never thinks about it. Like most Narcissists, he pays attention only to what he feels he might lose. Kristin is there for him, loving, solid, and therefore pretty much ignored. It hurts Kristin that Tyler seldom acknowledges her efforts, but making demands and playing hard to get are not part of her nature. If she were down, she'd want somebody to stand behind her.

Kristin is making the most dangerous mistake possible in dealing with emotional vampires. She's assuming that she understands Tyler based on what she knows about herself. Kristin sometimes has problems with low self-esteem. When she messes up on something, even on something little, she feels like a failure. Kristin imagines that Tyler feels as low as she would if she'd been fired from jobs and couldn't make any money. So, following the Golden Rule, she tries to give him what would help her.

When other people give Kristin affection, support, and encouragement, she can feel good enough about herself to get up and do what needs to be done. In this respect, Kristin is like most people, but she's not like a Narcissistic vampire.

Narcissism is definitely *not* a problem with low self-esteem. Despite the setbacks, Tyler has no doubts about his self-worth. When Tyler broods, he's not blaming himself. It's more likely that he's feeling hurt and abused because people are not immediately recognizing the quality of his ideas and moving him to the head of the class, where he thinks he belongs. The last thing a Narcissistic Legend is likely to consider is that his setbacks are the result of his own behavior. Even when he goes through periods of depression, during which he talks about what a terrible person he is, what Tyler is looking for is not advice on how to do things better, but someone to reassure him of what he knows in his heart—that he's just fine the way he is. Unfortunately, that's just what Kristin does.

What should Kristin do instead? To answer that question, we have to look more closely at what prevents talented and intelligent Narcissistic Legends from achieving their potential.

HOW NARCISSISTIC LEGENDS PREVENT THEMSELVES FROM SUCCEEDING

Often, Narcissistic Legends are bright and creative, but it takes more than that to succeed at a career. Specifically, two other things are required: *the ability to do things you don't want to do because the job requires them and the ability to sell yourself and your ideas to other people.* Raw narcissism stands in the way of learning and practicing both of these skills. Narcissistic Legends believe that their ideas are so great that they don't have to take care of all those annoying tasks themselves. The Narcissistic Superstars in the next chapter are willing to do whatever it takes to succeed. Legends believe that success should just be handed to them.

Like many Narcissistic Legends, Tyler started his own business because he couldn't handle corporate bullshit.

In order to succeed in any business system, you have to be perceived as being part of it. This usually means going through an initiation period of doing pointless work because somebody more firmly entrenched in the system wants it done. There's no way around paying your dues. Narcissistic Legends are quick to note that the work they're being asked to do is pointless, and generally believe that they, because of their superior intelligence, are the first to discover this amazing fact. Often, they will use this pseudo-insight as justification for not doing what they consider unimportant.

There are two problems with this approach. First, Narcissistic Legends are apt to confuse what they don't like with what is unimportant. Whether it's making cold calls, playing politics, or checking facts and figures, every job requires doing things that you'd rather not do. The first step toward success comes from learning to do them anyway, regardless of how you feel.

The second problem with the Narcissistic approach to menial tasks is that what's unimportant to Narcissists may be of critical importance to everybody else. To someone who's climbed an organizational ladder for 20 years, paying dues at every rung, it's inconceivable that a new hire who never gets paperwork in on time should expect the business to be reengineered in his or her own image.

Besides the forbearance to do necessary but uninteresting work, success requires the ability to sell. Selling, first and foremost, means paying enough attention to other people to know what they will buy. Narcissistic Legends couldn't care less about what other people want. They believe that they're better mousetraps, and that people should be beating a path to their door. This makes them terrible at selling. Their idea of a sales pitch is sketching out their idea and acting as if it would be stupid to consider anything else.

Tyler believes incorrectly that having his own business will free him from having to do all the things that make a business succeed.

Narcissistic Legends' disregard of how they affect other people makes them blind to the real contingencies in their lives. Like Antisocials, they can make the same mistakes over and over and still not learn from them.

Narcissists *can* change their behavior when they find out it's preventing them from getting what they want. The funny thing is that they seldom find this out because other people don't explain the problem to them in a way they can understand.

NARCISSISTIC LEGEND HYPNOSIS

Narcissistic Legends create alternate realities that push powerful people away and attract the weak.

Narcissists know that they're the best. People who doubt themselves are attracted to Narcissistic certainty. When these vampires want someone, they can make that person feel like the second most special being on the planet.

> *In the dark hallway, on her way to Tyler's office, Kristin remembers how it was when she and Tyler first met. He sent her texts, e-mails, and even actual handwritten notes in the mail. He wrote her poetry. It was awful, but she loved it anyway. He gave her flowers and those dippy stuffed animals that she still keeps on the dresser. They stared into each other's eyes over candlelit dinners (she cooked them and Tyler brought the candles), talking far into the night about his big ideas and wonderful dreams. Kristin had never known such an intelligent person. And Tyler loved her; he said it all the time. More than that, he needed her. She knew that from the moment she saw that pigsty of an apartment he lived in.*
>
> *Since that time, the love has been buried under the ruins of one big idea after another, but still, Tyler needs her.*

Narcissists who want something are willing to work hard and single-mindedly to get it. In the early stages of a relationship, when it's new and uncertain, these vampires can be enthusiastic, if not adept, at courtship. Their lack of grace doesn't matter. What really draws their victims in is Narcissistic need.

Prospective purveyors of Narcissistic supplies see Narcissistic Legends as talented, intelligent people who need someone to take care of them. These poor benighted souls dare to hope that in return for their hard work and affection, the vampires will feel enough gratitude to love them back.

Narcissistic Legends are blissfully unaware that anyone could see them as less than perfect. Once the relationship is certain, they stop making an effort. The Narcissist expects other people to be so thrilled by even a little attention that they will happily give anything for the pleasure of associating with such a superior person. Suppliers do little to discourage the idea.

In the beginning, both vampire and supplier see each other as bargains. For a while, their relationship seems to be a very sweet deal. Then it slowly goes sour.

No matter how hard suppliers work, Narcissistic Legends feel very little gratitude. They expect their suppliers to be grateful to *them*. After a while, even the most caring suppliers get sick of having their needs ignored. Then they create their own hypnotic bind. Either they keep on giving, and thereby continue to be good but exploited people, or they nag or leave or otherwise act in ways that they themselves consider selfish and hurtful. They can't win, so most often they do nothing but hurt inside.

If suppliers do allow themselves to ask for anything at all, it's usually something vague and after the fact, like appreciation. They never think of demanding specific behaviors with specific consequences for not complying. Unfortunately, ultimatums and contingencies, the very things that might help the relationship, are as alien to the suppliers as appreciation is to the Narcissist.

The situation continues to get worse. Narcissists do less and want more, because that's precisely what their suppliers have inadvertently taught them to expect. The relationship is marked by one crisis after another each time suppliers realize that, yet again, they've been had.

Kristin gets out of bed to be with Tyler as he makes his first sale. On bare feet, she tiptoes into the office. Tyler, as usual, is hunched over the keyboard. He doesn't see Kristin until she's standing right behind him. He seems to be studying an aerial view of a castle with an army of skeletons swarming over it.

"Tyler, what is this? It's one of those games, isn't it?"

He turns toward her, grinning like a little boy caught with his hand in the cookie jar. As he does, he hits a key and the Netmarket.com logo appears on the monitor. "Just taking a little break while I'm waiting for Bjorn in Norway to message me. Thought I'd check out the old castle. Bjorn said he'd get right back to me."

The instant messenger pops up. "See, this must be him now," Tyler says.

The message scrolls across the screen in capital letters, as if someone very far away were shouting to be heard.

"TROLLMEISTER, GET ON THE STICK. IT'S YOUR MOVE!"

Kristin feels a million things at once, none of them charitable. "You haven't been working at all," she says. The cold fury in her voice frightens even her. "You've been playing those stupid games again."

"No, you don't understand. I was just—"

"You don't have to lie about it, Tyler. From here on out, you can play all the computer games you want."

"What do you mean?" he asks. His voice is barely above a whisper.

For a long time Kristin stares at him and says nothing. She's never spoken the words before tonight. Tears fill her eyes and she begins gasping for breath. "I think maybe you should get a place of your own."

Tyler's lip quivers as he speaks. "Honey, please don't. I'm sorry. I'll do anything."

If you're applauding Kristin for finally throwing the bum out, you probably don't understand either her or Tyler very well. Kristin loves Tyler, and she believes strongly in the power and obligation of love. By turning her back on Tyler after all these years of hoping and helping, she is repudiating what, until this moment, has been the most important force in her life.

Tyler is inconsiderate, and he can't seem to earn much of a living, but he's not a bad man. He doesn't drink, run around, or beat her. The kids love him; when he has time for them, they play Wii together. What right does Kristin have to abandon him for playing a computer game in the middle of the night? Wouldn't that be more selfish than anything Tyler has done?

The chances are good that Kristin will let Tyler stay in return for a few vague promises to do better. This would be a huge mistake. Letting Tyler stay isn't the mistake; it's the vagueness of the promises. What Kristin needs to do is make their relationship contingent on Tyler's doing some very specific things.

As I said earlier in the chapter, Narcissists can learn to act differently, but they're usually not taught very well. There are two elements to effective teaching: a good lesson plan, which we'll discuss later in the chapter, and sufficient motivation for learning. The only thing that reliably provides enough motivation for Narcissists to change is the imminent loss of something they value.

Narcissists are insensitive, but they're not stupid. They may fume and fuss, but they do respond to ultimatums. If you tell them to shape up or ship out, and they believe you're serious, you'll have their attention in a way that is impossible to achieve by any other means. Obviously, they don't always shape up, but a clear ultimatum, contingent upon very specific behaviors, is the best, and only, chance you're going to get.

HOW TO SOCIALIZE NARCISSISTIC LEGENDS

With powerful enough motivation and a good lesson plan, it's possible to teach Narcissistic Legends to act in a more socialized manner. You may not be able to change their basic narcissism, but you can get them to act in ways that are not so destructive to relationships and careers.

First, the contingencies have to be crystal clear:

> *"You're saying you'll do anything to stay in this marriage?" Kristin asks Tyler at the end of a long and tearful night.*
>
> *"Anything," Tyler says.*
>
> *"All right," Kristin says. "Here are my terms. First, you can go on with the Netmarket project for three more months. If you aren't making the equivalent of minimum wage by then, I want you to get a real job and do whatever it takes to hold it for at least a year."*
>
> *"Three months? But it takes longer than that to get a thing like this off the ground."*
>
> *"Then work on it in your spare time. After you've done two hours of work around the house every day."*
>
> *"But—"*
>
> *"No buts. Take it or leave it."*

You're probably thinking that Kristin would never say those things in a million years, and you're right. It's what she should say, because it's the only approach that will have a ghost of a chance with a Narcissistic Legend like Tyler. Unfortunately, it flies in the face of the kindness and unconditional positive regard that Kristin thinks are essential to a loving relationship.

Can she be this cold and calculating, even to save her marriage? That's up to her. We leave Kristin struggling with her Narcissist and her own personal demons.

The only way to teach Narcissists basic human skills is to show them clearly that it is in their own self-interest to act differently. A strong contingency is essential. They can put out considerable effort if they believe that it is the only way they can avoid getting divorced, being fired, terminating a friendship, or going to jail. Most other contingencies are not compelling enough. Once the contingency is in place, you have to direct the effort toward two specific goals:

1. Narcissistic Legends have to learn to make themselves do things they don't want to do.

2. Narcissistic Legends have to learn to sell themselves and their ideas by paying enough attention to other people to know what they're likely to buy. I'm not talking just about selling at work. Every relationship involves transactions. Narcissists never expect to negotiate, but to make a relationship work, they have to learn.

Be clear that in offering suggestions for change, you're acting in your own self-interest rather than as the agent of a higher moral authority or out of simple kindness. Narcissists don't believe in your altruism. Most of them would argue that Mother Teresa's saintliness was at least in part an ego trip.

NINE WAYS TO PROTECT YOURSELF FROM NARCISSISTIC LEGENDS IN THEIR OWN MINDS

Here are some suggestions on how to teach Narcissistic Legends a little work ethic.

1. Know Them, Know Their History, and Know Your Goal

Narcissistic Legends are people who have trouble living up to their potential. You can find them everywhere: in break rooms at work, and in chat rooms on the Internet. They're always talking about how much brighter and more talented they are than people who are merely rich and famous.

Often they really are smart, but if you're considering hiring them into your life, you need to know more than their IQ numbers. Carefully examine their track record, and expect their future behavior to be similar to what they've done in the past. Narcissistic Legends are quick to explain that *this* time, things will be different. They are slow to grasp how their own hang-ups ensure that everything will stay the same. All they seem to learn from mistakes is that other people make them.

Your goal with Narcissistic Legends, as with all vampires, is to keep them from draining you. This is difficult, because they can drain you in so many different ways. Legends can dash your hopes or suck out every drop of support and affection you have, and still expect more. They can whip you into a froth of self-destructive outrage at their insensitivity, or they can alienate you to the point where you reject a really good idea just because it came from them. The list is endless, and Narcissists take no responsibility for any of it. Narcissism means never having to say you're sorry.

Narcissistic Legends demand a lot. Your most important goal is to make sure you're getting something back for what you give.

2. Get Outside Verification

Narcissistic Legends can tell wonderful stories about the great things they've done in the past. Often, the stories are huge exaggerations. Always check. This is the obvious use of verification.

A less obvious and therefore more important use is to get external verification of the value of their ideas. Often Narcissistic Legends present a good idea in such an obnoxious way that it's easy to discount it. Paranoid vampires do the same.

Virtually all really great ideas sound threatening or impertinent when you first hear them. Sometimes you need an outside opinion to keep your own ego from getting in the way of a real creative breakthrough.

3. Do What They Don't

Whatever the task, do the hard part first. In dealing with Narcissistic Legends, the hard part is demanding what you want from them clearly and up front. This is particularly difficult, and important, if you see yourself as a giver. With Narcissists, unless you're willing to take, you will be taken.

If you do have the capacity to give, you have a tremendous opportunity that is forever denied to Narcissists. You can be a part of the group, a regular person who plays by the same rules as everyone else. Rejoice in being part of something larger than yourself. Narcissists are condemned to live in a world where nothing can be bigger than their own egos.

4. Pay Attention to Their Actions, Not Their Words

If you have to deal with Narcissists, the word to remember is *accountability*. Build it into whatever relationship you have from the beginning. It will be far more difficult to tack on the notion later. Narcissistic Legends are famous for taking on projects that they never finish because they never get down to doing the difficult parts. They may look as if they're working hard, but they're really hardly working, at least at the things that pay off. If Legends are doing something for you or with you, specify tasks and set time limits and dollar amounts. Inspect deliverables carefully to make sure you're getting what you expected. Narcissistic Legends sometimes mistake cutting corners for art.

5. Pick Your Battles

If you think you can teach a Narcissist to care about what other people feel, it's probably best to sit in a dark, quiet room until the delusion goes away.

Narcissistic Legends don't understand empathy, and they're never going to understand by listening to what you tell them.

With well-chosen words and well-constructed contingencies, you may be able to get them to change annoying Narcissistic behaviors, but not the narcissism underneath.

6. Let Contingencies Do the Work

When you hear Narcissistic Legends talking big, ask yourself why, if they're so smart, they aren't rich. This isn't a rhetorical question. The answers you come up with will be essential in helping you deal effectively with these vampires.

The reason Narcissistic Legends don't succeed is that they can't make themselves do things they don't want to do. You need to know what these things are. Make sure your dealings with Legends are structured so that they get the biggest rewards for actually doing the difficult stuff rather than just talking about it.

7. Choose Your Words as Carefully as You Pick Your Battles

The words you have to use most carefully around Narcissistic Legends are any that sound even a little bit like criticism. No matter how constructive it is, to Narcissists, the tiniest criticism feels like the fiery sting of a crucifix. They'll scream, snarl, and rationalize until dawn, but unless the criticism is delivered exceedingly well, they will not learn anything.

To deal with Narcissistic Legends at home or at work, you have to learn to criticize effectively, because they make a lot of mistakes that they will never recognize on their own.

Criticism is a tool that is easy to use badly with vampires (or with anyone). Unless you're very careful, you can do more harm than good. Here are some ideas about how to maximize the positive effects and minimize the damage.

Give far more praise than criticism. If you want to use criticism well, especially with Narcissistic Legends, the first step is to use praise more often than blame. Narcissists need tons of praise, and to get anywhere, you'll have to give it. Just make sure you give it for the right things. Catch them being good and reward them.

Don't be spontaneous. Criticism given spontaneously usually takes the form of an emotional explosion—a way of expressing hurt or anger rather than a planned intervention to help the other person improve. There is a place for emotional expression, of course, but not as a method for getting other people to change their behavior.

Know your goal. What do you want the Legend to do as a result of what you say? You don't have to spell out what Legends did wrong to ask them to do it right next time. Sometimes a simple request is the best criticism.

Ask permission. Before you criticize, ask: "Are you open to some feedback?" If the vampire says yes, then you have at least a rudimentary agreement to listen.

Criticize the behavior, not the person. We all know this rule, but we break it every day. Focus on the words you choose. If you begin any statement with the words *you are* and the next word is not *wonderful*, whatever you say will be perceived as a personal attack, no matter what you intend. Be more effective by asking for what you want or saying what you feel.

Instead of saying, "You are insensitive," a better approach is to say, "When you answered before I finished talking, I felt put down. Is that what you intended?" Or simply ask the vampire to wait until you finish talking before answering. Remember, the word *interrupt* carries an accusation within it. For best results, use neutral language.

Give the vampire an out. Provide a socially acceptable reason for making a mistake before you say what the mistake was. Begin your criticism with, "I know you're busy" or some other statement that implies that the vampire was trying to do a good job.

Rehearse. Practice criticizing Narcissists the way you would practice an important speech. Listen to yourself and imagine how you would feel if someone said that to you. Then multiply by 10.

Give the vampire time to think. If a Narcissistic Legend responds immediately, it will most likely be with an attempt to explain why he or she is right and you are wrong. Saying, "I don't expect you to answer immediately— we'll talk about it tomorrow" is a way to discourage knee-jerk defensiveness. Remember to say it and walk away immediately.

Criticism is an important tool for changing vampire behavior. Like any other tool, if criticism is to work, it must be used with attention, skill, and forethought.

8. Ignore Tantrums

Most of the vampires we've met so far use temper tantrums to get their way. Narcissists practice tantrums as if they were a martial art. They hold black belts in both the endless lecture and the shoulder of ice. Despite their obvious skill, Narcissistic Legends throw tantrums that are relatively easy to tune out. Anger is a form of theater, and Legends are terrible actors. They don't pay enough attention to their audience to draw people into the performance. Remember, they can't sell much of anything.

They are creative, however. Narcissists have developed a form of manipulative emotional explosion all their own. Call it a guilt tantrum. When things go really badly, and these vampires sense that they are in major trouble, they may erupt into a torrent of self-blame. To the unwary, it may look as if these self-absorbed children of the night are finally catching on to what everyone has been trying to tell them for years. No way. The feelings are temporary, and if you scratch their newfound self-knowledge even slightly, you'll find self-pity just below the surface. And incredibly transparent guilt trips.

> *"I don't blame you for wanting to leave." Tyler's voice cracks, and his eyes fill with tears. "Who would want to live with a failure?"*
>
> *"You're not a failure," Kristin says. She's crying too. "You're just—"*
>
> *Tyler holds up his hand. "Don't deny it. We both know I'm a pretty sorry human being."*

Stick to your guns. It hurts, but in the end, it's kinder to everyone.

9. Know Your Own Limits

Narcissists require an enormous amount of praise, attention, and other supplies. Like pigeons in the park, when you run out of popcorn, they fly away. Sometimes it's best to let them.

Even with good intentions and good technique, sometimes there's nothing you can say or do to match the lure of Narcissistic Legends' grandiose internal fantasies. If the going gets too rough, they can create an alternate reality for themselves and retreat into it forever.

By day, Tyler is a ne'er-do-well who can't seem to hold a job, living alone in a grubby apartment. By night, as Trollmeister, he stalks the Internet, a bold warrior defeating all comers in fantasy games. He's a legend among a small, select cadre of gamers. Nobody knows his real name or where he's from. Only that he's the best.

18 Vampire Superstars

You've Got to Love These Guys!
Worship Them, Actually

Narcissistic Superstars play the lead in their own life story, which, to them, is indistinguishable from the history of civilization. At the depths of their souls, these vampires believe that they are the most important people on earth. If you understand and accept this one central fact, Superstars cease to be a danger and become merely an annoyance. If the fact that they believe themselves to be the crown of creation offends you and makes you want to point out to them that they're not so great as they think they are, get away quickly, because they will destroy you.

Unfortunately, there are few places you can get away to, because wherever you go, there will likely be a Narcissistic Superstar in a position of authority over you. So, what's it to be? Do you fight them, run from them, or learn how to deal with them?

Everything we've learned up to now about Narcissists is also true of Superstars, except that, unlike Legends in Their Own Minds, they know how to work, and they know how to sell. These vampires are willing and able to do what it takes to turn their grandiose dreams into reality. Almost. Superstars' dreams are always beyond their grasp. Whatever they are and whatever they have is never enough. They always want more.

Narcissistic Superstars' abilities, coupled with their tremendous hunger, may bring them success, but never satisfaction. They build empires, lead nations, create great works of art, and amass huge sums of money for one purpose only: to prove how great they are. Superstars may boast incessantly about what they have and what they've done, but once they have it or have done it, whatever it is loses value in their eyes. They always need more.

Whether it's money, honors, status symbols, or sexual conquests, Superstars always want something. They get what they want, too. Every one of them has a trophy collection. Adding to it is the sole purpose of Narcissistic Superstars' existence; there is no higher goal.

The most dangerous place you can be is between a Narcissistic Superstar and the next trophy.

> *With surgical precision, Vampire Antonio unpacks the boxes of photographic equipment spread across the dining room table.*
>
> *Oriana stands in the doorway, shaking her head. "Another camera?"*
>
> *Antonio holds up what looks like a futuristic gray box with a viewfinder on top. "This isn't a camera; it's a Hasselblad!" He removes a lens from a leather case and reverently connects it to the camera body. "See this? It's the finest lens made. The resolution is incredible. Here, look."*
>
> *He holds the camera out to Oriana, who dutifully looks through the eyepiece. "Very nice," she says. "But it doesn't seem that much different from all your other cameras."*
>
> *Antonio tenses up. "Here we go again," he says. "Let's hear the spending-too-much-money-on-cameras lecture. I know it's coming."*
>
> *"I didn't say—"*
>
> *Antonio puts the camera down. "What's the matter? You don't think I work hard enough?" He begins ticking off points on his fingertips. "Twelve years of round-the-clock training, 60 or 70 hours of surgery cases a week, plus the time I spend on publications. You'd think the least I could expect out of my life is to use some of the money I earn to give myself a little pleasure. It's not as if you and the kids are doing without anything. I mean, that* is *your Mercedes in the driveway, isn't it?"*
>
> *Oriana stands there quietly, waiting for Antonio to finish.*

DEALING WITH SUPERSTARS' INSATIABLE NEEDS

Superstars love expensive toys. They *have* to have the best, because this shows that they *are* the best. An unrelenting drive to achieve and acquire is the center of their personality. There is no point in asking Narcissistic Superstars why they need to have so much and do so much. They don't know, any more than a flower knows why it turns toward the sun.

Don't waste your time trying to figure it out. Use it. For all their talent, intelligence, and temporal power, Superstars are pathetically easy to manipulate. Here's how.

First, Kiss Up

There is no way around it. If you want to maintain any sort of relationship with Narcissistic Superstars, you have to admire them, their achievements, and their toys incessantly. Typically, it won't take much effort on your part to kiss up to Superstars. They'll be more than happy to come up with reasons to congratulate themselves. All you have to do is listen and look interested.

Know Your Needs

It's important to know what you want for yourself as clearly as Superstars know what they want for themselves. Superstars *always* know what they want, and they're always trying to figure out how to get it. If your own needs are unclear to you, or you wait for these vampires to give you what you deserve, you'll never get anything.

Tie Your Needs In with Theirs

Superstars are going to get what they want, whether you're a part of it or not. Make yourself a part of it. To get even slightly reasonable treatment from Superstars, you'll have to play all the angles, just as they do.

Oriana doesn't want her own camera, but there are many things she does want from Antonio. At the top of the list is for him to spend more time with her and the family, which is an almost universal desire among people close to Superstars. To get what she wants, Oriana will have to somehow tie it into Antonio's desire to do great deeds and own great things. Here's an example of how she might go about it:

> *"Can I hold it?" Oriana asks. Antonio hands the Hasselblad to her, and she cradles it gently. "So tell me," she says. "What does this camera do that makes it so special?"*
>
> *Antonio beams. "What doesn't it do is more like it. This is the most advanced camera made anywhere in the world today. Let's start with the lens mount . . ."*
>
> *Oriana listens patiently and enthusiastically throughout Antonio's lengthy presentation. Finally, she senses an opening. "This may be a dumb question, but can that camera take pictures of things that are moving, even though they're far away? Like maybe a sports event?"*
>
> *He removes a longer lens from its case. "With a lens like this, this camera can catch the beads of sweat on a quarterback's nose at a hundred yards."*

"Wow! You mean it can really pick up sports action, and even the expressions on the players' faces?"

"Absolutely! Why do you ask? Do you have some particular sport you want a picture of?"

"Well, the other day at Ramon's soccer game, I was looking at the boys. I started thinking about what a wonderful photo essay somebody could do on third-grade soccer. It was so cute how they were playing like grown-ups in the game, then playing in the mud puddles when they were on the sidelines. If somebody could catch those contrasts.... Of course, it would take a really good photographer and really excellent equipment to get the kinds of one-in-a-million shots I'm thinking of."

Antonio pats his new camera. "This is the baby that can do it, right here."

Is Oriana being manipulative? You bet. With Superstars, there's no way around manipulation. Vampires understand that most human interactions have a manipulative component, but that some techniques work better than others. Telling Antonio how sad Ramon is that his dad doesn't come to his soccer games is also a manipulative strategy, but it's one that won't work on Superstars. They never feel guilty about being too busy to meet anybody else's needs. If you can't get over the fact that Oriana has to stoop to trickery to get Antonio to do things a normal father would be happy to do, you probably shouldn't marry a Narcissistic Superstar. Or work for one. In order for Narcissistic Superstars to act like normal human beings, they generally have to be manipulated into it.

Superstars always seem to forget that someday the people who are beneath notice may have something to offer. Narcissists' paths through life are always marked by scorched earth and burned bridges.

Narcissists get away with utter disregard for other people's feelings because they can. If these vampires want to build a business, then drive off their best talent for lack of reverence or lack of political skill, there's no way to stop them. They have the money and the power to do what they want, and they certainly don't give a damn what others think about it.

Among numerous authors on the way of Narcissists, Christopher Lasch is by far the most eloquent.* He believes that narcissism is becoming an epidemic, especially in the worlds of business and politics. Lasch may be cor-

---

*Christopher Lasch, *The Culture of Narcissism: American Life in an Age of Diminishing Expectations* (New York: W. W. Norton, 1991).

rect, but that still leaves us with the question of what to do about it. Narcissists certainly won't change because some expert tells them it's bad to be Narcissistic.

No amount of negative press will change Narcissistic Superstars. They always have glee clubs of self-interested supporters to sing their praises. Narcissists prefer sucking up to reasoned criticism every time.

People tend to either love Superstars or hate them. There's no in between, and there's very little predicting who will feel what. Some people forgive any amount of Narcissistic behavior because of the vampire's talents and success; other people become outraged at even small amounts of entitlement. Remember that the next time you want to grumble about your Narcissistic boss.

SUPERSTAR HYPNOSIS

Superstars create an alternative universe in which they are special, and your success and happiness are contingent upon your indulging their every whim. If you work for them, their power over you may be sufficient to turn their alternative universe into the one you have to live in. To make things more confusing, these managerial vampires often create systems that they themselves don't understand, because they don't design them. Everything is jury-rigged by employees to compensate for deficiencies in the manager's personality. There is only one rule in such systems: humor the boss. Superstars like to spout off about teamwork, empowerment, and flattening the organization, blissfully unaware that when they're around, all real work stops because job number one is entertaining the boss. The comic strip *Dilbert* is a far better guide to this kind of organizational structure than any management text.

SEX AND THE SUPERSTAR

Superstars are famous for making fools of themselves over sex. Right now, you can probably name a dozen or so who have shot themselves in the foot by philandering. Well, maybe it's not the foot.

People marvel at how such bright people can act like such complete idiots when their pants are off. Why do they do it?

Sex is just one of the many forms of adulation that Narcissistic Superstars expect from other people. Superstars are major-league seducers and world-class adulterers, but absolute rookies when it comes to love. Often, they don't see sex as related to love. It's more like a sport.

High-profile womanizers are often misdiagnosed by the press as being sex addicts. Real sex addicts act like other addicts. They are consumed by their addiction. They build up a tolerance, which means that they have to have more sex, more often, usually several times a day. They don't much care with whom. Between partners, they masturbate. For them, sex is joyless, an insatiable need.

Narcissists are not addicted to sex, but to adoration in whatever form it takes. They can't tolerate anyone turning them down for any reason.

For Narcissists, it's not so much the sex; it's the keeping score. Antisocials pursue sex because it's fun. If a relationship gets too difficult, they tend to move on because there are other fish in the sea. Not Superstars; as a matter of principle, they want every fish, in every ocean, all the time. Sex for Narcissists is more important as a token of obeisance than because it feels good or is a form of human closeness. The problem is that the people they get the sex from don't always feel that way.

> *The hotel bar is quiet this late at night. In a dark corner, it's just the Candidate and Trish, one of the many staffers who are working so hard to get him elected.*
>
> *Trish can't believe her good luck. Face time with Him. She was so surprised when he asked her to have a drink; she didn't think he even knew her name.*
>
> *He smiles that campaign poster smile at her. "Trish, I think you have real potential, now and when this campaign is over. Of course, we have to win first, which won't be that easy. A lot is riding on what happens in the next few days. The speech tomorrow, how do you think we should play it? Is it time for me to take off the gloves?*
>
> *Trish is flabbergasted. The great man wants her opinion!*

Trish isn't flabbergasted; she's seduced.

When Narcissists want something from people, they actually see them as great and wonderful. That's why their hypnosis is so effective. Once Superstars get what they want, their perceptions return to what, for them, is normal—seeing ordinary people as, well, ordinary. The problem is that the people they seduce may still be laboring under the delusion that they are as special as the Superstars said they were.

Everyone is affected adversely by Superstars' peccadilloes: the people they seduce, their own families, the coworkers who are jealous of favoritism, and all the businesslike folks standing on the sidelines watching this soap opera proceed to its unhappy conclusion so they can get on with their jobs. And that's even before the press gets wind of it.

You've seen this story play out so many times with so many powerful characters. Each time, you probably wonder how such smart people can be so stupid.

Narcissists are very good at *compartmentalization*. They can draw a mental curtain around one area of their life, and pretend that it has nothing to do with anything else. It's easy for them, because what connects the areas in our lives are people's feelings, something that Superstars rarely notice. In more ways than one, that proves their undoing.

SUPERSTAR DEPRESSION AND ANGER

Remember the three requirements for mental health that I outlined in Chapter 2—perception of control, pursuit of challenge, and feeling connected to something larger than yourself? Narcissistic Superstars make top scores in two out of three. They stand proudly at the helm of their own lives, captains of their fate. They love challenge, the tougher the better. Their great deficiency is that they live in a miniature universe that is no larger than their own desires.

Superstars never seem to grasp the idea of connecting to something larger than themselves. It is this lack that ultimately makes their lives unsatisfying. Yet these vampires invariably believe that their lack of satisfaction results from other people criticizing them unfairly or just not making enough effort to please them.

> *Antonio has that pinch-browed look on his face when he comes through the door. Oriana knows that things have gone badly at the clinic. She also knows that within the next few minutes, Antonio is going to find something—anything—on which to vent his frustrations.*
>
> *Oriana looks around the living room, hoping that the kids remembered to take their backpacks upstairs. Marta's shoes are in the hallway. Oriana swoops down and whisks them out of sight before Antonio notices. "How was your day?" she ventures.*
>
> *Antonio doesn't answer. A bad sign.*
>
> *Oriana thinks about positive things to bring up. "Ramon got three goals at soccer practice."*
>
> *Antonio grunts, and continues flipping through the mail. "Did you pick up my tweed jacket at the cleaners?" he asks.*
>
> *Oriana feels an electric tingle along her spine. "I meant to," she says, "but I didn't have time."*

Narcissistic Superstars tend to experience two different kinds of anger that may be indistinguishable to the outside observer.

In the world of Superstars, incompetence is the gravest crime. Their standards for themselves are high, and even higher for the little people around them whose job it is to keep everything running smoothly so that the Superstars can do their jobs.

Needless to say, Superstars get angry quite often, especially if other people's mistakes cause even slight inconvenience. Narcissists' favorite tantrum is the condescending lecture on standards of minimal competence. Such lectures seldom have the desired effect of inspiring people to work harder and be more careful. Superstars often feel, correctly, that the little people around them are *purposely* ignoring their requests and instructions. This usually leads to more tantrums.

The other kind of anger that Superstars experience is at themselves when they don't win. Their spirits can drop like a stone at the slightest evidence that they've made a mistake. Superstars are their own severest critics, but when they begin criticizing themselves, they always seem to find things to criticize about other people as well. Being angry at everybody else tends to divert Superstars from their disappointment in themselves. It's hard to say whether Superstars get angry because they're depressed or get depressed because they're angry, but it's absolutely certain that when Narcissists get depressed, *everyone* gets drained.

If you're close to a Superstar, rather than cringing in fear at his or her irritability or retaliating, it's more helpful to try to find out what the real problem is and discuss it.

> *"Tonio, what do you say we get beyond the grumpiness and talk about what's really going on?" Oriana says.*
>
> *"What do you mean?" Antonio replies.*
>
> *Oriana puts her hands on her hips. "You tell me. All I know is that you don't get this upset unless something really big is bothering you. Has something happened at the clinic?"*
>
> *"I guess I am upset," Antonio says. His lower lip quivers almost imperceptibly as he pushes it into a fatalistic smile. "I mean, it's not that big a deal, but they, uh, put me on probation for yelling at a nurse in the OR."*

Passive-Aggressive behavior enrages Superstars, yet they draw it like a magnet. It makes sense. The way they whack people over the head with blunt criticisms, who could blame anybody for retaliating? Superstars, that's who.

Narcissistic Superstars and Passive-Aggressive Histrionics are a match made in hell. Each can cause the other to escalate into spasms of self-destruction. If you ever have to deal with Superstar anger, the most important thing to remember is not to respond the way a Passive-Aggressive Histrionic would.

Understate Superstars' transgressions rather than exaggerating them even slightly. Annoying as they are, Narcissists aren't sadistic like Antisocial Bullies; they don't enjoy inflicting pain for its own sake. Superstars are just a bunch of insensitive babies throwing very creative tantrums. Call them irritable, call them obnoxious, call them SOBs, but don't call them abusers. Abuse is a crime. If you use that word, all you'll get from Superstars is defensiveness. If you impugn their reputations, they'll be more interested in proving you wrong than in hearing what you have to say.

Histrionics tend to use the word *abuse* for anything that causes them discomfort, and that usage has moved into the vernacular. As a rule, the only time it's appropriate to use the term *abuse* is when you've consulted an attorney, or if you're going on a daytime talk show.

Even though Superstars' anger is different from that of Antisocial Bullies, the same strategies will work. If you have to deal with an angry Superstar, you might review the approaches suggested for dealing with Bullies in Chapter 8. Your goal, as always, is to get vampires to stop picking on you, not to have them acknowledge how much it hurts to be picked on.

In addition to the strategies outlined for Bullies, there's one more thing to remember about Superstars' anger.

Superstars, because of their competence, achievement, and general arrogance, are often more respected than liked. People who love these vampires, in a misguided attempt to humanize them, will sometimes share stories of funny little mistakes that Superstars have made. Don't even think of doing this! Superstars' mistakes are not little, and they are absolutely *not* funny.

NINE WAYS TO PROTECT YOURSELF FROM NARCISSISTIC SUPERSTARS

When you deal with Superstars, take care of business—your own.

1. Know Them, Know Their History, and Know Your Goal

Narcissistic Superstars draw you in because of their talents, abilities, and power. They are often special people, and you feel special being around them. You're not. For Narcissists, other people are sources of supplies, rather than real, full-blown human beings. Only Superstars are three-dimensional.

One of the easiest ways to spot Narcissists is to look around when you need help at an inconvenient time. They're the ones who aren't there.

Superstars' histories are often impressive lists of achievements. Don't be too impressed to find out how they've treated other people while they were doing their great deeds. Whatever happened to those other people is what will happen to you.

There will always be two kinds of people in Superstars' past. The people above them will always think they were wonderful, but if you really want to know what they were like, you have to talk to their peers and the bit players in their lives. There is no greatness without narcissism, and narcissism is caustic to human relationships. The question you want answered about Superstars' past is not whether they were Narcissistic, but how well they kept it contained.

Superstars run many businesses, perhaps even yours. If you work for them, they expect to be treated in a particular way, and you'd better know how. Watch the people who are successful and do what they do.

Your goal with Superstars is to get the best return on your efforts, whatever they are. This is true whether you are involved in a personal or a business relationship with them. I know this sounds mercenary, but it is the approach that works best. Narcissists of all types are famous for unbalanced relationships in which the other person does all the giving. It's harder to get caught if you keep an eye on the bottom line from the beginning.

If you want Superstars' attention, you'll have to sell yourself and your ideas. Whatever you're selling should be presented in the same way as a Rolls-Royce—as a top-of-the-line item that Narcissists *might* not be able to afford. They usually find a way to pay for high-status luxuries. As long as you're one of those, you'll do fine. With Superstars, there's no point in being a bargain.

2. Get Outside Verification

With Superstars, it's a bigger problem trying to give outside verification than to *get* it. Behind their backs, everybody agrees that Superstars make mistakes. Nobody wants to tell them to their faces, because Superstars have strong propensities both to ignore information that suggests they're less than wonderful and to kill messengers who bring them bad news.

If you do have to give a Superstar bad news, make sure that you have facts and figures to back it up, or opinions from people with status *much* higher than the vampire's own.

As to getting outside verification, Superstars are famous for paying off their debts with vague promises and lots of ego massages. The massages feel very good, so it may be helpful to check with other people to make sure you're getting substance rather than ambience.

3. Do What They Don't

Value the little people and listen to them. Also, help them understand what they have to do to be big people. This is especially important at work, where the temptation to emulate Superstars, rather than learning from their mistakes, will be strong.

For all their talents, Superstars are terrible at being team players or coaches of effective teams. In Superstar organizations, the word *teamwork* gets batted around like a softball at the company picnic, but the real emphasis is on individual incentives for top players. The star system, of course, cancels out any motivation to work as a team.

4. Pay Attention to Their Actions, Not Their Words

Superstars can talk the talk. They've read all the books, and they know all the buzzwords, but they're the guys who invented not walking the walk.

5. Pick Your Battles

The most important battle to win is the one for Superstars' respect. You won't get respect because you deserve it, or because of your own talents and achievements. No matter what Superstars say, they will always believe that they are better than you are. The only way to win respect from Superstars is by driving a hard bargain. If you hang around with these vampires, you have to show them that you're capable of playing in their league. If you don't constantly demonstrate that you're as tough as they are, they'll just take whatever they want from you and never give anything back at all.

With Superstars, there are some battles you don't want to win. Actually, these are battles you can *appear* to win, but in fact lose. To get you off their case, Superstars may tell you what you want to hear even though they don't actually feel it. The price for this kind of false deference is their respect.

Superstars never feel wrong, they never feel gratitude, they don't believe other people are entitled to the same rights and privileges as they are, and they seldom see other people's actions as worthy of spontaneous praise. If you demand any of these indulgences, Superstars will speak whatever words you want to hear and never again give you anything more than lip service. Superstars will formally acknowledge your worthiness at the price of genuine regard. In public, they will say whatever you deem to be politically correct, and laugh in private at your presumptuousness. If they praise you, either they're trying to sneak up on your Narcissistic side or they're indicating that you are one of the little people who needs occasional doses of praise to keep going, much as a car has to be filled with gas.

Be very careful what you ask of Superstars. They're famous for taking the best of what people have and giving back only hollow words, worth less than nothing. It's always up to you to know the difference between inconsequential trinkets and tokens of real respect.

6. Let Contingencies Do the Work

The most meaningful contingency with Superstars is the transaction. To keep from being sucked dry by these vampires, you must always think of yourself as a commodity, because that's the way they think of you. To survive with Superstars, you have to know what they want from you and what you want in return. Then you have to negotiate to get the best price you can. Superstars have absolutely no sense of fairness. If they want something, however, they will generally pay the price, provided it is demanded up front. Don't extend credit.

To negotiate a good price, you have to know what Superstars value. At the top of the list is whatever will make them look good. This can be anything from an impressive bottom line and employees who can do a bang-up job without much supervision, to trophy wives and fancy cars. Narcissistic supplies come in all shapes and sizes.

Next on these vampires' wish list is adoration. With Superstars, you just can't suck up too much. If you're selling an idea to Superstars, do it quickly. Always cut to the chase, and tell them what's in it for them if they give you what you want. Forget about snow jobs; Superstars are not easily fooled. Always do your homework. You can bet that the Superstars have done theirs.

The chance to make money is always a good bargaining chip. Sex might be worth something, if you're attractive and play hard to get. Superstars also like challenges and interesting company that stimulates their minds. They love a good argument, but you probably won't be able to convince them of anything they don't already believe. It's fine to try, so long as you don't resort to moralism to make your point. Superstars fall asleep during sermons.

Superstars *expect* loyalty, so they're usually not willing to pay much for it. They will, however, spend quite a bit of money and effort to get back at somebody they think has betrayed them.

What Narcissistic Superstars don't value at all is being fair to others, or being seen as nice. They pride themselves on not suffering fools gladly, and they destroy those who try to embarrass them.

What Superstars hate most is whining, unless they're the ones doing it. They absolutely do not care about the trials and tribulations of your life. They may take them on as a problem to solve, but they will never just listen quietly and sympathize.

No matter what they pretend to be, on the inside, Superstars are tough and cynical. If you can't be as tough as they are, stay away from them. They'll eat you alive.

7. Choose Your Words as Carefully as You Pick Your Battles

Superstars are even more sensitive to disapproval than Legends. It might be a good idea to review the section on how to criticize Narcissists in Chapter 17.

The words you should pay most attention to are the ones in your sales pitches. If you think that dealing effectively with Superstars is a lot like door-to-door sales, you're doing it right. Your most important products are yourself and your ideas.

8. Ignore Tantrums

Superstars regularly throw tantrums when other people make life difficult for them. They demand competence and severely punish tiny mistakes. It helps to get outside verification to decide whether the vampires actually have a point or are merely trying to manipulate you. If they're trying to manipulate you, stand up to them directly or lodge a formal complaint. If you try to get back at them in sneaky ways, you'll be the one who gets hurt. Don't call what Narcissists do *abuse* or *harassment* until you've checked with your attorney.

Superstars also throw another kind of tantrum that is quieter, but far more destructive. They use their power to frighten people into letting them have everything their own way. Over time, they make their worlds over in their own image.

Business is the Superstars' world; it bears their marks everywhere. In the darkness beneath their towering shadows, there can be no dreams greater than personal glory and this quarter's bottom line.

The numbers say business is prospering, yet in cubicles and on production floors, times are always hard and the lives of little people are cheap.

9. Know Your Own Limits

If you want to be successful with Superstars, you have to compete in their league and play by their rules. If you do, however, there is a very real danger that you will become like them. With their bites, Superstars create more new vampires than do all the other vampire types combined. Don't enter their world unless you know how to get out. Many have been lost.

19 Narcissists in Your Life

People either love Narcissists or hate them. Many of the people who once loved them end up hating them, and hating themselves for loving them. As I said in Chapter 16, Narcissists are, rightly or wrongly, the most despised of the vampire types. Perhaps they are not the most dangerous, but they do seem to be the most draining to the most people.

One of the reasons that Narcissists have such a strong effect on us has to do with the programming in the most primitive areas of our brains. We respond to dominance hierarchies in very predictable ways.

These rules of dominance are simple: the dominant get to be aggressive against the submissive, but the submissive can't be aggressive in return unless they are vying for the dominant role. These rules may be simple, but their effect is anything but.

Some hierarchies are clear and formal, but most are not. Any time two or more people get together, there is always some question as to who has ascendancy over whom.

Narcissists *always* take the dominant role, whether they have a right to it or not. The anger we feel at being treated like inferiors bubbles up from the depths of the oldest part of our brains.

This anger clouds our judgment. Instead of figuring out what we want to have happen in a particular situation, we just want to get back at them, or show them how it feels to be treated the way they treat us. Narcissists thrive in the confusion this kind of competition creates.

In order to deal effectively with the Narcissists in our lives, we must be able to override our primitive anger, think about what we want, and decide how best to get it. This process is similar to overriding the fight or flight response in dealing with Bullies. We need to understand Narcissists, and use that understanding to be as calculating in our dealings with them as they are with us.

Here is the most important thing to understand: though Narcissists treat you callously, they need you—maybe more than you need them. They don't need you in the way you might want to be needed, as a three-dimensional human being; but as a source of Narcissistic supplies. To protect yourself, you have to accept this, because you're not going to change it.

To be effective with Narcissists, you have to deal with them at their own level. You must be coldhearted enough to barter whatever it is they want from you for decent treatment, and strong enough to make them pay up front. If you can't do this, or if you get angry because you have to, you'd better get out now because they will eat you alive.

Here are some of the Narcissists you may encounter in your life. What you do with them is up to you.

PUNDITS FROM HELL

Everybody in the family thinks Uncle Ed and Uncle Walt should have their own political show on Sunday morning. That way, they could turn them off.

Ed and Walt actually are radio pundits, at least in their own minds. They make regular calls to local talk jocks, Ed to the conservative guy and Walt to the progressive.

Ed and Walt have ironclad opinions, based mostly on their own prejudices and bolstered by what they hear on the radio and TV and read on their favorite blogs. They both believe that anyone who doesn't agree with them is an idiot.

"Well, Mr. College Man," Uncle Ed says to Brian, his nephew. "What did you think of the president's speech?"

"Well," says Brian, who majors in economics, "I think his ideas about tax cutting don't make a lot of sense, based on any of the most accepted economic models."

"That's the problem with you liberals; you're always using models. I'm talking about the real world."

"And what real world is that?" Uncle Walt chimes in. "The one where the gap between the rich and poor is bigger than the one in Uganda? Of course, Ed, I know you don't believe in statistics. You think they're right up there with the Easter Bunny and global warming."

So it goes, ad nauseam. These Legends in Their Own Minds are experts in what logicians call the ad hominem argument, attacking the person instead of the idea. In formal debates, this is tantamount to admitting defeat. For Ed and Walt, it means they're just getting warmed up.

The ad hominem argument is the Narcissist's secret weapon. They use it all the time. Just listen to any blowhard on the radio. If you tangle with a

Narcissist, you can get trapped into defending yourself instead of your opinion. In the battle for dominance, the Narcissists usually win because they don't fight fair.

Here are some ideas about how to deal with pundits like Ed and Walt. I'm afraid there is nothing we can do about the ones on radio and TV.

Don't Engage

I'm not sure if the story of the tar baby, who trapped Br'er Rabbit by not saying a word, is still politically correct, but it is apropos. The easiest way to avoid a struggle with someone who is vying to be the smartest guy in the room is to play dumb. To do this, you will have to tamp down your own irritation at being treated like you don't know anything and just say, "Huh?"

As with any extinction strategy, once you start it, you have to stick with it. Narcissists will happily lecture you on their point of view for as long as you'll listen. Don't listen. Say, "I don't know anything about politics" and be on your way.

Invoke the Rotary Rule

I have been a member of Rotary for quite some time. It was founded a little over a hundred years ago by a group of business leaders who thought that fellowship and amiable discussion could benefit their community. They recognized that getting a group of high-powered people together might result in all sorts of dominance struggles, so from the beginning, they banned discussion of politics and religion. From that day to this, the rule has prevented millions of arguments and made it possible for Rotarians to stay focused on the stated goal of helping their communities.

Following the Rotary Rule will make all your family gatherings more civil, especially if there are Narcissists in the house. Invoking it will require some cooperation, but you will probably be able to recruit co-conspirators pretty easily. There is strength, and dominance, in numbers.

Turning the Tables

This strategy is risky at best. I don't suggest you try it at home. Nevertheless, if you want to score a point against a Narcissistic blowhard, take advantage of the fact that an ad hominem argument is logically indefensible.

The best protection against an ad hominem argument is to ignore it and stick to the subject at hand. Needless to say, this is hard to do when you or your sources are being called idiots.

To use this tactic, begin by stipulating whatever you're being accused of—stupidity, racism, or dewy-eyed idealism. If you take the bait and try to defend yourself, you're toast.

Instead, steal the position of dominance. In any discussion, questions are far more powerful than statements. Try asking a blowhard Narcissist where he gets his facts.

> *"Global warming? Give me a break!" Uncle Ed fumes. "That's just a load of manure that the Democrats are trying to shove down our throats. There's no such thing as global warming. It's just natural climate cycles."*
>
> *"So, what's your source?" Mr. College Man Brian asks. "How do you know there's no such thing as global warming?"*
>
> *"What do you mean, 'what's my source'? That sounds like the kind of thing those liberal PhDs up at the university are always whining about. You mean to tell me you believe those guys? I thought you were smarter than that."*
>
> *"Okay, I admit that there are a lot of liberal profs up at the U. I may be stupid for taking classes from them. So educate me. How do you know there's no such thing as global warming?"*
>
> *"It's like the Ice Age."*
>
> *"How is it like the Ice Age?"*
>
> *Ed just shakes his head. "Kids these days."*

Would it really work? Can you actually win an argument with a blowhard?

Probably not, but you can dream.

Meanwhile, try to invoke the Rotary Rule.

TIGER MOM

> *Gwendolyn calls herself a Tiger Mom, but she seems to have confused tigers with racehorses. She has two beautiful daughters, ages 8 and 12, who are talented, gifted, and driven to the very limit. They are the top students at prep school. They excel in sports, music, art, and whatever else there is to excel at.*
>
> *Evan, their dad is very proud of them, but he is worried that they're missing out on childhood.*
>
> *He knows why Gwendolyn does it. She is scary bright, but had to make do with a local college. She's a successful real estate developer, but could have been . . . well, who knows?*

> *What Evan suspects is that she is re-creating her own youth through them.*
>
> *He tries to bring it up casually. "Gwen," he says one evening, "don't you think you're pushing the kids kind of hard?"*
>
> *Gwendolyn's stare is colder than Antarctica. "Those girls that you think I'm pushing too hard are happiest and healthiest when they are doing their best to make something of themselves. But you wouldn't understand that, would you?"*
>
> *Evan hears a damp thump as his testicles hit the floor.*

When criticized, Narcissists quickly escalate to tactical nuclear weapons. They lash out, not caring how much pain they are causing. You probably recognized the ad hominem argument, and know it is merely a diversion. Let's hope Evan did.

Here are some guidelines that might help Evan in this situation. They might also help you if you have to discuss a controversial subject with a Narcissistic vampire:

Do Not Criticize!

It's not that Narcissists like Gwendolyn don't deserve criticism; they just won't hear it. You have to try something different.

Know Your Goal

Ask yourself what you want to have happen. Think long term.

Evan wants Gwendolyn to ease up on the girls, which is a good place to start. If he stops there, he will have to have this discussion again every time Gwendolyn gets pushy.

In order to ease up with any consistency, Gwendolyn needs to be able to consider someone else's feelings as well as her own. This is a hard thing to teach a Narcissist, but it is possible, especially if you are dealing with someone she dearly loves.

Evan should use every opportunity to ask the girls how they feel, not just about their achievements, but about everything. Making feelings a regular part of the family discourse will remind Gwendolyn that other people have feelings, and may encourage her to consider them in the name of being mother of the year, which is the title she seems to be vying for.

Retake the High Ground

Gwendolyn put Evan down hard, and unfairly. Most people would consider him to be a pretty successful guy, but in competitive achievement, Gwendolyn is a pro and he's an amateur. To accomplish his goal of getting her to consider the girls' feelings, he needs to change the sport to who is the most concerned parent, one in which he is a viable contender.

SEASON'S GREETINGS FROM THE NARCISSIST IN YOUR LIFE

Narcissists are difficult at any time of the year, but during the holidays, they can be even bigger pains in the butt.

Sarah looks forward to the holidays; she also dreads them. The problem is that every year, Connor's lack of enthusiasm hangs over the season like a damp blanket. He doesn't actually yawn and look at his watch, but he might as well.

Getting him a gift is a nightmare. Last year, the kids picked out a shirt and tie that they thought looked really cool. When Connor started tearing off their homemade wrapping, the children were so excited that they were literally jumping up and down—that is, until he lifted the lid.

He said, "Thanks kids; these are great!" But the way he tossed the box aside made it seem like he'd gotten a lump of coal. Even the four-year-old knew that he was disappointed.

Narcissists often see themselves as easy to get along with because they never yell. They don't need to; they can convey displeasure eloquently without saying a word. A cold shoulder, a look of disdain, or just not being there says more than words can ever express. Sarah's heart aches. There is nothing she can say, either. She just lets it be, thereby rewarding Connor for being a jerk and making it more likely that he will continue to act like a pouty child when he doesn't get exactly what he wants. He does stuff like this all the time, but it seems so much more painful during the holidays, when everyone else is full of love and good cheer.

If there is a Narcissist in your life, here are some suggestions that may make your holidays a little bit brighter (not to mention the rest of the year as well).

Make the Nonverbal Verbal

Don't let a Narcissist, or any other kind of vampire, get away with nonverbal disapproval. Unspoken communication has much more power than mere words because it is ambiguous. If a Narcissist says you did something wrong, you can at least disagree. If he only hints at it, you are left wondering if what you're seeing really means what you think it does, or if the whole thing is somehow your fault, or whatever else you might be imagining.

By trying to avoid conflict with a Narcissist, you set up a conflict within yourself, and he gets off scot-free. If there are children around, they are probably feeling the same things, and wondering why adults never say what they really mean.

What do you do instead? This technique will work, but it requires some finesse and quite a bit of courage. Here are the steps to follow:

Observe.   People have characteristic ways of expressing nonverbal disapproval—a snort, a frown, eye rolling, changing the subject, or damning with faint praise. Watch closely, and identify these characteristic behaviors well enough to be able to describe them out loud.

Translate rather than pointing the finger.   This is the tricky part because it is subtle, but it will make all the difference. An unsubstantiated accusation of an internal state, like, "You're bored," invites defensiveness. A translation, like, "You keep looking at the clock; I'm assuming you're bored," is much harder to deny. A Histrionic might try, but other kinds of vampires will have to concede that they are indeed looking at the clock.

> *Sarah takes a deep breath. "From the way you set that box aside, it seems like you don't like the shirt and tie."*
>
> *Connor tries to smile. "No, uh, it's just that . . . well, the color doesn't go with any of my suits."*

This is what it sounds like when you score a point against a Narcissist. The goal is not guilt induction, but clarification. When you make the nonverbal verbal, Narcissists lose the refuge of silence. They have to admit to their childish behavior. This makes it less likely that they will try the same stunt again, and it validates the perceptions of any real children who might be present.

You Have Something a Narcissist Wants; Bargain for It

Narcissists need narcissistic supplies. Connor wants to be seen positively, so name your price in advance. This is the sine qua non of dealing effectively with Narcissists.

> *"Connor, the holidays are coming. We want them to be fun for everyone, so I'll ask you now: do you want to participate?"*

> *"Of course. What makes you think I wouldn't?"*
>
> *Sarah presses on, ignoring the hook that might get her into a useless argument at this point.*
>
> *"Okay, here's a list of the things we typically do over the holidays. Tell me which of them you want to do with us."*
>
> *Connor glances at the list. "All of them."*
>
> *"Okay, if you want to be a part of things, here's a list of dos and don'ts."*
>
> *"Are you kidding?"*
>
> *"Not in the least."*

For a normal person, this approach would be outrageous, but you may be surprised at how well Narcissists respond. They will pay to play, but only if you ask for it up front.

There will likely be an argument about you being controlling or treating him like a child. Cop to it. The only position he will have left will be to argue for his right to act like a Grinch.

Do Not Expect a Narcissist to Actually *Like* Anything He Does Not Choose for Himself

As with all vampires, you have to focus on behavior, not feelings. If you want to see a Narcissist's eyes light up, ask him what he wants, and give it to him. If you feel that a gift must be a surprise, remember that for a Narcissist, it's the expense that counts, not the thought. Always go for the top of the line.

To get a Narcissist to participate in holiday festivities, you need to do pretty much the same thing you'd do for a four-year-old: give him his own part of the celebration to plan and execute however he wants.

If there is a Narcissist in your life, you know what it's like to feel love, hate, fear, and anger tangle and intertwine inside you until you are so confused you don't know what to do.

In those dark moments, trust yourself. In the end, Narcissists need you more than you need them.

20 Therapy for Narcissistic Vampires

What should you do if you see signs of Narcissistic behavior in yourself or someone you care about? This section is a thumbnail sketch of the sorts of self-help and professional therapeutic approaches that might be beneficial. Always remember that attempting psychotherapy on someone you know will make you both sicker.

THE GOAL

Most of all, Narcissists have to develop a sense of connection with the rest of humanity. Until Narcissistic vampires learn empathy, they are condemned to walk the night in search of one victim after another. Unfortunately, learning empathy takes years. The immediate goal for Narcissists is to act, in public and in private, *as if* they value other people's needs, thoughts, and feelings. With sufficient effort at pretending, Narcissists may eventually discover that their tiny souls can grow to match the size of their egos.

PROFESSIONAL HELP

Narcissists do better with old, rather frumpy therapists who are not impressed with them. These are, of course, not the sorts of therapists that Narcissists would typically select for themselves. They want young, well-dressed yuppies or eminent and important experts in the field. One of the first therapeutic lessons Narcissists have to learn is that getting what they want may not be what's best for them.

SELF-HELP

Listen!

If you're a Narcissist, the most important thing you can do for yourself is to try to understand and value other people. It's especially helpful to listen quietly when people are talking. Work hard to avoid tuning them out or composing your response before the person has finished speaking.

Listening is particularly important if someone is criticizing you. Never answer immediately; take at least 24 hours to consider your response. During that time, think about all the ways the criticisms could be accurate.

Avoid Talking About Yourself

You can listen to other people only if you're not trying to convince them of how great you are. If you must mention yourself, talk about your mistakes.

Play by the Rules

Whatever the rules are in the situation you are in, follow them to the letter. The more ridiculous and arbitrary you think they are, the harder you should strive to follow them. This includes speed limits; the signs don't say "50 mph unless you are important." Do whatever the little people are supposed to do.

On the highway, pick one lane and stay in it. It's not a race.

Practice the 360-Degree Empathy Drill

Whenever you're around people, stop every few minutes and mentally go around the room asking yourself what each person is feeling and thinking. Empathy takes practice. If you imagine that everyone is thinking about you, try again.

Be a Follower

In as many endeavors as possible, let other people lead and just do what they tell you. If you have children, play with them, letting them structure the activities.

Spend Time with People Who Are Different from You

Take a class or join an organization that is made up of good people who are different from you. Do your best to participate. The goal of this exercise is to learn that being a good human being is independent of politics and social standing.

Do Charity Work

Charity work does not mean fund-raising at fancy affairs! I'm talking about actual get-your-hands-dirty, menial work. Pick up trash, build houses, or serve soup. Wash your hands before doing that last one.

Most of all, *never miss an opportunity to do an anonymous good deed.*

WHAT WILL HURT

Narcissists will be further damaged by just about any situation in which they are treated as special or different from ordinary people.

21 Too Much of a Good Thing

The Obsessive-Compulsive Types

Can you imagine a vampire who drains you by working hard, being conscientious, and always doing the right thing? I'm sure you can, if an Obsessive-Compulsive has ever caught you making an insignificant mistake or going out to play before all the work was done. Obsessive-Compulsives are the living embodiment of too much of a good thing. In their world, no mistake is insignificant, and all the work is never done.

These vampires have characteristics of Obsessive-Compulsive personality disorder. In the minds of the public, this is hopelessly confused with Obsessive-Compulsive disorder, which is a brain dysfunction characterized by ritual repetitions, such as hand washing and door locking.

Obsessive-Compulsive *disorder* probably involves some disruption in brain chemistry and is often treated with medication. An Obsessive-Compulsive *personality* is a pattern of overly rigid and detail-oriented thoughts and actions that typically doesn't respond to drugs. To make things more confusing, obsessive-compulsive *disorder* sometimes occurs in people with obsessive-compulsive *personalities*.

Colloquially, people often speak of being "a little OCD" when they mean having a slight tendency toward the *place for everything and everything in its place* characteristics of Obsessive-Compulsive personality. This is almost as annoying to people in the field as calling Histrionics who act as if they had two competing personalities "schizophrenic." As you can already see, dealing effectively with Obsessive-Compulsives means keeping your details straight. You might also see that most professionals are a bit Obsessive-Compulsive.

The engine that runs both the disorder and the personality is fear. Obsessive-Compulsives are deathly afraid of doing anything wrong. To them, the smallest crack in their perfect facade leaves them open and vulnerable to all the seeping horrors of the universe.

Obsessive-Compulsives see their existence as a battle against the forces of chaos. Their weapons are hard work, adherence to rules, scrupulous attention to detail, and the capacity to delay gratification into the next life if need be.

Without Obsessive-Compulsives to do the unpleasant and painstaking tasks that make the world go, nations would fall, businesses would grind to a halt, and households would collapse into utter confusion. At least, that's what these vampires think, and it may well be true. We *do* need them. We trust in their honesty, we depend on their ability, and we rely on their tireless effort. You could almost believe that *we're* the ones who drain *them*. There is, however, more to the story.

Obsessive-Compulsives want to create a secure world by making everybody Obsessive-Compulsive. Only then can they be safe from themselves.

Here's their secret: inside every Obsessive-Compulsive is an Antisocial trying to claw its way out. These overly conscientious vampires distract themselves from the scrabblings and scrapings of the unacceptable creature within by keeping their hearts in the right place and their noses to the grindstone. The internal battle is too terrifying for them to face, so they force their gaze outward—at you. As long as Obsessive-Compulsives are protecting you from your base impulses, they never have to look at their own.

WHAT IT'S LIKE TO BE OBSESSIVE-COMPULSIVE

Imagine your entire future riding on a single critical action—an examination, a presentation, a sports event, or perhaps a job interview. You can't stop thinking about it. You go over every detail to make sure it's perfect, punctuating your thoughts with jolts of adrenaline when you envision making a mistake. One part of Obsessive-Compulsive consciousness is this sort of incessant anxiety over even the smallest of performances.

For the other part, picture yourself walking into your office with your mind already filled to overflowing, then checking your e-mail and finding a hundred new messages marked urgent, then looking up to see lines of people in the hall bringing in more work. Next, imagine looking around the office and noticing that everybody else is talking, laughing, and generally goofing off. This is the Obsessive-Compulsive's consciousness: always rehearsing something, terrified of mistakes, overwhelmed by trivial tasks, and resentful of other people's lack of attention to detail. Can you imagine how terribly lonely you'd feel being the only competent person on the planet?

All the incessant work and mental activity is designed to keep Obsessive-Compulsives from thinking about that frightening creature inside them. It's not as if these people would be serial killers if they let themselves go. The monster inside is little more than a rebellious teenager, so long walled off from the rest of the personality that it has taken on the aspect of an alien menace. Obsessive-Compulsives, like Histrionics, attempt to get rid of the unacceptable in themselves rather than learning how to live with it. Histrionics can just ignore what they don't like. Obsessive-Compulsives have to bury it in piles of work or drive it off with a flaming sword.

HOW MUCH IS TOO MUCH?

There is no success without compulsion. Since you're reading a book on improving your interpersonal skills instead of watching TV, you probably know this. Being a little Obsessive-Compulsive leads to an accomplished and virtuous life. Being too Obsessive-Compulsive leads to defeating yourself and draining other people.

How much is too much? As we saw in the case of Narcissistic Legends, one of the elements of socialization is learning how to make yourself do things you don't want to do because they need to be done. Obviously, that has to stop somewhere, but where? There must be a point at which a person works too hard or is too good.

Unfortunately, the answer can't be expressed as some sort of optimum good-to-evil or work-to-play ratio. The difference between normal conscientiousness and Obsessive-Compulsive behavior lies not in how much work people do, but in the strategy they use to keep themselves working when they'd rather play. Obsessive-Compulsives use psychological violence—jolts of fear, pangs of guilt, and sharp, icy threats of punishment. And that's just on themselves.

PUNISHMENT, WHERE GOOD AND EVIL MEET

Obsessive-Compulsives believe punishment is synonymous with justice. Punishment is the only strategy that Obsessive-Compulsives know for controlling their own behavior or that of other people. It is also the only one they want to know.

Punishment has two distinct purposes. First, it's a way to keep people from doing bad things. In that respect, it's not particularly efficient. Any psychologist will tell you that punishment causes all sorts of unintended side effects, and that rewarding people for positive behavior is far more likely to get them to do what you want.

It is the second use of punishment that makes it so popular with Obsessive-Compulsives. Punishment is a clever device that allows good people to do bad things without seeing themselves as evil.

Obsessive-Compulsives have the same kinds of innate violent tendencies as everybody else, but they deplore them as uncivilized, dangerous, and definitely outside the fence. Unless, of course, they're doing violence to somebody who is *bad*. The secret reason that Obsessive-Compulsives keep themselves from sin is so they can be first in line when it's time to throw stones.

Obsessive-Compulsives use punishment in all its forms, from condescending lectures and poor performance ratings to witch burning. They always see their actions as altruistic, done for the person's own good, rather than sadistic.

No matter how and how often they use punishment, Obsessive-Compulsives never seem to grasp its true nature, or understand that it just doesn't work. The only predictable effect of punishment is that it creates more need to punish.

Obsessive-Compulsives coined the phrase, "This hurts me more than it does you," and they believe it absolutely. There is no clearer window through which to see the murky confusion of their souls.

Obsessive-Compulsives are always trying to establish order. The problem is that the human mind is basically disorderly. Along with noble impulses, our thoughts are full of mixed feelings and uncivilized urges. These overtaxed vampires must hide from this reality behind enormous piles of work. From there, they can safely throw stones.

WHAT THE QUESTIONS MEASURE

The specific behaviors covered on the checklist relate to several underlying personality characteristics that define an Obsessive-Compulsive emotional vampire.

Love of Work

Forget about simple carnality. The great passion in the lives of Obsessive-Compulsives is work. It is their pride; their joy; their obsession; their drug; the alpha and omega of their existence. It is their gift, and the cross they have to bear. When Obsessive-Compulsives are working, they feel good about themselves and safe. If you want to feel safe, you'd better be working, too.

THE OBSESSIVE-COMPULSIVE VAMPIRE CHECKLIST: VICE MASQUERADING AS VIRTUE

True or False   Score one point for each *true* answer.

1. This person is a workaholic.   T F
2. This person has a hard time relaxing.   T F
3. This person believes there's a right way and a wrong way to do everything.   T F
4. This person can usually find something wrong with other people's way of doing anything.   T F
5. This person takes an inordinately long time to make up his or her mind, even about small matters.   T F
6. Once this person has made up his or her mind, it's almost impossible to change it.   T F
7. This person seldom gives a simple yes or no answer.   T F
8. This person's attention to detail may be annoying, but it has saved people from making dangerous or costly mistakes.   T F
9. This person has a very clear moral code.   T F
10. This person never seems to throw anything away.   T F
11. This person runs his or her life according to the adage, "If you want something done right, do it yourself."   T F
12. This person can spend almost as much time organizing a task as doing it.   T F
13. This person always looks neat and well organized.   T F
14. In meetings, this person will often suggest delaying action until more information can be obtained.   T F
15. This person balances his or her checkbook to the penny.   T F
16. This person is controlling.   T F
17. This person does not see himself or herself as controlling, only as right.   T F
18. When asked to give input on something written, this person will always correct the grammar and spelling, but sometimes make no comment on the overall idea.   T F
19. This person expresses anger by asking hostile questions that he or she sees as simple requests for information.   T F
20. This person becomes irritated or upset if asked to deviate from his or her routine.   T F

(continued on next page)

21. This person often feels overwhelmed by all the work he or
    she has to do.   T F

22. Although this person never says so directly, it's clear that he
    or she takes pride in working harder than everybody else.   T F

23. This person takes as much pride in a perfect attendance
    record as he or she does in any other achievement.   T F

24. This person has a hard time finishing tasks.   T F

25. This person will go through any amount of personal difficulty
    to make good on a promise, and expects you to do the same.   T F

Scoring   Five or more true answers qualify the person as an Obsessive-Compulsive emotional vampire, although not necessarily for a diagnosis of Obsessive-Compulsive personality disorder. If the person scores higher than 10, don't get too close or you'll get zapped.

Reliability

You can trust Obsessive-Compulsives. They keep their promises, and they're honest to a fault. Their word is as good as a legal contract, and often as labyrinthine and confusing. In their world, the law is all letter and no spirit.

Rigidity

Black-white, right-wrong, good-bad—Obsessive-Compulsives invented the dichotomy, which, like the straight line, does not exist in nature. (Obsessive-Compulsives also invented the straight line.) Though these vampires love complexity, they have a hard time with ambiguity, especially moral ambiguity. They struggle all their lives to impose order on a capricious universe.

Preoccupation with Details

Obsessive-Compulsives are famous for not seeing forests because of all the trees. They dash frantically from one detail to the next, never quite grasping that all the little details fit together into some sort of big picture.

Perfectionism

Perfectionism is a vice that masquerades as a virtue. It can lead to excellence, but it usually doesn't. Doing everything correctly can become the top priority, eclipsing the importance of the task or the feelings of other people. The wake of Obsessive-Compulsives is an orderly row of insignificant tasks done to perfection, and significant people leaving in frustration because they don't measure up.

Emotional Constriction

Most Obsessive-Compulsives suffer from emotional constipation. Freud thought this was caused by strict toilet training. He called them *anal-retentives*, because not going potty on demand was how they gained control of their overly demanding universe.

For anal-retentives, holding back is a creative act. Emotional control is their major art form. They take pride in it the way any artist would. Obsessive-Compulsives all seem to come from the same planet as *Star Trek*'s Mr. Spock, a place where irritation at illogical thinking is the only feeling allowed.

Indecisiveness

Obsessive-Compulsives try to keep their options open long after the windows of opportunity have shut. Their basic life strategy is minimizing loss rather than maximizing gain. This strategy is reflected in every conscious decision these vampires make, or rather fail to make.

One of the most common manifestations of Obsessive-Compulsive indecisiveness is the amount of stuff that these vampires accumulate, because they can never bring themselves to throw anything away. Often these people require more space to store useless items in than they do to live or work in. The extreme of this behavior is hoarding, which is likely a manifestation of the brain dysfunction rather than the personality. Obsessive-Compulsives keep useless things for a reason: they think they might have a use for them. Hoarders are just terrified of throwing anything away.

Unacknowledged Hostility

Obsessive-Compulsives secretly resent people who are not as hardworking and upstanding as they are. That turns out to be almost everyone. This resentment is hidden only from them; everybody else knows about it all too well.

THE OBSESSIVE-COMPULSIVE DILEMMA

Say what you will about Obsessive-Compulsives being difficult and draining, you have to admit that they put their money where their mouth is. Without their hard work and stern example, all of us would probably go over the edge.

22 Vampire Perfectionists and Puritans

Can the Undead Be Anal-Retentive?

Under the skin, the two major subtypes of Obsessive-Compulsive vampires are similar enough that the same general strategies work for both of them. Perfectionists and Puritans are obsessed with control. They're most draining when they try to reduce their own anxieties by managing your life. Perfectionists attempt to control your actions, what you do, and especially how you do it; Puritans try to control your soul.

At first, these vampires don't appear in the least dangerous. They're intelligent, responsible, and hardworking, if a bit uptight. They seem mild-mannered, surely not the sort of people who would lose their tempers or make a scene. They draw you in with their competence and reliability. You may even look up to them. Only later, when you make a mistake, or try to get them to do something *your* way or, perish the thought, give you a little praise, do you come to realize how vicious Obsessive-Compulsives can be.

Perfectionists and Puritans drain you by withholding approval, giving in its place petty criticisms and unsolicited comments about the error of your ways. No matter how hard you work, how good you are, or how carefully you try to follow the rules, it won't be enough. The first time you make a mistake, Obsessive-Compulsives will imply that you are lazy, immoral, or, at the very least, careless. They don't lose their tempers. Their words seem to come from a place of rectitude and moral authority, but they sting like fire and carry the scent of brimstone. Obsessive-Compulsives are not above using the powers of hell to achieve what they consider to be heavenly goals.

WHY DO THEY ALWAYS SEEM ANGRY?

Though they never admit it, Perfectionists and Puritans are angry much of the time. They carry around a good deal of free-floating resentment that they can easily attach to anyone who doesn't follow the same rules about work and morality that they do, which is virtually everyone. Obsessive-Compulsives always feel overwhelmed, underappreciated, and disappointed at the laxity of others. They're famous for sighing, shaking their heads, and muttering under their breath as they work themselves up for their next lecture. To hear them tell it, no one even *tries* to help them.

Inside, Obsessive-Compulsives want to rebel just as much as other people want to rebel against them. They never leave the straight and narrow path, however, because their own cruel consciences keep prodding them along and holding their feet to the fire. The pain they cause for you is nothing compared with what they inflict on themselves.

To make matters worse, Obsessive-Compulsives are unaware of their anger, their urge to rebel, or any other untoward thoughts they may be having. Unlike Histrionics, whose bad thoughts just disappear, Obsessive-Compulsives have organized minds, in which everything unacceptable is buried under stacks of rule books and piles of work.

Perfectionists and Puritans are angry because they're good people who are somehow stuck in a bad world.

OBSESSIVE-COMPULSIVE HYPNOSIS

Beware of confusion! Obsessive-Compulsives purposely fog their minds with minutiae to obscure the objectives of their own actions. If you don't watch out, they'll do the same to you. They create an alternate reality in which even the simplest tasks are fraught with hundreds of confusing and esoteric details that must be kept under tight control lest everything fall apart. What they're really trying to keep under control are their own aggressive impulses.

As we have seen throughout our study of emotional vampires, unacceptable impulses forced out of awareness always come back in a darker and more dangerous form. Obsessive-Compulsives could be the poster children for this process. The last thing these children of the night would consider doing consciously is taking hostile action in their own self-interest. Their aggressive impulses are relegated to their unconscious mind, where they're pursued with a vengeance. They seem to be the only ones who can't see their hidden agendas.

Perfectionists and Puritans try to hypnotize you into believing that their anger is praiseworthy, since it is in the service of goodness and light. Don't be fooled; behind all the moralizing and responsibility, under the piles of rules, and beneath the rationalizations, Obsessive-Compulsives are bullies. As long as you remember that, they can't sneak up out of the fog and bite you.

PRODUCT VERSUS PROCESS

To deal effectively with Obsessive-Compulsives, *you* have to know what they're doing even when *they* don't. This statement, like everything else relating to these complex and confusing vampires, has meanings on several different levels. To keep the levels straight, let's consider the notions of product and process.

Product is *what* you're trying to do. Process is *how* you do it. The two are separate—a point you need to remember, because Obsessive-Compulsives won't.

Think of all actions as having a product or goal. At work, the products, in addition to what gets sold, include improving quality, reducing costs, writing marketing plans, and making specific decisions. At home, the products may be getting the dishes washed, keeping the house clean enough for unexpected company, and raising moral and responsible children.

Obsessive-Compulsives habitually confuse process with product. To them, *how* something is done can become more important than whether it gets done at all. It always helps to use well-constructed questions to keep these anal-retentive vampires focused on the product rather than getting lost in the forests of process, which in their view surround everything. Questions like, "What's our overall goal here?" and, "What would you like me to do?" are extremely useful in dealing with Obsessive-Compulsives.

Product-clarifying questions can help you keep tasks in focus. Obsessive-Compulsives tend to think that there is only one way to achieve any goal. The more clearly the end point is defined, the more likely these vampires are to allow a number of ways of getting there. If you are unfortunate enough to work for an Obsessive-Compulsive boss, you'll make your life more bearable by contracting to produce specific deliverables on specific dates. When the boss starts checking to see *how* you're going about your task, you can gently point out that the product will be on the boss's desk by the due date. If the boss quibbles about process (and any Obsessive-Compulsive will), you can go back to the original contract and say that *what* you're supposed to do is in it, but *how* is not. Does this mean the boss is changing the terms of the agreement? By taking this approach, you make the *how* a subject for negotiation rather than a foregone, but unstated, conclusion.

Needless to say, this strategy will work only if you put out deliverables that are on time and up to previously agreed-upon specifications.

By the way, the technique of asking questions to clarify the product works almost as well on Obsessive-Compulsives who only *think* they're your boss.

At home, if you can get Obsessive-Compulsives to specify in advance who is in charge of producing what and when, they're a little less likely to quibble about process. Unlike other vampires, Obsessive-Compulsives have a strong sense of fairness. Their own internal logic dictates that if there are rules, they have to play by them. Your best bet is to do everything you can to get the rules on the books before the game starts.

For this reason, the *on duty* strategy described in Chapter 6, on Daredevils, works well, but in almost the opposite direction. You'll remember that the strategy has two parts: specifying who is responsible for what task and when, and the requirement that the person on duty is completely in charge of *how* the task is to be done. This second part is what will protect you from Obsessive-Compulsives.

DEMANDING PRIORITIES

For Obsessive-Compulsives, product is a moving target. When you ask, "What do you want me to do?" their list grows longer and longer the more they think about it. In their minds, as soon as a product is specified, it begins to turn back into process. You can actually see it happening. Before your eyes, overall goals morph into smaller and smaller tasks of ever-decreasing relevance.

At that point, you need to ask your second question: "What's the top priority?" For Obsessive-Compulsives, being in control is always the main goal. The easiest way for them to maintain control is by making products and priorities vague, and keeping all discussion fixed endlessly on process. By asking what specifically they want you to do, and in what order they want it done, you may be able to gain some control over your own destiny.

This brings us to a consideration of *your* hidden goals. If your top priority is demonstrating to these vampires that they can't tell you what to do, you are apt to make more than your share of mistakes. Unfortunately, Obsessive-Compulsives are often right. If you want to deal with them effectively, you have to put aside your own inner teenager, with its proclivities toward rebellion for its own sake, and learn from them when they know more than you do. We will discuss your inner teenager in more detail later in this chapter.

The other goal you may be trying to achieve in your interactions with Obsessive-Compulsives is winning their approval. Give it up. Before Obsessive-Compulsives can give a compliment, they have to figure out all the possible ways you might have messed up, and then make sure you didn't do any of them. By the time they've assembled enough information to justify praise, you'll probably have forgotten what it was that you did in the first place.

If there are Obsessive-Compulsives in your life, you have to learn to evaluate your own performance and praise yourself for your achievements. They never praise you, even when they love you.

PERFECTIONISTS

Perfectionism is a vice that masquerades as a virtue. For people who only want everything to be right, Perfectionists can cause an incredible number of things to go wrong.

> *Sunday at 6:32 p.m., Keith startles the cat by jumping up and shouting, "Yes!" far more loudly than he'd intended. Finished at last! Vampire Rebecca and the kids have been at her mom's for a long weekend, and he's spent the entire time taking care of a whole to-do list of little jobs that have been piling up for months. He's also managed to clean the house from top to bottom. Rebecca always says she wants him to take some initiative about chores, and this time he has. As Keith drives to the airport to meet her 7:30 plane, he thinks about how pleased she'll be.*
>
> *At 8:47 p.m., Keith pulls into the driveway with his family. He's anticipating the surprised expression on Rebecca's face when she sees the house. Before he even turns off the ignition, Rebecca looks at the curb and shakes her head. "Tomorrow is garbage day. Will you put the cans and recycling out while I get something for the boys to eat? They're starving."*
>
> *"Sure," Keith says. "Damn it," he thinks. "She would have to notice the one thing I forgot."*
>
> *As soon as he has carried the suitcases into the entryway, Keith hurries into the kitchen to take out the garbage.*
>
> *Rebecca is leaning over the sink, scraping at a plate with her fingernail. "Keith," she says, "I've asked you to rinse the dishes off*

before you put them in the dishwasher. Once the food gets caked on, you know it's almost impossible to get off."

Instead of saying anything, Keith shuffles into the family room and turns on the TV.

Perfectionists, bless their neurotic little hearts, don't have a clue about what a pain they are to everybody around them. It's not that they don't care what the people close to them feel; it's just that they get so distracted by little details in the process of living that they miss the overall product. If Keith also loses sight of the big picture, he will make the situation worse for himself, and for Rebecca.

Keith needs to realize that Rebecca's withholding of praise, no matter how much it hurts his feelings, isn't in itself an attack. It's an oversight that he can correct if he stays focused on the product he wants to achieve. If he blows up, withdraws, or refrains from helping around the house in the future, Rebecca *will* attack because there will be good reason to dump some of her free-floating resentment onto him.

To understand how Keith can avoid further disaster, we have to go back to the beginning and see how he got into this unfortunate situation.

For his hard work, Keith expected a spontaneous expression of delight from Rebecca. This is unrealistic, to say the least. Perfectionists never do anything spontaneously, except perhaps notice mistakes. To Obsessive-Compulsives, the notion of a pleasant surprise is an oxymoron. Spontaneity means a loss of control, which is usually too threatening to consider. If Keith thinks back, he'll probably remember that most of his attempts to surprise Rebecca have not come to good ends.

Keith should also realize that to a Perfectionist, few jobs are done well enough to warrant unsolicited praise. He *can* get Rebecca to acknowledge his efforts and his intent to please her, but he will have to ask for what he wants directly. Instead of sulking in the family room—a response that Rebecca will interpret, correctly, as typical male withdrawal—Keith needs to tell her that she hurt his feelings by her lack of attention to his labors. She will understand this because she's felt the same way most of her life. They can both agree that it hurts to be overworked and underappreciated, and that they ought to do something so neither of them has to go through this sort of thing again. The stage is set for a deal.

Keith can offer to take care of more jobs around the house if Rebecca will agree to specify the product—washed dishes, a vacuumed rug, a mowed lawn, or whatever—and let him be in charge of the process.

I'm not naive enough to believe that Rebecca can stick to this agreement, but the important thing for Keith is to establish it as a rule on the books. Perfectionists usually play by the rules, whether they like them or not. By clarifying product and process, Keith can turn a difficult and painful situation with a Perfectionist into a template for further productive discussion. As a solution, it beats TV.

HOW THE IMPERFECT CAN DEAL WITH PERFECTIONISTS

If you have to live or work with a Perfectionist, here are some ideas that may lead to productive discussions instead of heated arguments and cold shoulders.

Ask for What You Want Directly

Saying, "You always tell me what I do wrong, never what I do right," won't get you anywhere, even if it's true. Instead, ask, "What did you like about what I did?" Consider three criticisms or less to be an A+.

If Your Feelings Are Hurt, Say So

Don't try to make your point indirectly by rebelling, withdrawing, "accidentally" making mistakes, or griping to friends, family, and coworkers. Passive-aggressive behavior just makes Perfectionists feel more justified in their anger. There's no point in throwing gas on the fire.

Don't Criticize Perfectionism

Perfectionists may *say* that their perfectionism is a problem, but they don't really believe it. Secretly, they're very proud of how hard they work and what they accomplish. Also, if you're pointing the finger at their faults, they'll feel justified in attacking yours. Their overriding fault is being too good. Do you really want to compete with that?

Negotiate for Product

This is the ideal to strive for, rather than a real goal. Not meddling in the process is the one thing Perfectionists can't do perfectly. Nevertheless, the more clearly you can specify in advance the product you're responsible for, the easier your job will be.

Demand Priorities

With Perfectionists, tasks have a way of mounting up. You always have the right to ask which should be done first. Exercise it. It will help you, and it will encourage Perfectionists to maintain perspective. The primary task of management is to set priorities for those managed. Always make sure that the people who try to manage you are doing their job.

Show Some Appreciation

You can be sure that, however hard they are on you, Perfectionists are twice as hard on themselves. Face it, they're better than we are. They have to be.

PURITANS

Puritans try to perfect the world using their favorite tools—criticism, punishment, and censorship. They see evil everywhere, except in their own actions. If there's a Puritan in your life, you know that it's far easier to be a saint than it is to live with one.

Mirror, Mirror on the wall, who's the greenest of us all?

That would be Martha. She's also the neighborhood expert on fitness, nutrition, housecleaning, and parenting. There's no question that she knows her stuff. Everyone respects her and goes to her for advice, but sometimes being her friend is like being audited by the IRS.

Yesterday, outside the school, Kinesha asked Martha to stop by for coffee. Martha had invited her over a couple of times, and Kinesha had been putting off reciprocating.

Since the moment she asked, Kinesha has been working her butt off, getting ready. She keeps asking herself, "Why am I doing this?" but she keeps working on into the night.

The next day, the house is clean, the recycling bins are lined up neatly in the kitchen, and the freshly ground, organic, fair-traded coffee is hot, with Public Radio mugs next to the pot. Just as Martha arrives, Kinesha takes a loaf of whole-grain zucchini bread out of the oven.

"What's that heavenly smell?" Martha asks.

Kinesha smiles. "Just some zucchini bread. I got the recipe from Splendid Table." She goes on to recite the ingredients, knowing that Martha is very particular about what she eats.

Kinesha serves the bread with cinnamon-tofu spread and pours the coffee.

The visit is going great. Kinesha actually begins to relax as they talk about their favorite cardio workouts and volunteering for voter registration.

Suddenly, the boys burst in from outside, wearing their Star Wars *helmets and swinging light sabers. When they see Martha, they stop to say hello politely, then run off to their room.*

"They're really getting big," Martha says. Then she frowns. "Kinesha, as smart as you are, I'm really surprised you let them play with weapons."

Kinesha feels hurt, like a failure as a parent. At the same time, she has an urge to take one of those light sabers and shove it someplace where the sun don't shine.

Why is Kinesha so upset?

If you think the answer is perfectly obvious, and it has the B word in it, you're probably listening to the little devil on your shoulder, the one with dreadlocks, tattoos, and piercings.

MEET YOUR INNER TEENAGER

Being an adolescent is so traumatic that most people never fully get over it. Most of us have a leftover teenager inside us who reacts just the way we did in middle school, when we had no idea who we were, but were absolutely certain who we were not.

The task of adolescence is to separate our identity from that of the parents who have loved us, cared for us, and controlled us all our lives. We accomplish this by getting irrationally angry at parental figures who try to tell us what to do and who to be. The anger is followed by guilt and confusion, which leads to even more erratic behavior.

If you let them, Obsessive-Compulsives can trigger flashbacks to adolescence. With a critical word, they can make you feel like lashing out, running to your room, slamming the door, then crying because nobody approves of you.

You can prevent your inner teenager from taking over by reminding yourself that you are a grown-up now, and you do not have to act on your immediate emotional response. There are other ways to solve problems.

In the moment, Kinesha pulls it together and decides not to lash out at Martha. For all her faults, she is a good friend, trustworthy and generous. Still, holding back on her anger makes Kinesha feel like a wimp.

The rest of the visit is tepid as the half-empty mugs of coffee sitting unnoticed on the table.

Martha finally leaves. After a good cry, Kinesha calls her friend Mindy to ask for advice.

"You've been friends with Martha for years. How do you do it?"

"She can be judgmental," Mindy says. "We had a few kerfuffles over the years, and finally agreed to disagree.

"Maybe that would work for you. If she's hurting your feelings, you can't just sit there fuming. You have to say something."

Mindy's advice is excellent. Since she sought it out, Kinesha can accept it as coming from a peer rather than a parent.

So now, Kinesha has to say something, but what?

Here are a few suggestions for her, and for you if an Obsessive-Compulsive ever brings you face-to-face with your own inner teenager:

First, Give Yourself Time to Think

When you're upset, it is generally not a good idea to go with the first thing that pops into your head. Like Kinesha, you may decide not to say anything when you're in the situation, but to bring it up later when you've had a chance to think.

Know Your Goal

Think about what you want to have happen as a result of your comment. Kinesha wants Martha to mind her own business when it comes to parenting, but she doesn't want to say so in a way that will end the relationship.

Don't Expect an Apology

Trying to get Obsessive-Compulsives to apologize is a waste of time. Their biggest fear is of being wrong. So if you accuse them, instead of an apology, you will get an explanation of why they were right, or at least innocent. They never *mean* to hurt you. In their opinion, it's the truth that hurts you, not them. If you press for an apology, the very best you'll get is, "I'm sorry you feel that way."

Obsessive-Compulsives are not heartless. It does matter to them that they hurt your feelings, but it matters more to establish that they did not do it on purpose.

Choose Your Words Carefully

Let's review. When Obsessive-Compulsives insult you, you need to tell them how you feel and what you want without accusing them of doing anything wrong. This is not an impossible task, but it must be done carefully, in two separate steps. The first is establishing that they hurt you, but it was unintentional. The wording for this should be precise: "When you said [fill in the words], I felt [fill in the emotion]. Was that what you intended?"

The answer to this question will always be no, followed by an explanation of what the Obsessive-Compulsive actually intended, which is most often to be helpful by informing you of the error of your ways. Do not dispute this; merely reiterate that you were hurt. This puts the Obsessive-Compulsive into a slightly one-down position, which you can exploit by telling her what you want her to do in the future if she sees you doing something wrong—namely, don't comment and respect your right to make your own mistakes. Let's see how Kinesha does it:

> *"Martha, when you commented on my boys playing with light sabers, it hurt my feelings. Is that what you intended?"*
>
> *"No, I didn't mean to criticize you. I just wanted to let you know about how violent games lead to violent behavior. There's a lot of research—"*
>
> *"I'm sure there is, and I may be totally wrong, but my feelings were still hurt. In the future, unless I ask you, please don't comment on how I raise my kids, and I won't comment about how you raise yours."*

Kinesha could have pointed out that when Martha's boys come over, they make a beeline for the light sabers and toy guns. Censorship always makes whatever is censored more attractive. One of the reasons that Puritans like Martha can be so mean is that nobody seems to heed their wise advice, even though they're going to hell in a handbasket. It never occurs to them that you can't get people to do the right thing by hitting them over the head with how wrong they are.

If, like Kinesha, you override your inner teenager and follow the steps outlined here, Obsessive-Compulsives will probably not make any immediate comment, but they will be more likely to do what you ask in the future.

Don't be surprised if at some point later on when they see you doing something they disapprove of, you hear their inner teenager making snotty comments like, "I'm not supposed to say anything about how you raise your kids, but . . ."

Ignore it; it's just a tantrum. Be the adult. Say nothing and realize that you've won.

NINE WAYS TO PROTECT YOURSELF FROM OBSESSIVE-COMPULSIVES: WHAT TO DO WHEN THE GOOD GUYS ARE AFTER YOU

Convince Obsessive-Compulsives that you're not really one of the bad guys.

1. Know Them, Know Their History, and Know Your Goal

It's easy to recognize Perfectionists. They'll walk right up to you and identify themselves. Then they'll probably tell you what's wrong with whatever you're doing. Puritans are also easy to spot; they seldom go for long periods of time without getting offended at something. Both of these vampire types try to control whatever situation they're in, down to the tiniest details. Especially the tiniest details. Obsessive-Compulsives contain their anxieties about bigger issues through overconcern with the small. If you let them, they'll manage their own anxieties by delegating them to you.

It's easy to play right into their hands. If you go along with their demands, they'll just pile on more. If you rebel or get angry at their pettiness, they'll try to put you under even tighter control, because it's clear that you're the one with the problem.

Your goal should be negotiation, not recrimination. Every task has an end product—whatever it is that needs to be done. A task also has a process—the actual behaviors through which the end product is achieved. Negotiate to deliver a very specific product at a very specific time. If you hand over the goods, there is less motivation to quibble about how you got them. Not that Obsessive-Compulsives won't try. Treat attempts to control the process as requests to change the end product, which means reopening the whole negotiation. If the end product isn't affected, why change the process? Needless to say, you have to have some history of delivering the goods for a strategy like this to work.

Bottom line: if you do what you say you'll do when you say you'll do it, these overcontrolling vampires will go and drain somebody less reliable.

2. Get Outside Verification

Obsessive-Compulsives tend to structure their lives to minimize failure rather than to maximize success. As a result, they will be quick to tell you what's wrong with any new idea. Don't let them be your only source of information on what's possible. They are the ones who told Leonardo da Vinci that his flying machine would never get off the ground.

If you work with Obsessive-Compulsives, you can make them less draining and more focused by getting clarification of goals and priorities from above—the higher above, the better. Take advantage of the fact that the Obsessive-Compulsive code of conduct often precludes arguing with authority figures.

At home, you'll never win an argument with an Obsessive-Compulsive on the strength of your ideas alone. For Perfectionists, the documented opinion of an eminent expert might open up the discussion. For Puritans, a few biblical quotes may help. They tend to forget the ones about mercy and forgiveness.

3. Do What They Don't

Look at the big picture, paying attention to details as they fit into the over-all pattern. Know what you want, and realize that there's always more than one way to get it. Have a sense of humor about yourself. Most important, use punishment only as a last resort.

4. Pay Attention to Their Actions, Not Their Words

Obsessive-Compulsives want you to pay attention to how hard they work, how much they do, and how well they do it. Don't be distracted by the quantity or even the quality of their work. Pay attention to how relevant what they do is to achieving the overall goal.

There are some words you can ignore, sermons. Perfectionists run on about the terrible problems that will result if you don't do everything exactly as they say. Puritans tell you that if you don't believe exactly as they do, you'll burn in a lake of fire. Both vampire types secretly enjoy inflicting pain because they've hypnotized themselves into believing it's for your own good.

These vampires are not heartless. Sometimes you can break the spell by telling them that they're *unintentionally* hurting your feelings. If you try to convince them that they're hurting you on purpose, believe me, you'll fry.

5. Pick Your Battles

Forget trying to talk Obsessive-Compulsives out of being controlling. Even seasoned therapists have trouble with that. (Between you and me, at least part of the difficulty lies in the fact that it's always hardest to cure people who have the same neuroses that you do.)

Never expect Obsessive-Compulsives to see anything selfish or purposely hurtful in their own actions. They are experts both in self-deception and in the letter of the law. If certain actions have made it past an Obsessive-Compulsive's internal censors, it means they've been thoroughly rationalized and are, in the vampire's mind at least, completely legal, moral, and altruistic.

As we've seen already, the battles you're most likely to win involve having Perfectionists and Puritans specify products and priorities and negotiating some latitude in how to achieve them.

6. Let Contingencies Do the Work

Always understand that Obsessive-Compulsives are sincerely trying to be good people and do a good job. The problem is that they're pretty naive about how human beings operate. They let their beliefs about how things should be blind them to the way things really are. Consequently, these vampires are sometimes dead wrong about what process leads to what product.

You may be able to help them make better choices by explaining the contingencies that are actually operating. Gently remind them that rewards go for results rather than for good intentions. Tell them that it's human nature to want to see what you're not supposed to see and do what you're not supposed to do. Deferentially suggest that the more you criticize people for messing up, the angrier you make them—and the more incentive you give them to mess up even more as a way of getting back at you.

Finally, respect the fact that Obsessive-Compulsives structure their lives to minimize losses rather than to maximize gains. In order for these vampires to risk doing anything differently, the benefits have to be very clear and very large.

7. Choose Your Words as Carefully as You Pick Your Battles

Perfectionists and Puritans are never wrong. If you criticize these vampires, they're likely to respond with a list of incidents in which you did something worse—complete with time, date, and witnesses.

One of their favorite defenses is explaining how whatever they did was the result of your miscommunication about what you wanted. They will, of course, twist your words unmercifully. Unless you have a tape recording, don't bother trying to explain what you actually said.

When Obsessive-Compulsives criticize you, don't try to use their own strategies on them. They're better at them than you are. Instead, ask questions that invite them to focus on the product that they are trying to create.

"Why are you telling me this?" is a good beginning, followed by "What would you like me to do?"

In any difficult situation involving an Obsessive-Compulsive, it's always more effective to ask questions than to make statements that can be disputed. If you let vampires start questioning you, it will turn into a cross-examination followed by a swift conviction.

8. Ignore Tantrums

Obsessive-Compulsive tantrums are nothing if not subtle. These vampires express their feelings of overwork and underappreciation with sighs and disdainful snorts at the less industrious. They'll swear it's just a sinus problem. Don't waste your time trying to get them to take responsibility for nonverbal editorial comments. You'll need all your energy for their major tantrums, which usually take the form of long and exhausting guilt trips.

Always remember that although their words may sting like scorpions, they're still only words. In the end, the only weapons these vampires have are verbal attacks on your perception of yourself as a moral and effective person. *If you know who you are, they can't hurt you. If you need their approval to maintain your self-esteem, you're dead.*

9. Know Your Own Limits

It's better to know your own limitations. Perfectionists and Puritans always have something to teach you about the areas in which you don't measure up. Their lessons are hard, but valuable. Obsessive-Compulsives are the world's toughest audience. If you can convince them, you're probably right. If you feel the need to hide something from them, it's probably wrong. They can help you be a better person, but you alone have to decide how good you want to be.

23 Obsessive-Compulsives in Your Life

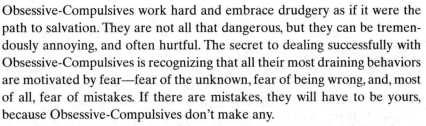

Obsessive-Compulsives work hard and embrace drudgery as if it were the path to salvation. They are not all that dangerous, but they can be tremendously annoying, and often hurtful. The secret to dealing successfully with Obsessive-Compulsives is recognizing that all their most draining behaviors are motivated by fear—fear of the unknown, fear of being wrong, and, most of all, fear of mistakes. If there are mistakes, they will have to be yours, because Obsessive-Compulsives don't make any.

When these vampires attack, if you can see the fear beneath their harsh words, you will be better able to defend yourself.

CONTROL FREAK

Nobody can remember how many times Linda has been named Volunteer of the Year. Since time immemorial, she has been Empress of the Benefit Auction. The events she puts on are successful and beautiful, but a little dull because they are exactly the same year after year.

If you are on her committee, you get a list of the tasks you are to do and when you need to do them. You'll get a reminder e-mail and a call to make sure you've done your job on time. Everything must be done in a particular way, or Linda herself will redo it.

Rosa has been volunteering for a couple of seasons and has some ideas about how to liven things up a bit and maybe even raise some more money. She brings them up at the planning meeting.

"What about a raffle for something really big, like a car? We could charge $200 a ticket, and we could limit the sale to say 500. We could make, maybe—."

Linda interrupts. "We considered that a few years ago, but we decided there's too much risk and a possible liability. Are there any other ideas?"

Obviously, the planning meeting has nothing to do with planning; it's just Linda telling people what to do.

Rosa's job is finding sponsors for the auction items, and she's really good at it. Still, she gets daily e-mails from Linda telling her who to contact and what to say. Rosa has considered just quitting the committee, but she is devoted to the organization, and the auction is where most of the money comes from.

Every day, Rosa gets more irritated at Linda. Over and over, the same questions keep running through her mind: Why won't Linda listen to any new ideas? Why won't she let me do things my way? Does she think I'm stupid? Why is she such a control freak?

Before Rosa gets too worked up, she should stop and consider: why *would* a person have such an overwhelming need to control? The answer is, simply, fear.

Frightened people devise frightening systems to keep themselves at a safe distance from whatever it is they fear. What they do to protect themselves often causes more damage than what they were afraid of.

As Linda becomes more controlling, the performance of the people on her committee deteriorates. Irritation at being controlled and worrying about being criticized makes people anxious, so they make more mistakes. Then there is always passive-aggressive retaliation from people who don't like to be told what to do. Whatever their causes, the mistakes that ensue increase Linda's need for control, and performance deteriorates further. Many highly motivated and competent people have burned out on Linda's committee. Rosa is well on her way.

If Rosa can turn the situation around enough in her mind to see Linda's fear rather than her own irritation, she might be able to make some headway, or at least stop wearing herself out with all the internal muttering.

Here are some suggestions that may help in dealing with control freaks like Linda.

See Their Fear, Not Your Irritation

This is the secret to dealing effectively with micromanaging control-freak Obsessive-Compulsives like Linda. If you want them to be less controlling, you have to calm them down rather than making them more upset.

Deactivate Your Internal Teenager

Power struggles will only make the situation worse. Listen to the adult on your other shoulder.

Don't Call Them Control Freaks

Getting irritated and calling them control freaks, whether out loud or in the privacy of your mind, will make the situation worse. Controlling people pay attention to tiny details. They will see your irritation as clearly as if you'd posted it on a billboard outside their window. Your attitude will serve as evidence that they should watch you even more closely.

Even if you bring it up in the kindest way possible, discussing the issue of control directly will backfire. Control freaks, even if they joke about it, never see themselves as *overly* controlling. They are only protecting an ungrateful world from the inevitable mistakes that result from not paying close enough attention. Forget trying to talk them out of it. They will only see this as criticism, which is what they are afraid of in the first place.

Remind Yourself That It's Not About You

Even though control freaks may make very critical comments, they are not really personal. They criticize everybody. Obsessive-Compulsives are not thinking about you or your specific abilities, but about all the things that might go wrong. Most of their harsh comments are just worrying out loud.

Use Reassurance, Not Recrimination

The process of getting a control freak to lighten up is similar to training a squirrel to eat out of your hand. It must be done slowly and patiently, or you are likely to get bitten.

Listen to the Lecture

Control freaks love to give lectures. Listen attentively, respectfully, and, most of all, visibly. Take copious notes.

There are two reasons for doing this. The first is simple reassurance. If you look like you are taking their instructions seriously, control freaks will worry less about you misunderstanding and making mistakes later on.

The second reason for listening closely is to come away with clear specifications of the end product required. If at all possible, at the end of the initial lecture, negotiate to deliver a very specific, measurable product at a very specific time. This will be crucial later on when Obsessive-Compulsives try to control the process.

Give Progress Reports Before They Are Due

Nothing allays control freaks' fears like excess information. Remind them that you are taking the project as seriously as they do.

Keep Up the Good Work

If you actually do what you say you are going to do when you say you are going to do it, control freaks will be less worried about your performance, and may go off to micromanage somebody less responsible.

Over the long run, when you have shown yourself to be reliable, control freaks may not be eating out of your hand, but they may occasionally listen to a few of your ideas.

CONTROL FREAK PARENTS

If by chance you are an actual teenager, regardless of what your parents are like, you will probably see them as control freaks. The strategies just given will still work for you, if you care to use them.

MARRIED TO A CONTROL FREAK

If your spouse is a control freak, you may be able to use most of the suggestions I've outlined here and in the previous two chapters. In addition, you might want to go back and read about the on-duty procedure as described in Chapter 6.

Being as close and personal as you are with an Obsessive-Compulsive, you may also have an opportunity to deal directly with the fear that underlies overly controlling behavior. Just be sure that your inner teenager is deactivated.

> *Linda's husband, Peter, dreads auction season. For months Linda gets uptight and snaps at everyone. Nothing is right. She grumbles about having to supervise her committee so closely. At home, everything has to be neat and tidy—no, make that sterile—or it drives her insane. She says that her mind is so cluttered with details about the auction that she can't stand any more clutter around her.*
>
> *Peter tries to help out, but what he does is never enough. If the kitchen is not antiseptically clean, she redoes it, sighing like a steam locomotive. If he leaves part of the newspaper lying by his chair, or his biking gear by the door, it is a Major Issue. He feels like he is not allowed to live in his own house.*

When he says something about her criticism, Linda agrees that since she's so stressed out, she may occasionally go over the top, but she has good reasons for everything she says and does. She says she needs his help to get through this stressful time, which means doing everything her way. Nothing changes.

When Peter is not feeling irritated, he worries about all the pain and excess work Linda is creating for herself. He'd like to help her, but nothing he tries seems to have any effect.

Anybody who lives with a control freak like Linda can see clearly that what's driving her crazy is not the work she has to do, but the obsessive way that she worries about it. Getting her to see that she is making herself and everybody else miserable is very difficult. If Peter tells her she is overreacting, she will see it as accusing her of making a mistake, and we know how Obsessive-Compulsives react to *that*.

If you, like Peter, are married to a control freak, here are some ideas that may help.

Make Love, Not War

Even though control freaks are totally unreasonable and tend to irritate everyone close to them, confronting them gets you nowhere.

Peter is at a choice point. He can't help her and be mad at her at the same time.

If he wants to help, he needs to view situations through Linda's eyes rather than his own or his inner teenager's. This does not mean that he has to do everything her way, but it does mean that he has to communicate with her in her own language.

Call It Stress

Psychologists make a distinction between *stress*, which is what's happening out there, and *anxiety*, which is the internal reaction to external events. Most people, especially Obsessive-Compulsives, do not make this distinction. They think that the worry, irritation, and overall misery they feel is a direct and inevitable result of the external stress, and everything that they are doing is the only possible response to the situation. This is a good working definition of a neurosis. To help Linda deal more effectively with her anxiety, Peter will have to operate within her belief system. He will have to speak and act as if the source of her pain is actually the external stress. This can be tricky.

Don't Accommodate Their Neurosis

Obsessive-Compulsives see their anxiety as a handicap that should be accommodated. They will expect you to accede to their demands and tolerate their irritability because they are under so much stress. On the face of it, this sounds reasonable, but it isn't. What they are really asking you to do is to reward them for managing their own anxiety badly.

A handicap is something a person can't do anything about, like being in a wheelchair. If you accommodate a handicap, say by building ramps and making tables the right height, it makes the handicapped person's life better. If you accommodate a neurosis, you make it worse by reinforcing the person's belief that she is the way she is, and there is nothing else she can do. You might think of this as the *don't upset your mother syndrome*, which transfers the responsibility for managing anxiety from her to you.

Another way of accommodating a neurosis that has been unsuccessfully used by well-meaning spouses is saying, "Just quit." There is absolutely nothing positive to recommend this strategy. It does damage in every way imaginable. It will be seen as insulting and condescending by most Obsessive-Compulsives, who feel honor bound to live up to their responsibilities. What they will hear is an unsupportive spouse saying that what they are putting all their time and effort into is trivial enough to just toss away. Even if they do take the advice, it teaches them to avoid anxiety rather than deal with it.

Yet another way of accommodating a neurosis is medicating the symptoms away. A prescription for benzodiazepines can temporarily get rid of the anxiety, allowing control freaks to continue their neurotic behavior with less pain, but the possibility of addiction. Antidepressants are less dangerous, but without behavior change, they treat only symptoms, leaving the cause of the problem untouched. The value of these medications is that they may alleviate crippling symptoms enough to make it possible for people to learn different techniques for dealing with anxiety.

Not accommodating a neurosis doesn't mean attacking it directly. We have already seen that confronting Linda's demands and irritability directly doesn't work. Peter will have to entice her into changing her behavior, which will also change her way of thinking. To do this, he can make use of her Obsessive-Compulsive tendencies in a positive way.

Make Stress the Target

Peter will have the most success if he encourages Linda to deal with the physiological aspects of stress rather than the external factors, like the incompetence of volunteers or the mess in the house, that she believes are causing her problems. Talking about how stressed out she is will only make her worse. Managing the physiology of stress might make her better. Luckily, there are hundreds of books and articles on how to do this. All of them advise the same things: exercise, eating right, getting enough sleep, and learning relaxation techniques.

Do It Together

Whether it's going for walks, changing the diet, going to bed at a reasonable hour, or signing up for a yoga class, Linda will at first claim that she doesn't have time. Peter will gain much more traction if he organizes the stress management program and follows it with her, hand in hand, encouraging her at every step. Obsessive-Compulsives don't give out much praise, but they do respond to it.

24 Therapy for Obsessive-Compulsive Vampires

What should you do if you see signs of Obsessive-Compulsive behavior in yourself or someone you care about? This section is a thumbnail sketch of the sorts of self-help and professional therapeutic approaches that might be beneficial. Always remember that attempting psychotherapy on someone you know will make you both sicker.

THE GOAL

The goal of all treatment for Obsessive-Compulsives is to help them move away from fear of bad consequences as the prime mover in their lives and the lives of the people around them. Obsessive-Compulsives need to focus on the big stuff and not sweat the small, and not make other people sweat at all. The big stuff for them is their relationships, which they can unwittingly destroy by trying to make those close to them into better people. Obsessive-Compulsives need to learn to love people for who they are.

PROFESSIONAL HELP

Essentially, anything that will hurt a Histrionic will help an Obsessive-Compulsive, and vice versa. Obsessive-Compulsives can profit from techniques that focus on expressing feelings and generally being positive. New Age approaches, art and dance therapy, and random exploration of emotions may damage other vampires, but they can help Obsessive-Compulsives. A useful rule of thumb is: if the Obsessive-Compulsive thinks the approach is scary or stupid, it will probably do some good.

Avoid approaches that analyze thoughts in great detail or that require a lot of written work, like homework exercises or journaling. Obsessive-Compulsives love these techniques, but seldom change as a result.

Self-Help

If you recognize Obsessive-Compulsive tendencies in yourself, the following exercises will be very difficult for you, but they will make a difference.

Always Know Your Top Priority

Not for the moment, but for your whole life. Think about what you'd like to have carved on your tombstone, and work toward that. The other details will take care of themselves.

Judge Not, Lest Ye Be Judged

Pay attention to the negative judgments you make about people and things. Every time you catch yourself thinking that something is bad, quickly, in your mind, list two good things about it. If you can't come up with two, ask somebody to explain the good parts to you.

Goof Off

Spend a little time every day just sitting and doing nothing. Computer solitaire was invented for this purpose. Learn some sort of relaxation technique and practice it every day, especially on the days when you think you're too busy.

Specify Products and Don't Meddle in Process

Define the final product you want from other people as clearly as possible, then step back and let them do their best. Performance never improves when you stand over someone's shoulder. Let people learn from their mistakes rather than from your lectures.

Criticize Only on Thursdays

The rest of the week, use praising people for what they do right as your only device for behavioral control. If you save all your criticisms for one day of the week, you may be surprised at how few will be needed by the time Thursday rolls around. Remember, the Thursday rule applies to your own actions as well.

Publicly Acknowledge at Least One Mistake per Day

Maybe you could acknowledge two on Thursdays.

WHAT WILL HURT

Obsessive-Compulsives love psychoanalysis and other process-oriented approaches. They can doggedly pursue them for years, trying to comprehend the underlying reasons for everything they do, and never changing anything. They can do pretty much the same thing with highly structured behavioral and cognitive techniques, because they do all the exercises perfectly but forget to learn anything from them.

25 Seeing Things That Others Can't

The Paranoid Types

Another confusing name. To most people, *paranoid* means having delusions of persecution. The word really describes an exquisitely simple way of perceiving a complex world. Paranoids can't tolerate ambiguity. In their minds, nothing is accidental or random; everything means something, and everything relates to everything else. This sort of thinking can lead to genius or to psychosis, depending on how it's used.

There's no question that Paranoids see things that other people can't. But do the things they see actually exist? *That's* the question.

These vampires have tendencies toward Paranoid personality disorder, which, like the vampires themselves, is often misunderstood, even by the people who treat it. The word *paranoia*, which means "thinking beside oneself," has been used to describe virtually all forms of craziness, especially those involving false beliefs. The problem with the concept, as any Paranoid will tell you, is that it's not all that simple to determine which beliefs are false and which are true.

Paranoia is easier to understand if you look at the patterns of thinking that lead to false beliefs, rather than at the beliefs themselves. Paranoids are blessed and cursed with the ability to perceive very tiny cues. Unlike Obsessive-Compulsives, who compartmentalize small details, missing the big picture, Paranoids drive themselves crazy by trying to organize details into a coherent and unambiguous whole.

Paranoids' perceptive ability and compulsion to organize may have their roots at the neurological level. Wherever they come from, these behaviors create tremendous problems in relating to human beings. When Paranoids look at other people, they see too much for their own good—and everybody else's.

Paranoids long for a simple world in which people can be trusted to mean what they say, particularly when those people are talking about them. Instead, Paranoids see the human condition in all its ambiguous detail. People exist on many different levels at the same time. No human thought is singular, and no feeling is pure. Many of the conflicts that people experience are observable in slight hesitations, small changes in expression, slips of the tongue, and the like. Most people ignore these tiny cues, but Paranoids try to sort them into either-or categories—yes or no, love or hate, truth or falsehood. Sometimes, in their search for simple answers, Paranoids can see through all forms of subterfuge to the heart of a matter. Just as easily, they can rip that heart out and tear it to pieces—especially when it belongs to someone close to them whose only crime is being human.

Paranoids draw you in with their perceptiveness; they see the confusing and uncertain details of life so clearly. Later, they drain you with endless probing of the uncertainty they perceive in you.

What Paranoids never see is their own role in creating the ambiguity that so terrifies them. Their distrust invites duplicity. Their suspiciousness keeps people from telling them the whole truth. Their incessant doubts drive away the people who say they'll always be there. Paranoids can feel like they're at the center of a vast conspiracy to rob them of the certainty they so fervently desire. Naturally, they become even more guarded and suspicious.

What Paranoids really fear is the uncertainty at the center of their own souls. They desperately want to be close, but are terrified at the ambiguity that comes with closeness. They try to drive the desire for intimacy out of their hearts. In place of love, Paranoids search in vain for purity and truth.

PARANOID PURITY

Paranoids try to remove the ambiguity from their lives by organizing everything around a small number of black-and-white principles. In the minds of Paranoids, truth, loyalty, courage, honor, and the like are not abstractions. They are living, breathing presences that they live by, and will kill or die for if called upon to do so. At least, that's the way the Paranoids themselves imagine it. The reality is, of course, more complex. Paranoids are just as likely as anybody else to justify their self-serving actions in terms of high-sounding principles. More likely, actually. The most dangerous thing about Paranoids is their utter certainty of their own virtue.

Even Obsessive-Compulsive Puritans are aware enough of their own failings to grudgingly forgive others their trespasses—if they acknowledge the error of their ways. Paranoids seldom forgive. Puritans try to punish only the sin; Paranoids happily consign sinners to the flames.

Aside from their questionable approach to morality, Paranoids are capable of extreme purity of thought. Many discoveries of the organizing principles that bind the universe together are the products of Paranoid thinking. So is every crackpot theory you've ever heard of.

Paranoids vacillate between extreme naiveté and utter cynicism. Their goal is to achieve a happy world (or family or business) in which everyone follows the same simple and rigid rules as they do. When people go along, Paranoids are happy, loving, and giving. If by some chance other people want to think for themselves, Paranoids take it as a personal insult. They feel disappointed and hurt when people try to leave their little paradises. When Paranoids get hurt, they hurt others.

Of all the vampire types, Paranoids are the most determined and conscious hypnotists. They invented cults and the brainwashing that keeps them running. Whenever Paranoids put together any sort of organization, be it a cult, a family, a business, a political party, or a religious movement, they use their persuasive power to create unambiguous alternative realities in which all rewards are dependent on belief and loyalty. Obsessive-Compulsives tell you to work hard if you want to get into heaven; Paranoids say all you have to do is believe in them. If you stop believing, there will be hell to pay.

WHAT IT'S LIKE TO BE PARANOID

Imagine a date with the man or woman of your dreams. You talk of nothing in particular, yet you desperately search your companion's every word for clues to what he or she *really* thinks about you. Your heart soars at tiny signs of acceptance and falls to the pit of your stomach at the slightest hint of rejection. This is business as usual for Paranoids, who analyze every conversation with the same degree of scrutiny. Awash in a flood of ambiguity, they grasp at straws, often clutching them so tightly as to make them break up and drift away.

To Paranoids, many of the straws turn out to be anvils. Paranoid existence is one perceived betrayal after another. Their suffering is exquisite, the sorrowful and pretentious center from which their entire universe radiates. Being Paranoid hurts.

Some of them give up and withdraw completely into a world of delusion. Those with better social skills can attract friends and lovers, on whom they rest the entire burden of keeping them safe and sane.

Even thinking about Paranoids is exhausting; imagine what it's like being one. That, strangely enough, is one of their saving graces. Paranoids

THE PARANOID EMOTIONAL VAMPIRE CHECKLIST: NEXT STOP, THE TWILIGHT ZONE

True or False   Score one point for each *true* answer.

1. This person is overly suspicious. T F
2. This person has very few close friends. T F
3. This person can make a big deal out of nothing. T F
4. This person tends to see many situations as struggles between good and evil. T F
5. This person never seems to let go of a hurt or a mistreatment. T F
6. This person seldom takes what he or she is told at face value. T F
7. This person cuts people out of his or her life for tiny slights. T F
8. This person is able to detect deception in one or two parts per billion, and sometimes sees it when it isn't there at all. T F
9. This person demands absolute loyalty in thought and deed. T F
10. This person is fiercely protective of his or her family (or one or two close friends). T F
11. This person sees connections among things that most people would consider unrelated. T F
12. This person sees little mistakes, such as lack of punctuality or forgetting instructions, as indications of disloyalty or disrespect. T F
13. This person tells people to their face what others say only behind their backs. T F
14. This person may have a good sense of humor, but cannot seem to laugh at himself or herself. T F
15. What will make this person angry seems completely unpredictable. T F
16. This person sees himself or herself as a victim of multiple discriminations. T F
17. This person believes that trust is something to be earned. T F
18. This person is known to take ill-considered actions "on principle." T F
19. This person often talks about suing people to redress wrongs. T F
20. This person questions people to determine their loyalty and fidelity. T F

21. This person collects little details that seem to prove his or her pet theories.   T F

22. This person believes in the literal interpretation of the Bible or some other religious text.   T F

23. This person believes in UFOs, astrology, psychic phenomena, or other concepts that most people consider to be on the fringe of credibility.   T F

24. This person openly advocates cruel and unusual punishment for certain classes of people. A typical comment might begin, "They should take all the bigots and . . . ."   T F

25. Though I won't always admit it, this person is sometimes embarrassingly correct in his or her assessment of me.   T F

Scoring Five or more true answers qualify the person as a Paranoid emotional vampire, although not necessarily for a diagnosis of Paranoid personality disorder. With twelve or more true answers, watch out for imperial storm troopers.

long to make sense of themselves and to be understood by others. That totally selfish quest can bring suffering to the rest of humanity, or provide generous gifts in the form of art, philosophy, and religion. Paranoia and Narcissism are the world's two main sources of creativity.

The internal struggle of Paranoids is the subject of much of the world's great literature. Science fiction is a particularly pure example. How many times have you read about regular-seeming folks who discover mysterious powers in themselves that place them at the center of a cosmic battle? They win, of course, with a little help from a few loyal and loving friends. The force that draws people to Paranoids is the same urge for moral simplicity that attracts them to *Star Wars*. Needless to say, that force also has a dark side.

WHAT THE QUESTIONS MEASURE

The specific behaviors covered in the checklist relate to several underlying personality characteristics that define a Paranoid emotional vampire.

Perceptiveness

Paranoids see things that others can't. They may even see more than you want them to. They're always looking below the surface for hidden meanings and deeper realities. Sometimes they discover great insights, but more often they find reasons to doubt the people whom they should be able to trust. In the world of Paranoids, the line between perceptiveness and suspicion is as thin as a spiderweb and sharper than a razor blade.

Intolerance of Ambiguity

Paranoids need answers, even when there are none. They love to explain how complex situations boil down to a few black-and-white concepts. For Paranoids, everything is simple and clear. The only reason everyone doesn't know what they do is that someone, somewhere is conspiring to cover up the truth. Paranoids love nothing more than a good conspiracy theory.

Paranoids' oversimplification of the world can also lead to great courage and dedication. They are fierce defenders of themselves, their principles, and the few people and things they consider closest to them. Paranoids have been known to give their lives for what they believe in. They've also been known to take lives.

Unpredictability

Paranoids can shower you with affection one minute and with ice water the next. Their moods are dependent on their momentary perceptions of the honesty and faithfulness of the people around them. If Paranoids sense treachery, they attack so fast that you won't know what hit you. Or why.

They can back off just as quickly. Many of their attacks are tests of loyalty. If you pass, they calm down immediately. If you don't, brace yourself to argue all night.

Unlike most other vampire types, Paranoids have the ability to say that they're wrong. They accept criticism and can make changes in a limited way for a short period of time. Often they will shift slightly to get some sort of concession from you. If you don't live up to your end of the so-called bargain, the Paranoid will add one more perfidy to your list of betrayals.

Bombast

Paranoids long to be understood. Their idea of intimacy is to spend six or seven hours sharing their theories of life or explaining how your actions have hurt them.

Jealousy

Paranoids don't understand the concept of trust. They never seem to realize that trust is supposed to be in their own minds, rather than in the actions of other people. Consequently, if you're close to one of these vampires, you'll have to re-earn his or her trust every hour on the hour. This is especially true if your relationship is sexual. A Paranoid's idea of foreplay is 20 minutes of questioning you about exactly what you were thinking the last time you made love.

Ideas of Reference

In their search for truth, Paranoids connect everything with everything else, then take it all personally. To poor virtuous Paranoids, the universe is a conspiracy designed to make them miserable.

If you associate with Paranoids, it won't be possible for you to say or do anything that does not relate to them.

Vindictiveness

Paranoids believe that revenge is the cure for what ails them. They never seem to see that it is also the cause. It's not that Paranoids never forgive; they just do it at the same rate as glaciers melt.

26 Vampire Visionaries and Green-Eyed Monsters

Inspiration Always Involves Blowing Things out of Proportion

Paranoids fall into two subtypes: Visionaries and Green-Eyed Monsters. Again, the strategies for dealing with these subtypes are similar enough for them to be included in the same chapter. Although the things they say and do may be very different, Paranoids themselves are remarkably similar. For you, they can create two very distinct sorts of problems. The first arises if you pay too much attention to them; the second, if you don't pay enough. Either way, Paranoids can be very draining.

To protect yourself, you need to know which ideas arise from Paranoids' unique way of looking at the world and which are just characteristic representations of their own internal conflicts, or yours. The discrimination is difficult; it will require all the wisdom you've gained studying the other emotional vampire types, and more. To be safe from Paranoids, you must know them well, but you must know yourself even better.

THE PARANOID QUEST

Paranoids are always searching for their Holy Grail, the one simple idea that explains everything. These vampires hate ambiguity so much that they refuse to believe it exists. Whether they're confused about the movements of the stars, the fluctuations of the stock market, or why other people just aren't as caring as they would like them to be, Paranoids believe that the answers are out there, and they're willing to do what it takes to find them.

Paranoids are always looking for clues. They'll peer into microscopes, sift through volumes of forgotten lore, or cross-examine their loved ones as to exactly where they went, when, and with whom.

Paranoids' greatest weakness is that they are much more willing to believe in conspiracy than ambiguity. They can draw you in with elegant theories that are often more convincing than mere facts. Paranoids can drain you by demanding that if you care about them, you must believe in their dubious hidden truths. That, however, is nothing compared with what they'll do to you if they suspect that you're the one who's hiding the truth from them.

PARANOID HYPNOSIS

Paranoids have delusions, but they can also delude. They can hypnotize you with their dogged determination to make you believe in the hidden realities they've discovered. They get to you by relentlessly hammering away at your resistances. Sometimes, however, Paranoids' craziest ideas sound eerily sane, as if they had cut through all the garbage to a shining nugget of truth that somehow you've known was there all along. Those are the ideas to watch out for. People who tell us what we want to hear always have more power than people who tell us the truth. Use your own feelings to guide you. The more you want to believe, the more skeptical you should be.

One of the most reliable warning signs of Paranoid hypnosis is that the vampire will discourage you from getting outside opinions. In Paranoids' simple world, the very idea that another person's opinion might carry more weight than theirs is tantamount to treason. Don't let their hurt feelings prevent you from checking out their ideas with someone you trust. Always remember the rule about not letting a vampire be your only source of information.

Unlike Used Car Salesmen, Paranoids actually believe what they tell you. Don't let the force of their conviction persuade you to ignore the facts. As we've seen many times, the most effective hypnotists are those who have hypnotized themselves.

VISIONARIES

At this point, you might be wondering why you should have to worry about Paranoids at all. Maybe you should just stay away from them.

It's not that simple. You may try to stay away from Paranoids, but they won't stay away from you. Maybe the Paranoids themselves will keep away, but not their ideas. You'll hear them everywhere—by the watercooler, over the back fence, and, most of all, on the Internet. A good portion of the new ideas you hear every day are products of Paranoid thinking. Some of them are crazy—just old Paranoid standbys dressed up in different outfits. Some Paranoid ideas are really novel, useful, and profitable. The trick is knowing the difference.

Vampire Waylon takes a pull on his second beer and laughs, snorting a bit through his nose. "Whoa," he says. "I can't remember the last time I had two in a row. It's been a great week."

Gary raises his own beer in a toast. "It's about time somebody had a good week," he says. "What happened?"

Waylon looks around to see if anyone is eavesdropping. "Well, for years I've been working on this formula to predict changes in the stock market. And, I can't believe it, the damn thing finally seems to be paying off."

"Really?" Gary says, taking a sip of beer.

"Yeah," Waylon says. "You know how they talk about expansion and contraction cycles that correspond to Fibonacci numbers? Well, everybody knows they're great for estimating overall market trends, but, until now, nobody's been able to apply the number to the movements of a single stock. At least not well enough to make solid predictions, anyway. The thing they haven't gotten is this." Waylon grabs a cocktail napkin and writes down a long equation, then turns it around so Gary can read it.

Gary has no idea what a Fibonacci number is. He taps at the scribblings on the napkin with his finger. "Are you telling me you can predict the stock market with this?"

"No, this is just the algorithm. I've used it to generate a mathematical model and then written a program to crunch the numbers and make the actual predictions."

"And it works?"

"Let's put it this way," Waylon says. "A month ago I invested $1,000. I put it in three stocks that the model predicted were going to go up, and every one of them did. In two weeks I had just about tripled my initial investment. Then, I put it all into a stock that the model said was just about to go through the roof, and this afternoon it started taking off."

Gary wonders if Waylon should be showing his equation to Scully and Mulder on The X-Files, *but he decides to keep his mouth shut. Instead, he asks if Waylon will tell him the name of the stock.*

> *Waylon thinks about it for a minute or so while he takes another*
> *pull on his beer, then he writes a name on the napkin, cupping his*
> *hand around it so that no one else can sneak a peek. FibreCom.*
> *Two days later, Gary sees a headline in the business section:*
> *COMMUNICATIONS STOCKS SOAR*
> *FibreCom leads the pack with 15-point gain.*
> *"Mulder, I think you should see this," he thinks to himself.*

Before you laugh and say Gary should just go home and forget about Waylon's crazy ideas, remember that people like Bill Gates and Steve Jobs probably had a few weird barroom conversations when their radical visions were little more than crackpot schemes. What if you had been there and they'd offered you the chance to buy in? How would you feel today if you'd laughed?

On the other hand, how would you feel if you'd decided to invest your life savings in something that later turned out to be a delusion?

HOW TO RECOGNIZE CRAZY IDEAS

With the advent of the Internet, Paranoid ideas travel almost as fast as off-color jokes. Every day, chat rooms and inboxes overflow with health fads, investment schemes, rumors about people, and warnings of impending doom. Some are the insights of true Visionaries, and some are just the rantings of fools. The good news is that crazy ideas, whether dangerous or merely silly, tend to follow predictable patterns. To know what's sane, you must first disregard what is definitely crazy. This isn't easy, because sometimes your own needs can get in the way. Here are some ways of sifting through the daily pile of new ideas.

Know the History of the Idea

From time immemorial, the same attractive but incorrect ideas have resurfaced from the depths of the Paranoid unconscious and reached out to grasp the unwary. Some well-known delusions include perpetual motion, turning base metals into gold, astrology and other psychic phenomena, ancient predictions of current events, secret drugs that cure cancer, effortless ways to lose weight, and "evidence" that particular people are planning to take over the world using subterfuge. These ideas have a great deal of power because people would like to believe them. Unfortunately, they are seldom true. It's not that these ideas can never be true; it's just that in the past, they've been proved false on many occasions. If they are to be true now, there has to be some very convincing new reasoning that gets around the ancient fallacies.

Be especially wary of ideas presented as secret or forbidden knowledge, or of any theory that explains everything.

Understand How the Idea Works

Just because an idea is complex and difficult to understand doesn't mean it's good. Remember that confusion is one of the warning signs of hypnosis. The first step in evaluating an idea is to understand it. In order to test Waylon's theory about using Fibonacci numbers to predict the stock market, Gary needs to know what the numbers are. This task will take time and effort, but it is essential. A good rule of thumb is never to throw money at something you don't fully comprehend. The important part to understand about any idea is the mechanism, *how* it's supposed to work. Most crazy ideas are weakest at this point.

Fibonacci numbers are sequences in which each term is the sum of the two terms immediately preceding it. Many natural processes seem to correspond to this progression, which is quite interesting, but not definitive. To evaluate Waylon's idea, Gary needs to know *how* the relationship between Fibonacci numbers and the stock market operates, not just that there seems to be a connection.

Get Outside Verification

The angrier a Paranoid becomes when you suggest a second opinion, the more you need one. A good rule of thumb for evaluating a new idea is: if you can get two Obsessive-Compulsives to accept it, you probably should also.

Understand the Motivation

Always ask yourself who would gain what if you were to buy into the idea. Look at financial considerations, of course, but remember that, more than money, Paranoids want disciples to validate their theories.

The most important motivation to understand is your own. The world is full of tempting Paranoid ideas that we wish were true, but aren't. Miracle diets, mysterious cures, and offers of salvation through belief alone prey on our fervent hope that health and happiness can be achieved without effort.

If an idea taps into your own secret fantasies, you're more likely to believe it without question. Paranoid Visionaries know this, because they have the same fantasies. They'll be happy to confirm that anybody who has more than you do got it by unfair means, or that only a select few people really know what's going on in the world, and you're one of them.

Visionaries can also come up with ideas we wish weren't true, but are. Doomsaying economists try to persuade us to save more. Annoying doctors tell us that our bad habits can kill us. Futurists have been saying for years that we need to become technology-literate more quickly. Environmentalists keep hammering away at the simple, though much disputed, truth that we all need to make personal sacrifices to protect the planet. Many of us are inclined to doubt these Paranoid ideas, not because they lack supporting evidence, but because belief would require us to make unpleasant changes in our lives.

Put the Idea to the Test

The best way to evaluate an idea is to make predictions based upon it and see whether the predictions come true on a regular basis. This is the principle behind the scientific method. Waylon's Fibonacci number theory is unusual among Paranoid ideas in that it actually generates predictions that can be checked. If Gary wants to know how valid the idea is, he needs to know some of Waylon's predictions in advance and keep a box score on his hit rate. One prediction doesn't mean anything. A list of accurate picks from the past isn't enough to prove the theory, either, because Gary won't be able to tell how many bad picks were in with the good. If Waylon should want to charge for his predictions, Gary should regard the transaction like any other form of gambling and not spend any more than he can afford to lose.

Before you buy into ideas, check them out to see how well they work. This is what scientific studies are all about. You don't have to do the research yourself, but you do have to know it. Scientists are as slow as anybody else in accepting ideas that make them change the way they think, but they *are* persuaded by evidence. Even though we've all heard of ideas that were rejected by science but later turned out to be true, the fact is, there aren't that many.

The craziest Paranoid ideas are usually untestable. They're better at explaining the past than at predicting the future, and their acceptance depends more on the needs of the believers than on the objective merits of the belief. Just because an idea *sounds* good doesn't mean that it *is* good.

If creativity means looking at things differently, Paranoid Visionaries are certainly the most creative of the emotional vampires. Some of what they create exists only in their own minds, but sometimes their ideas can let you in on the ground floor of a new way of looking at the universe. You have to decide.

PARANOIDS AND RELIGION

It would take a whole book to examine the relationship between Paranoids and religion. Religion is their greatest invention, the shining triumph at the end of the Paranoid quest. Without Paranoids' faith in hidden truth, none of us would know God. Religion is also the black hole that sucks the Paranoid soul into cruelty unimaginable to the rest of humanity. With Paranoids in the world, there's no need for Satan.

GREEN-EYED MONSTERS

Next to religious fanaticism, jealousy is the most dangerous Paranoid idea. It's also the most universal. Who among us has never suspected that people don't love us as much as we love them? Most of us tolerate the ambiguity, but Green-Eyed Monsters cannot. Loyalty is everything to them, so important that they can't simply accept it on faith. They poke it, prod it, and all too often question it to death.

The last stragglers from rush hour make for slow going downtown. Still, there's plenty of time for a leisurely dinner and a movie. Lisa leans against the door and relaxes, grateful that Vampire Joseph is doing the driving. He always drives when they go out. When they first started dating, Lisa wondered whether she should offer to drive half the time, to be politically correct and all. Now she's glad she didn't. It's such a luxury being driven around. It makes her feel taken care of. Joseph is such a nice man. A little stiff, maybe, but always kind and considerate.

At a long intersection he turns toward her and smiles. "So, how was your day off?"

Lisa thinks back on her hectic day—getting her hair done, grocery shopping, dropping off the dry cleaning, and grabbing a quick lunch with her sister. "Oh, the usual," she says, trying in vain to find something interesting enough to talk about. "You know, errands. Stuff like that. Nothing special."

"I figured you had a really busy day."

"I guess I did. But how did you know that?"

"Well, I called a couple of times, and your phone went right to voicemail."

"Oh, the battery keeps losing its charge. I have to get it fixed."

"I called your landline too."

"You did? There weren't any messages on the answering machine."

Joseph shrugs. "I didn't leave any. It wasn't anything important. I just thought I'd call you back later."

"Oh."

"You were gone quite a while."

"Yeah, first one place, then another. You know how it is. I always seem to be busier on my days off than when I'm at work. It's nice to finally have a chance to sit down."

"So, where did you go?"

"Let's see," Lisa says, surprised that Joseph would have any interest in the dumb details of her day. "Haircut. Grocery store. Cleaners. Lunch. Cash machine. And I bought some new panty hose." She pulls her skirt up an inch or so above her knee. "Like them?"

"Yeah, they're great," Joseph says. "Where did you go for lunch?"

"The Bagel Shop over on Forty-fifth. It's right next to Annie's office, and she only gets a half hour break, and—"

"So you had lunch with your sister?"

"Yes." Lisa's voice comes out as a nervous giggle. "Joseph." She laughs again, this time at the preposterousness of the idea that just popped into her head. "It sounds like you're checking up on me."

Joseph laughs too. "No," he says. "Nothing like that. I'm just interested, that's all."

This is how Paranoid jealousy begins, with small, almost innocent questions. At first, the prospective victims might even be flattered that someone cares enough about them to worry that they might be seeing someone else. The feeling of being flattered disappears quickly when the innocent little questions become a regular part of the relationship, and the victim realizes that there will never be enough answers.

Many Green-Eyed Monsters, like Joseph, play to their victims' fantasies of being swept off their feet and taken care of. In relationships, Paranoids endear themselves by protecting people, giving them gifts, and doing little things for them without being asked. All they expect in return for these services is absolute loyalty and complete devotion that must be proved and re-proved forever. Often, people like Lisa accept the care without knowing its terrible price.

Paranoids are always on the lookout for the tiniest hint of perfidy in word, deed, or thought. Inevitably, they find what they're looking for, not because it's actually there in any objective sense, but because they continually focus on smaller and smaller details. No regular human can live up to a Paranoid's standards for purity of mind.

One reason Paranoid jealousy is such a problem is that people usually handle it in exactly the wrong way: by trying to appease and reassure. Think of the contingency here. This approach teaches the Green-Eyed Monster that jealous questions are appropriate in the relationship, and will be rewarded with answers. The Lisas of the world would do better to respond to the first jealous questions with something like this:

> *"Joseph, I may be overreacting here, but it sounds like you're checking up on me, and that's kind of frightening. Let me tell you this once and forever: I'm a one-man woman. As long as we're dating, you can be sure that I'm not seeing anybody else. You don't need to check up, and I won't allow it. Either you trust me to be faithful or we need to end things right here."*

Unfortunately, people like Lisa who have fantasies about being taken care of are seldom willing to risk a whole relationship by making such an assertive demand at the beginning. A time will come when she'll wish she had.

Here are some ideas for dealing with the Green-Eyed Monsters in your own life. Like many of the approaches for protecting yourself from emotional vampires, these strategies rely on doing the opposite of what you feel. Think carefully before deciding that they won't work in your life. Jealous Paranoids can be very dangerous.

Answer the Big Question, Not the Little Ones

The big question is: "Are you faithful to me?" Answer that one truthfully, then refuse to submit to further cross-examination.

The most dangerous thing about jealousy is that the more you do to make it better, the worse it gets. Answers about little details will only lead to more suspicion and questions. The only way to win the jealousy game is not to play. Jealousy has to be the Green-Eyed Monster's problem, or there will never be an end to it.

Never Agree to Tests of Love

There is no way to prove affection. Only a vampire would suggest that giving up your autonomy has anything to do with love. If someone you care for suggests that you can prove your love by taking a certain action, ask that person to prove his or her love by trusting you. This may help you explain that trust lives in the other person's mind, not in your behavior.

Being Paranoid means having problems with trust. Your actions cannot fix those problems. Paranoids will offer up the painful betrayals in their past as reasons for you to reassure them now by doing their will and answering their questions. Take their pain seriously, but don't believe for a minute that anything you can do will heal it.

Never Try to Deceive a Paranoid

If a Paranoid catches you in even the tiniest of white lies, it will provide justification for all further questions. Don't think that concealing anything will spare anyone's feelings or get you out of an argument. Paranoids have no compunctions about going through your drawers or checking your cell phone bill or the odometer of your car. Whatever evidence they find, however slight, will convince them that they were correct in making the search.

Green-Eyed Monsters will also search through your words and actions to find out exactly what you think of them. If your interest in them has begun to wane, there's no point in trying to hide it. They'll know. It may be less painful for all concerned if you end the relationship at that point or find a really good couples therapist. If you ever doubt that you'll be able to answer the big question correctly, it's definitely time to leave. Paranoids believe in eternal punishment, even for fantasies of infidelity.

If the Relationship Ends, Avoid the Person

When you leave, or even when they throw you out, Paranoids will usually want you back. Typically this has more to do with vengeance than love. They will scrutinize your words and actions for the slightest sign that you've changed your mind. Don't be polite! Hopeful Paranoids will always mistake civility for rekindled love. If you're ending a relationship with a Paranoid, don't discuss it. Just go. Once you've gone, don't accept phone calls or visits. If you're divorcing one, let your lawyer do the talking.

THE NINE ELEMENTS OF VAMPIRE-FIGHTING STRATEGY: HOW TO GIVE PARANOIDS A GLIMPSE OF REALITY

Don't lecture, transcend.

1. Know Them, Know Their History, and Know Your Goal

To Paranoids, nothing other than their own virtue is ever as it seems. They try to make the world fit the narrow bed of their beliefs, chopping and stretching reality to conform to their procrustean standards. Sometimes this process cuts away illusion and reveals the underlying structure of the universe. More often, it creates monstrous distortions. Your goal with Paranoids is to know which is which.

2. Get Outside Verification

Paranoid ideas fester in darkness. They have to be dragged kicking and screaming into the light of day and verified according to consensual standards of reality. Paranoids will regard this as the ultimate betrayal. To them, loyalty means keeping their secrets.

If you are involved with a Paranoid, don't accept this vow of silence. Affirm your right to discuss anything with the people you trust. There may be some slight validity in asking you to avoid discussing the relationship with your cousin. There is absolutely no validity in demanding that you don't talk about certain things with your doctor, your lawyer, or your accountant.

3. Do What They Don't

Look for complexity in everything that Paranoids say is simple. Real morality has to factor in human nature as something more than a miscalculation by God. It can never be as absolute as Paranoids would have you believe.

Look for simplicity in everything that Paranoids hold to be complex, like the reasons why they're so cruel and unforgiving. They're just mad because everybody doesn't do everything their way.

Also, trust others until there's a reason not to, and always be open to second opinions.

One of the things Paranoids want is to be understood. You can give them that without giving in to their pressure. Always listen, but never confuse listening with obedience.

4. Pay Attention to Their Actions, Not Their Words

Paranoids always see their own actions as completely virtuous. They often justify rage, rancor, and emotional abuse as conforming to a higher morality, applicable only to gods and Paranoids. Don't bother to ask them why they do anything. The answer will always be the same: because it was the right thing to do. Once Paranoids start rationalizing, anything is possible except their admitting that their motives were less than pure.

The fact is that Paranoids, like most emotional vampires, behave like infants. They want the few people they trust to meet their needs immediately, and they punish those people severely for not coming through. Paranoids' reasons for doing so are elaborate, twisted, tortuous, intricately contrived, and ultimately irrelevant. Focus on what they actually do, not why they say they do it.

5. Pick Your Battles

The battle you can never win with Paranoids is proving that you are trustworthy. You could die for them, I suppose, but even then they'd probably still have their doubts. There will always be tiny scraps of conflicting information that Paranoids want you to explain. Don't start down this path, because it has no end. Paranoids have trouble tolerating the normal ambiguity of human relationships. This is not a handicap to be accommodated, but a deficiency that the Paranoids themselves must correct. Demand that they do so. Fight for the idea that trust is in their mind, not in your behavior. It's a difficult battle, but it's one you can win.

6. Let Contingencies Do the Work

With Paranoid Visionaries, the important contingency for any idea is: does it work or not? It is not disloyal to ask.

With Green-Eyed Monsters, use your attention as a reward for trust, not for jealousy.

The kinds of "If you do this, I'll do that" contingencies that work with other infantile vampires also work with unruly Paranoids. For example, you might say, "If you ask me any more questions about where I was and what I was doing, I'm going into the other room so we can both cool down." Often, the most effective argument against Paranoid thinking is silence from behind a closed door. As I've said before in describing this sort of time-out technique, its value is completely negated if you take a parting shot before leaving.

The important contingency with Paranoids is to disrupt their tirades rather than reward the behavior by listening or fighting back. Paranoids love to argue; they can do it for hours without tiring or learning anything. The best way to stop them is not to let them start.

By the way, if you try the time-out strategy, even with full agreement, you'll probably still need to leave the premises, or at least lock the door. Paranoids consider it your duty and privilege to hear every bit of what they have to say. They'll try to convince you that not wanting to be yelled at is a kind of betrayal. Don't stay to argue the point. If they won't let you leave, recognize that as a form of violence—one that will most likely escalate over time.

7. Choose Your Words as Carefully as You Pick Your Battles

First and foremost, never ask why. Paranoids can explain anything, and they will persist until you accept what they say out of sheer exhaustion.

Paranoids are sensitive to criticism, but unlike many other vampires, they will listen to it, and sometimes learn. They would really like to be admirable people in your eyes and in their own. To criticize a Paranoid effectively, take your cue from the very best of sermons. Ignore the hellfire-and-brimstone kind beloved by Obsessive-Compulsives, and pay attention to the kind that remind humans of the divinity within their own souls.

Most Paranoids have a small number of very important concepts by which they try to live their lives. Honor, loyalty, honesty, and love are real enough for Paranoids to kill or die for. In the darkness of the Paranoid mind, however, these grand concepts can quickly shrivel into vindictive pettiness. The most effective criticisms redefine the Paranoid's core concepts to include trust, mercy, and open-mindedness. Needless to say, this task requires tapping into your own Buddha nature. It can't be done when you're angry.

For the less saintly, it is also effective to ask Paranoids how their core concepts relate to the present situation. A question like, "What is the honorable thing to do here?" or, "Doesn't love require you to forgive?" or, "Does loyalty mean never disagreeing?" can open doors in the Paranoid mind. If this sort of question doesn't work, you may be dealing with a different kind of vampire.

8. Ignore Tantrums

Tears, lectures, sermons, rambling rationalizations, jealous questions, displaying anguish as if it were a work of art—once Paranoid tantrums begin, they usually go on all night. If you give in, they'll go on for the rest of your life. As we have seen throughout this chapter, the best time to stop Paranoid tantrums is before they start.

9. Know Your Own Limits

Paranoids are in many ways the most difficult and dangerous of the emotional vampires. They will protect you, cherish you, and possibly illuminate your life. All they ask in return is absolute loyalty. No discounts; with Paranoids, it's all or nothing. For some people, it's the most wonderful deal of their lives. For others, it leads to nothing but exhaustion and endless suffering. Only you can decide whether you have what it takes to be close to a Paranoid emotional vampire. One thing is certain, however: before you attempt to understand Paranoids, you must first know yourself.

27 Therapy for Paranoid Vampires

What should you do if you see signs of Paranoid behavior in yourself or someone you care about? This section is a thumbnail sketch of the sorts of self-help and professional therapeutic approaches that might be beneficial. Always remember that attempting psychotherapy on someone you know will make you both sicker.

THE GOAL

The goal for Paranoids is to learn how to tolerate ambiguity, especially ambiguity in others' feelings toward them. A second, related goal is to forgive perceived betrayals. It usually takes a well-trained professional to help Paranoids achieve these goals.

PROFESSIONAL HELP

Paranoids require experienced professionals who have been in the therapy business long enough that they won't be intimidated or overwhelmed. The kind of therapy is almost irrelevant, because developing a trusting relationship is the most important part of treatment. However, to maintain control over the process, Paranoids often choose therapists who are less experienced, who are not trained as therapists at all, or whose only qualification is membership in the same cult. Paranoids try to hypnotize inexperienced therapists into accepting their alternate reality at least enough to prevent them from asking embarrassing questions. Sometimes Paranoids succeed at this, but more often they just get kicked out of treatment. Either way, the Paranoids get worse.

SELF-HELP

If you recognize Paranoid tendencies in yourself, the following exercises will be very difficult for you, but they will make a difference.

Check Reality

The most important thing you can do for yourself is to understand that some of the things you see or suspect are not actually there. You need a trusted confidant with whom to discuss your perceptions. The person should be strong enough to tell you when he or she thinks you're wrong. The confidant should *never* be a family member or someone with whom you are romantically involved.

Recognize That What Other People Do Has Little to Do with You

A common Paranoid tendency is to believe that if the people around you were appropriately loyal and respectful, they would automatically do everything the way you want them to. This borders on the delusional. Most of the time, other people are not thinking of you at all. This is not disloyal; it is normal. Allow the people close to you to have parts of their lives that have nothing to do with you, and don't feel threatened by it.

Forgive and Forget

Paranoids' memories tend to turn slights and oversights into betrayals and humiliations. As you run over small transgressions in your mind, they get bigger and more painful. If you catch yourself doing this, stop! You are creating anguish for everyone, yourself most of all. Let them all go. Forgive and forget. If you can't, maybe you ought to talk to a therapist.

WHAT WILL HURT

Paranoids often choose therapists on the basis of similarities of political or religious beliefs rather than training and experience. If Paranoids go to therapy to discuss politics or religion rather than their own behavior, it generally leads to increased suffering for everyone.

28 Sunrise at Dracula's Castle

Congratulate yourself. You've faced the vampires and come away unscathed. So far.

Emotional vampires can be the most difficult and draining creatures on earth. But, as you now know, their powers come from weakness, not strength. Vampires' personalities are distorted by simple, immature needs that make the children of the night both attractive and dangerous. If you know the need, you know the vampire.

Antisocials are addicted to excitement. They draw you in with devilish charm and the promise of thrills in the dark. You'll be drained if you expect them to remember their promises in the morning.

Histrionics live for attention. They beguile you with their stunning performances, but when the curtain falls, they fall apart. Between shows, you'll have to put them back together.

Narcissists think they're God's gift to the world. They'll tell you you're as special as they are, but as soon as they get what they want, they'll hardly remember your name—until the next time they need something.

Obsessive-Compulsives seem too good to be true. They strive for perfection by working hard, playing by the rules, and attempting to control everything within a 10-mile radius. Including you.

Paranoids prowl the night, searching for answers that are simple and true. Their certainty is so reassuring—until they start having questions about you.

It's misleading to think that emotional vampires are sick. Personality disorders aren't caused by microbes or lesions in vital organs, but by the misguided and sometimes predatory choices of the sufferers. There's a danger in perception of illness as well. Civilized people make accommodations for the sick, and accommodation is the last thing that vampires need. To deal effectively with the children of the night, you must know them for what they are. You must also know yourself.

Here is what you must always remember.

You, Not the Vampires, Are in Control

Vampires try to convince you that there are no options other than submitting to their will. This is never true. *When you're dealing with vampires, there is always another choice, even if it's only walking away.*

Strength Comes from Connection

Vampires are isolated by their insatiable needs. The only way they can drain you is by isolating you as well. They use hypnosis to pull you away from people you trust and convince you that the rules you believe in no longer apply.

Don't listen! Throw back the curtain and let the sunlight in.

Your power against vampires comes from your relationship with the rest of humanity and anything else larger than yourself. *When you're dealing with vampires, trust your oldest friends and hold tightly to your values. Secrets can hurt you; the things you're most embarrassed to discuss are the things you most need to share.*

Safety Means Facing Your Fears

Vampires use fear and confusion to control you. If you ever find yourself running scared, stop and turn around. The path to safety always goes *through* fear rather than away from it. *When you're dealing with vampires, the choice that seems most frightening is usually the right one.*

Crosses and garlic won't save you from emotional vampires. Your best defenses are knowledge, maturity, and good judgment. You now have the knowledge; the maturity and judgment you must supply for yourself.

Index

AA (Alcoholics Anonymous), 90–91
Abuse, 79, 120–121, 173. *See also*
    Substance abuse
Accountability, 32, 160
Achievements, 146–147, 167, 174
Acting, by Histrionics, 93
Ad hominem argument, of Narcissist
    Legends, 180–181
Addiction:
    anger as, 67
    Antisocial need for stimulation and, 25
    overcoming addition to excitement, 89
    picking battles in dealing with
        Daredevils, 33
    sexual, 170
    therapy for Antisocials, 90–91
Adolescent qualities, of Obsessive-
    Compulsives, 207–209. *See also*
    Teenagers
Adoration, Narcissists addicted to, 170, 176
Adultery, Narcissistic Superstars and, 169
Aggression. *See also* Anger
    avoiding hooks, 84
    Bullies and, 63–64
    history of, 68
    in Passive-Aggressives, 111, 113
Alcohol. *See also* Substance abuse
Alcoholics Anonymous (AA), 90–91
Ambiguity:
    black-and-white principles of Paranoids
        and, 228–229
    goals of therapy for Paranoids, 249
    Paranoids desire to banish, 7
    Paranoids intolerant of, 227–228, 232
American Psychiatric Association, 2
Anal-retentiveness, of Obsessive-
    Compulsives, 6, 197
Anger. *See also* Bullies
    as addiction, 67–68
    of Bullies, 63, 80–81
    clouding judgment in relating to
        Narcissists, 179
    fear response to, 65
    of Histrionics, 115
    how angry people think, 82–83
    instinct for aggression and, 63–64
    of Narcissistic Superstars, 171–173

of Narcissists, 163
of Obsessive-Compulsives, 200
strategies for dealing with angry
    people, 83–88
therapy for Antisocials, 90
Antisocials:
    anger control, 90
    Bullies. *See* Bullies
    Daredevils. *See* Daredevils
    facing consequences of behaviors, 92
    goals of therapy, 89–90
    Lovable Rogues. *See* Lovable Rogues
    qualities of, 4
    self-help, 91–92
    summary of, 251
    types of lies, 76
    Used Car Salesmen. *See* Used Car
        Salesmen
Anxiety, 119, 192, 219, 220
Apologies, dealing with Obsessive-
    Compulsives, 208
Appearance, Histrionics concern for, 98
Approval. *See also* Praise
    Histrionics need for, 5, 93–94, 97
    Obsessive-Compulsives and, 203
Attention:
    dealing with Passive-Aggressives, 123
    Hams need for, 101, 103
    Histrionics need for, 5, 93–96, 251
Attention to detail:
    of Obsessive-Compulsives, 7, 191, 196
    in relating to Hams, 108
Attractiveness, of Antisocials, 22
Authority, 29, 60–61, 165

Bargaining, 84, 175, 185–186. *See also*
    Negotiation
Behavior, focusing on behavior not feeling
    in relating to Narcissists, 186
Betrayal, Paranoids and, 229, 250
Black-and-white principles, of Paranoids,
    228–229
Boredom:
    Antisocial need for stimulation, 25
    Antisocials aversion to, 4, 23
    Daredevil behavior and, 28
    enduring, 89, 91

ex-husbands as, 44–47
female, 29–30
holding accountable, 32
hypnotic strategies of, 32–33
ignoring tantrums of, 37
influencing questionable decisions by, 30–31
knowing your own limits when relating to, 38
as liars, 42–43
maintaining love relationship with, 39–42
no used in communication with, 36–37
overview of, 27
physiology of excitement and, 27–28
types of lies, 76
as unfaithful lovers, 43–44
verifying claims of, 32
Day-to-day tasks, Hams difficulty in dealing with, 109
Deceit, 53, 244. *See also* Lies
Decision making, 7, 26, 30–31
Dependency, of Histrionics, 98
Depression, 28, 119, 130–132, 171–173
Detail-orientation. *See* Attention to detail
Dissociation, by Passive-Aggressives, 113
Dogma. *See* Authority
Dominance, 40–41, 179, 181, 182
Drama, 93, 128–129
Drugs, 27–28, 33. *See also* Substance abuse
Duplicity, Paranoid behavior inviting, 228
Duty/duty rosters. *See* On duty strategy

Emotionality, of Histrionics, 97–98
Emotions:
    anal-retentiveness of Obsessive-Compulsives, 197
    communicating hurt feelings to Obsessive-Compulsives, 205
    focusing on behavior not feeling in relating to Narcissists, 186
    goals of therapy for Obsessive-Compulsives, 223
    of Histrionics, 105
    of Narcissists, 148
    use of tantrums by emotional vampires, 17
    vampires thriving in emotional situations, 19
Empathy, 10, 148, 188–189
Entitlement, 17, 143, 146–147
Excitement:
    Antisocials addicted to, 4, 251
    bonding with Daredevils, 42
    Bullies and, 63, 68
    Daredevils addicted to, 27

exploitative nature of emotional vampires, 17–19
overcoming addition to, 89
physiology of, 27–28
understanding Daredevil behavior, 31
Used Car Salesmen partial to thrill of deceit, 53
Extinction burst, tantrums and, 37
Eye contact, lies and, 78

Fairness, 10, 124, 181, 202
Fans, Hams as, 106
Fantasy, 5–6, 27, 79
Fear:
    of being ordinary in Narcissists, 142, 148
    challenge of facing, 10
    of doing something wrong in Obsessive Compulsives, 191–192
    goals of therapy for Obsessive-Compulsives, 223
    need to control and, 216
    response to anger, 65
    safety in facing, 252
    using information to allay, 218
Feedback, in dealing with Passive-Aggressives, 124
Feelings. *See* Emotions
Females, 93
    as Daredevils, 29–30
    as Histrionics, 40, 93
    pathological giving by, 115
    socialized to pay attention to needs of others, 41
Ferrari-Toyota dilemma, 22–23
Fight or flight response, 64, 68–69, 70–71
Flatterers, Narcissists as, 148
Followers, Narcissists learning to be, 188
Forgiveness, 229, 233, 250
Freud, 94
Friendliness, strategies of Used Car Salesmen, 56
Frustration, of Histrionics, 115
Fun, Antisocials need for, 21–22, 28–29

Gambling, Daredevil behavior and, 33
Give and take, social systems based on reciprocity, 10
Golden Rule, 144
Gossip, Histrionics and, 93, 129–130
Grandiosity, of Narcissists, 146–147, 151, 165
Gratification:
    Antisocial need for stimulation, 25
    Antisocials demanding immediate, 21
    emotional vampires wanting it now, 17
    internal contingencies in delay of, 35
    learning how to delay, 89